Bishop of the Goths Ulfilas

The Gospel of Saint Mark in Gothic

According to the translation made by Wulfila in the fourth century

Bishop of the Goths Ulfilas

The Gospel of Saint Mark in Gothic
According to the translation made by Wulfila in the fourth century

ISBN/EAN: 9783337282288

Printed in Europe, USA, Canada, Australia, Japan

Cover: Foto ©Thomas Meinert / pixelio.de

More available books at **www.hansebooks.com**

Clarendon Press Series

THE

GOSPEL OF SAINT MARK

IN GOTHIC

ACCORDING TO THE TRANSLATION MADE BY

WULFILA

IN THE FOURTH CENTURY

*EDITED, WITH A GRAMMATICAL INTRODUCTION
AND GLOSSARIAL INDEX*

BY THE

REV. WALTER W. SKEAT, M.A.

ELRINGTON AND BOSWORTH PROFESSOR OF ANGLO-SAXON IN THE UNIVERSITY
OF CAMBRIDGE

Oxford

AT THE CLARENDON PRESS

M DCCC LXXXII

CONTENTS.

PREFACE.

THE following pages are intended to serve as a Gothic Primer, and to introduce the beginner to fuller and more complete works upon the subject. There is no lack of good editions in German, such as those by Gabelentz and Löbe, Massmann, and Stamm (as revised by Heyne). The price of the last of these is so moderate as to render it unnecessary to reprint all the fragments of the extant Gothic literature; but it appeared to be desirable to select a certain portion of it, which might be explained, by the help of notes, glossary, and grammar, for the benefit of English readers. As the best MS. contains the four gospels only, the choice was practically limited to one of these; and the gospel of St. Mark was chosen, because it is the least mutilated. Of the other gospels, whole chapters are wanting, but the missing portions of St. Mark are comparatively small, viz. vi. 30–53, xii. 38–xiii. 16, xiii. 29–xiv. 4, xiv. 16–41, and xvi. 12–20, amounting to not more than 95 verses.

The notes call attention to such difficulties of construction as are most likely to cause perplexity. The glossary not only explains all the words occurring in St. Mark's gospel, but is extended so as to contain all the more important words of the language, especially such as are most required by the student of English etymology. The introduction gives all necessary elementary information concerning the MS., the author, and the sources of the alphabet; with some account of the pronunciation, phonology, and grammar. Numerous references to the text have been introduced into the grammar, and several remarks are made relative to points of philological interest. The student who has already some knowledge of Middle English and Anglo-Saxon will not experience much difficulty in gaining, in a short time, some elementary and very useful knowledge of Gothic. A study of this language is absolutely indispensable for the student of Teutonic philology, and the number of points of English etymology which cannot be fully understood without it, is surprisingly large. A knowledge of Gothic ought to be as common among Englishmen as it is now rare; and I trust, for the sake of English scholarship, that the present attempt to smooth the way for those who wish to understand more about the formation of the Teutonic part of our own language, may meet with some success.

The Glossarial Index, which I have carefully revised, was almost wholly written by my eldest daughter. For several hints as to the phonology I am indebted to Mr. Sweet.

A more complete Glossary, with references to *all* the extant writings of Wulfila, was published for the Philological Society by Asher and Co. in 1868, and was written by myself. It is remarkable that no glossary or grammar of Gothic has ever appeared with explanations *in English*, except that volume and the present one.

INTRODUCTION.

§ 1. THE language in which the text of St. Mark's Gospel, as here printed, was originally written, is commonly called 'Mœso-Gothic;' or, as no confusion with any other Gothic dialect can arise—for no remains of other dialects are extant—it is often called by the simpler and sufficient name of 'Gothic.' The Goths consisted of numerous tribes, the most important being the Ostro-Goths or Eastern Goths, and the Visigoths (Wisigoths) or Western Goths, who, at the beginning of the fourth century, occupied the country to the north of the Danube, then called Dacia, but now Wallachia. Some of the Visigoths, who had been converted to Christianity and experienced persecution on account of their religion, were allowed to cross the Danube into Mœsia, the modern Bulgaria, before A. D. 337; but it was not till A. D. 376 that vast numbers of them, amounting to nearly a million of people of all ages and of both sexes, were permitted by the emperor Valens to establish themselves in that province. The cause which drove them to implore the Emperor's protection was their fear of the Huns, whose attacks they were unable to resist. When once firmly established in Mœsia, quarrels arose between them and the Roman empire; finally, they revolted, gained several battles against the Romans, sacked Rome under the leadership of Alaric in 410, and even extended their conquests as far as Gaul and Spain. We must therefore take 'Mœso-Gothic' to denote a dialect spoken by some of the Visigoths who at one time were settled in Mœsia; its exact bounds are uncertain, and the fragments of it which have survived are almost all due to the writings of a celebrated Christian bishop named Wulfila[1], though he is better known as Ulphilas (or Ulfilas), a form due to a Græcised spelling.

§ 2. The parents of Wulfila were Christians, of Cappadocian origin, having been carried away as captives by the Goths in one of their raids into Asia; and it would seem that the Goths first acquired a knowledge of Christianity from their captives. Wulfila himself was born among the Goths, A.D. 311, so that Gothic was his native language; but 'he was able in after-life to speak and write both in Latin and Greek[2].' It was under the conduct of Wulfila, then quite a young man, that some of the Christian Goths were allowed to cross the Danube (as above stated) by the favour of Constantine. He was consecrated bishop by Eusebius of Nicomedia at the early age of thirty, A.D. 341. He was still alive when the Visigoths, under Fritigern, inflicted a crushing defeat on the forces of Valens at the great battle of Adrianople, A.D. 378; and he died at the age of seventy, A.D. 381[3]. Little more is known about his life, except that he adopted the Arian heresy, which doubtless exposed him to attacks from the followers of Athanasius.

§ 3. The industry of Wulfila has conferred one of the

---

[1] *Wulfila* means 'little wolf,' and is the diminutive of *wulfs*, a wolf, formed like *magula*, a little boy, from *magus*, a boy. The actual spelling *Wulfila* occurs in Jornandes, as cited by Gibbon, Decline and Fall of the Roman Empire, c. xxxvii, note.

[2] Max Müller, Lectures on Language, vol. i. lect. 5; see, in particular, his quotation from Auxentius, in note 11.

[3] The three dates, of Wulfila's birth, consecration, and death, in 311, 341, and 381, are easily remembered. Waitz gives 388 as the year of his death; but this seems to be wrong.

highest benefits upon philology, whilst at the same time
it did excellent service in the cause of religion.   He con-
ceived the bold idea of translating the scriptures into the
'vulgar tongue,' and actually succeeded in this important
task.   He translated the whole of the Old Testament, with
the exception of the Book of Kings, from the Greek
(Septuagint) version, and the whole of the New Testament
from a Greek version closely resembling that from which
our own 'authorised version' was made.   It is much to
be regretted that only fragments of his work have come
down to us in various imperfect MSS. ; but to possess even
these fragments is a very great gain.

§ 4. The most important of these MSS. is not contem-
porary with the author, but is a good and early copy written
in the sixth century, and known as the Codex Argenteus, or
'Silver manuscript,' being written chiefly in letters of silver,
occasionally of gold, upon a parchment stained so as to
present a rich mulberry-tinted colour.   It was taken from
Prague by the Swedes in 1648, and is now carefully preserved at Upsal.   This MS. is imperfect, but contains large
portions of the Gospels, and is the one upon which the text
here printed is founded.   A most carefully printed copy of
it was edited by Uppström, and published at Upsal, 1854–
1857.   It represents the MS. just as it stands, being printed
line for line in double columns; and it is to this edition that
nearly all the other numerous editions are most indebted.
The best modern edition is, upon the whole, that by Stamm
and Heyne, which I have closely followed[1].

§ 5. Other MSS. are extant at Wolfenbüttell, Milan,

---

[1] The title is—Friedrich Ludwig Stamm's Ulfilas, oder die uns er-
haltenen Denkmäler der gothischen Sprache . . . Neu herausgegeben von
Dr. Moritz Heyne.   Siebente Auflage.   Paderborn, 1878.

Vienna, and Rome, and preserve various fragments of the same translation. In this way we possess fragments of Genesis, Ezra, Nehemiah, the four Gospels, and parts of many of St. Paul's epistles. In the same language are also found an explanation or commentary upon a part of the Gospel of St. John, entitled by Massmann *Skeireins aiwaggeljons thairh Johannen* (explanation of the gospel by John), some title-deeds to property, found at Naples and Arezzo, and a fragment of a calendar. Some have attributed to Wulfila the authorship of the above commentary; but there is no proof that it is his. The other documents are of little consequence.

§ 6. For further information about Wulfila, see Max Müller, Lectures on the Science of Language, vol. i. lect. 5, which should by all means be consulted; Gibbon's Decline and Fall of the Roman Empire, capp. 26 and 37; cap. 7 of the preface to Bosworth's Anglo-Saxon Dictionary, London, 1838; Waitz, Ueber das Leben und die Lehre des Ulfila, Hannover, 1840; Bessell, Ueber das Leben des Ulfila, Göttingen, 1860; and the various editions of Wulfila's translation. In the introduction to my Mœso-Gothic Glossary (Asher & Co., 1868), I give an account of all the MSS. and editions. The best editions are the following. Ulfilas, by Gabelentz and Löbe, 2 vols. 4to., Lipsiæ, 1836–1843; a very complete work, with a full Glossary, Grammar, &c. Ulfilas, Urschrift, Grammatik und Wörterbuch; by I. Gaugengigl, Passau, 1849, 1856. Ulfilas; by H. F. Massmann, Stuttgart, 1857. Vulfila; by E. Bernhardt, Halle, 1876. The edition by Stamm and Heyne has been already mentioned. One excellent feature of Massmann's edition is that it gives, not only the Gothic text, but also the Greek and Latin texts of the gospels and epistles, in parallel columns. Another very useful volume is 'The Gothic and Anglo-Saxon

Gospels, in parallel columns with the versions of Wycliffe and Tyndale; by the Rev. J. Bosworth, D.D. and G. Waring, M.A.; London, 1865.' A handsome quarto edition of the four Gospels, which had been prepared by Dr. Eric Benzelius, was published by Lye at Oxford in 1750[1]; it was printed at the Clarendon Press with the 'Gothic' type which Junius presented to the University of Oxford after it had been employed for his own edition, published at Dordrecht in 1665. This type, in which the letters of the Gothic alphabet are closely imitated, is still preserved, and I am enabled by means of it, to give the specimens on pp. xviii. and xxi.

§ 7. It is highly probable that Wulfila himself is to be credited with the invention of the so-called Gothic alphabet. It has long been observed that the alphabet is a compound one, being imitated partly from the Greek and partly from the Latin alphabet; but some uncertainty has existed as to the exact history of a few of the letters. The late publications of the Palæographical Society have enabled me, as I believe, to illustrate this matter in a very simple manner. If it be the case that the Gothic alphabet was thus compounded of two others, it would obviously be a great gain to find *bilingual* MSS. exhibiting the exact form of the Greek and Latin letters *at the same moment of time.* A few such exist, one of them being the well-known Codex Bezæ at Cambridge, a MS. of the sixth century, exemplified in plates 14 and 15 of the Palæographic Society's facsimiles. Another is a MS. of the Acts of the Apostles, of the seventh century, known as MS. Laud 35, and preserved in the Bodleian Library at Oxford. There is a beautiful facsimile of a page of this MS. in plate 80 of the same series;

---

[1] Though this book is generally said to be out of print, I am told that three copies of it still remain at Oxford.

and a fair imitation of it at the top of plate 10 in Westwood's Palæographia Sacra Pictoria.   When this plate 80 was first published in 1877, I well remember that, at the very first glance, it occurred to me that the letters presented an extraordinary resemblance to those of the Codex Argenteus, not merely in shape, but in actual size.   On a closer examination, I found that the plate contained all the Gothic letters but one, viz. *o*; and it was at once obvious that the Gothic letters denoted in this edition by *a, b, g, d, e, z, th, i, k, l, m, n, p, t, w, ch*, and *hw*, corresponded to the Greek capital letters A, B, Γ, Δ, E, Z, Φ, I, K, Λ, M, N, Π, T, Y, X, and Θ respectively; whilst the Gothic *kw, h, j, u, r, s*, and *f*, corresponded to the Latin capital letters U, H, G, U inverted, R, S, and F respectively.   In order to enable the reader to see this for himself, I have prepared the illustrative diagram printed upon the opposite page, which I now proceed to explain.   Line 1 contains the Gothic letters, copied from the facsimile of a page of the Codex Argenteus given in Plate 118 of the Palæographic Society, and marked 'Gothic Gospels.—(6th cent.) Upsala, Univ. Lib. Cod. Argent.'   It will be understood that the written letters of the codex are not all precisely alike, but it will be found that the letter *a* in my illustration agrees exactly with *one* of the examples of the letter *a* in Plate 118; and so of the other letters.   Line 2 contains Greek letters, copied from Plate 80, column 2, in which again, though the letters are of variable size, I have exactly copied the best example of each letter.   Lastly, line 3 contains Latin letters, copied from Plate 80, column 1.   The similarity is sufficiently close in every instance, and any dissimilarity may be readily accounted for by the slight difference in the date of the MSS.   If we had more numerous Greek and Latin bilingual MSS. of an early date, it is probable that all dissimilarity, such as now appears in the

I. *Gothic.*

ΛΒΓΔΕ ᚒ ᛉΖᚺΨΙΚΛΜ

a b g d e   kw z h th i k l m

II. *Greek.*

ΛΒΓΔΕ · Ζ · ΦΙΚΛΜ

α β γ δ ε   ϛ   φ ι κ λ μ

III. *Latin.*

· · · · **ᚒ ᚺ** · · · · ·

u   h

I. *Gothic.*

ᚾᏀᚷᚿᛈᚱᛊᛏᚤᚠᚷᛟᛉ

n j u p r s t w f ch hw o

II. *Greek.*

ᚾ · Π · ΤΥ · ΧΘ ·

ν   π   τ υ   χ θ

III. *Latin.*   IV. *Gk. ου.*
                                      inverted.

· **ᚷᚿ · ᚱᛊ · · ᚠ · · ᛉ**

g u (*inverted*) r s   f

H.W.S.

case of *a* and *d*, would disappear. We can, moreover, easily see how the Gothic alphabet was formed. Letters were first selected from the Greek alphabet, as far as seemed advisable; and, where no good representatives of the Gothic sounds appeared in that alphabet, Latin letters were added. In selecting Greek letters, Wulfila (if we may suppose the scheme to be his) had no difficulty with *a, b, g, d, e, z, i, k, l, m, n, p, t*; but the rest require a word of comment. *Ch* is not a true Gothic letter, being only used in the word Χριστός (Christ); hence the Greek χ, not being otherwise wanted, was at once adopted. Next *h* and *f*, not being represented in Greek, were taken from Latin. The Greek φ[1] and θ, having (apparently) no exact Gothic values, were arbitrarily chosen to stand for *th* and *hw*; and it is remarkable that θ was purposely dissociated from *th*, as if to mark more plainly some difference between them. The writer's choice of the Latin R and S instead of the Greek letters, need not surprise us; for both the Greek symbols are ambiguous. The Greek P (*r*) might be mistaken for the Latin P (*p*); whilst the Greek C (*s*) might be mistaken for the Latin C (*c*). As he had taken the Greek Γ for his *g*, he of course took the Latin G for the nearly related sound of *j* (German *j*, English *y*). It is difficult to see why the Latin *u* was taken to represent the Gothic *kw*, but the identity of the letters cannot be doubted. This decision led to the curious device of gaining a new symbol for *u* by *inverting* the Latin letter; whilst the Greek *u* (Υ) being thus set free, was adopted for the Gothic *w*.

We have now seen the origin of all the letters except that

---

[1] The Gothic *th* is φ, not ψ; the latter was widely spread at the top, and had straight sides. The question is settled by comparing other Gothic MSS. In one of the Milan MSS., the φ is quite distinct, and closed at the top. See the plate in Gabelentz and Löbe.

of the Gothic *o*. For this we should have expected that Wulfila would have chosen either the Gk. *omicron* (identical in form with the Latin O) or the Gk. *omega*. Some have indeed supposed that the Gothic *o* is, in fact, the latter, but a glance at the facsimiles will dispel that illusion; for the Gk. *omega* was not, at that time, written like our modern printed Ω, but was merely a magnified ω, a sort of *rounded* W. It seems to me clear that, being dissatisfied with *o* and ω, the writer had recourse once more to the principle of inversion, and chose for this purpose the symbol ȣ, well known as a contraction for *ου*, and originally due to placing *υ* above *o*. The last symbol in my illustration is not a good example, but was the best I could find among the Society's facsimiles; it occurs several times in Plate 27, my example being taken from l. 14 of the first column. This Plate 27 represents a page of a Greek Evangelistarium (MS. Harl. 5598 in the British Museum), written A.D. 995. Considering the great difference in the date, the resemblance is, I think, sufficient. Other examples of this symbol may be found in l. 14, col. 2, of the same plate; and I have since found another in l. 28 of Plate 84, the likeness of which to the Gothic symbol is *perfect*, though the MS. was not written till A.D. 1111. It seems to me that, thanks to the Palæographical Society, the history of the Gothic alphabet may be considered as settled.

§ 8. It so happens that Plate 118, exhibiting a specimen-page of the Codex Argenteus, contains a brief extract from St. Mark's Gospel, c. vii. vv. 3–7. By way of further illustration, I now give the words of c. vii. v. 6 (see p. 16) *exactly as they are written* in the MS., using the Gothic types above referred to. The extract necessarily includes the last word (*hlaif*) of v. 5, and the first word (*Ith*) of v. 7. The word *hairto* is divided between the *r* and *t*.

hᛚᚨᛁᚠ · ïᚦ ïs ᚨᚾᛞhᚨᚠᚷᚨᚾᛞs uᚨᚦ
ᛞᚾ ïᛗ · ᚦᚨᛏᛖᛁ ᚥᚨᛁᛚᚨ ᛔᚱᚨᛒᚠᛖᛏᛁᛞᚨ
ᛖsᚨᛁᚨs ᛒᛁ ïᛉᚥᛁs ᚦᚨᚾs ᛚᛁᚾᛏᚨᚾs
sᚥᛖ ᚷᚨᛗᛖᛚᛁᚦ ïsᛏ · sᛉ ᛗᚨᚾᚨᚷᛖᛁ
ᚥᚨᛁᚱᛁᚨᛉᛗ ᛗᛁᚴ sᚥᛖᚴᚱᚨᛁᚦ · ïᚦ hᚨᛁᚱ
ᛏᛉ ïᛉᛖ ᚠᚨᛁᚴᚱᚨ hᚨᛒᚨᛁᚦ sᛁᚴ ᛗᛁs · ïᚦ

Now if we substitute Greek and Roman letters for the above
(with the exception only of the Gothic *o*, which is retained),
we shall find, even though the ordinary modern type be
employed, a striking resemblance. The following is the
result of the experiment.

    HΛAIF · Iφ IS ANΔHAFGANΔS UAφ
    ΔΠ IM · φATEI YAIΛA ΠPAΠFETIΔA
    ESAIAS BI IZYIS φANS ΛIΠTANS
    SYE ΓAMEΛIφ IST · SϪ MANAGEI
    YAIRIAϪM MIK SYƐRAIφ · Iφ HAIR
    TϪ IZE FAIRRA HABAIφ SIK MIS · Iφ

With the transliteration which I have adopted this becomes :—

    hlaif.   Ith is andhafjands kwath
    du im.   thatei waila praufetida
    Esaias bi izwis thans liutans
    swe gamelith ist, so managei
    wairilom mik swceraith, ith hair-
    to ize fairra habaith sik mis.   Ith

The corresponding modern English is, literally, as follows:—loaf. But he answering quoth to them, that well

prophesied Isaiah by[1] you the deceivers, so[2] spoken is:
the multitude with-lips me honour, but (the) heart of-them
far hath itself from-me.   But—.

For a further account of the letters, see the explanation of
the Alphabet on p. xxi.

§ 9. The resemblance of Gothic words to English is often
striking.   In the above brief extract we may notice *hlaif*,
loaf; *kwath*, quoth; *waila*, well; *managei*, many; *fairra*,
far.   This leads us to a consideration of the position of
Gothic among the Aryan languages.

Its close affinity with English and Dutch is not to be
mistaken, and it evidently belongs to the Low-German di-
vision of the Teutonic dialects.   In Dr. Morris's Historical
Outlines of English Accidence, p. 4, we are told that ' the
Teutonic dialects may be arranged in three groups or sub-
divisions: (1) the Low-German; (2) the Scandinavian; (3)
the High-German.'   Of these, the first includes Gothic,
English,[3] Frisian, Dutch, Flemish, and Old Saxon (the language of the Heliand); the second includes Icelandic,
Swedish, Danish, and Norwegian; and the last includes
only the language usually known by the simpler name of
German.   Morris describes Gothic as ' the oldest and most
primitive of the Teutonic dialects, of which any remains are
known; spoken by the Eastern and Western Goths who
occupied the province of Dacia, whence they made in-
cursions into Asia, Galatia, and Cappadocia.'   It seems
necessary to add that Wulfila has only preserved for us
specimens of the language of the *Western* Goths, though that

---

[1] I. e. concerning.   [2] I. e. as.

[3] Dr. Morris puts English the *sixth* in the list; it may just as well
come *second*, considering its importance and the antiquity of some of its
remains.

of the Eastern Goths was doubtless very similar; also that the Western Goths were allowed by Valens to cross over the Danube into Moesia, at a time when the Eastern Goths remained behind. Morris proceeds to call attention to the marked distinction between German and all other Teutonic languages as regards the use of many consonants. 'Thus a *d* in English corresponds to a *t* in German, as *dance* and *tanz*; *day* and *tag*; *deep* and *tief*; *drink* and *trink*.' But there is no such difference between English and Gothic, which has *dag-s* for *day*; *diup-s* for *deep*; and *drigkan* (i. e. *drinkan*) for *to drink*. Still more curious is the resemblance between Gothic and English in certain phrases, such as *Ik im thata daur*, I am that (the) door; *hardu ist thata waurd*, hard is that word; *hweitos swe snaiws*, white as snow. It follows that the acquirement of some knowledge of Gothic is, for an Englishman, rather an easy matter; and, considering the great philological importance of the language, especially in matters of etymology and phonetic change, few linguistic studies are more remunerative. It may, however, be here remarked that many English words have substituted *r* for a more primitive *s*, which the Gothic has retained; good examples appear in the words *auso*, an ear; *basi*, a berry; *hausjan*, to hear; *hazjan* (for *hasjan*), answering to Chaucer's *herien*, to praise; *laisjan*, answering to A.S. *læran*, M.E. *leren*, to teach; *wasjan*, to clothe, allied to E. *wear*.

GRAMMAR.

§ 10. THE ALPHABET.

It has already been shown that the forms of the Gothic letters were imitated from various letters of the Greek and Latin alphabets. We also find that the Gothic letters were

used (as in Greek) with a numerical value; this enables us
to determine their alphabetical order. Some of the letters
are variously represented by modern editors, as will be
explained presently. The following is a table of the cha-
racters (col. 1); with their equivalents in the editions (col. 2);
their originals (col. 3); and their numerical values (col. 4).

1.	2.	3.	4.	1.	2.	3.	4.
`𐌰`	a	A	1	`𐌽`	n	N	50
`𐌱`	b	B	2	`𐌾`	j (y)	G*	60
`𐌲`	g	Γ	3	`𐌿`	u	U*†	70
`𐌳`	d	Δ	4	`𐍀`	p	Π	80
`𐌴`	e	E	5	`𐍂`	r	R*	100
`𐌵`	kw (kv, q)	U*	6	`𐍃`	s	S*	200
`𐌶`	z	Z	7	`𐍄`	t	T	300
`𐌷`	h	Η*	8	`𐍅`	w (v), y	Υ	400
`𐌸`	th (þ)	Φ	9	`𐍆`	f	F*	500
`𐌹`	i	I	10	`𐍇`	ch (x)	X	600
`𐌺`	k	K	20	`𐍈`	hw (hv, w, wh)	Θ	700
`𐌻`	l	Λ	30	`𐍉`	o	ϒ†	800
`𐌼`	m	M	40				

Remarks. *Col.* 1. The symbol ï is only used when the vowel
begins a word or a syllable. This use is peculiar to Gothic.

Col. 2. German editors write *v* for *w*, and consequently *kv, hv,* for
kw, hw. For *kw* some (including Stamm) write *q,* in order to obtain
a symbol expressed by a *single* character.

For *th,* many editors use the thorn-letter (þ). Here again, the object
is to obtain a single character; and there is a faint objection to the use
of *th* from the fact that a few words contain *t* and *h* (separate letters) in
juxta-position. Examples of this are seen in *athabaidedun* (10. 35),[1]
athaffan (15. 36), *athaihait* (3. 13); but an extremely slight acquaint-
ance with the language will enable any reader to recognise in such

---

[1] See note 1 on p. xxxix.

words the fact that *at-* is the usual prefix. Englishmen are quite accustomed to this second signification of *th*, as e. g. in *malthouse, left-handed*, and *Greatheart*.

For *j*, Dr. Bosworth and Mr. Cockayne write *y*, which certainly expresses the sound; but this English symbol has been so little used for the purpose that the German *j* is perhaps better. Added to which, the letter *y* is required to express the Gothic Ⅴ when it occurs, in a few rare instances, as a *vowel*. Examples are seen in *Tyre* (7. 24), *spyrei-dans* (8. 8), *Iairusaulyma* (11. 11).

For *ch*, some write *x*, as being a *single* symbol.

For *hw* Gabelentz writes *w*, as being a *single* symbol; but this is very unsatisfactory. Dr. Bosworth writes *wh*, as in modern English, but it is far better to use the A.S. *hw*, with which we may compare the Icelandic and Swedish *hv*. His sole objection to the use of *hw* is that *h* and *w* are separate letters in the word *hwssopo*, hyssop; but as (in common with the German editors) I denote the vowel-sound of Ⅴ by *y*, and write *hyssopo*, this objection altogether disappears.

The system of transliteration adopted in this book, and in my Mœso-Gothic Glossary (1868), precisely agrees with that adopted by Massmann, except in the use of *w, hw*, and *kw* for his *v, hv*, and *kv*. This one change was worth making, for *w, hw*, and *kw* represent the probable sound of the Gothic letters.

Col. 3. The letters in this column are Greek capital letters, with the exception of those marked *, which are Latin. Of the 25 Gothic letters, 18 are Greek, and 7 are Latin. The symbols for *kw, th, hw* are arbitrarily chosen, and have purely conventional values. The Gothic **h** obviously answers rather to the form of **h** than of **H**. The symbols for *u* and *o*, marked † above, are purposely *inverted*, as if to mark some slight difference in the sound.

Col. 4. We have examples of the *numerical* use of the symbols in Mark iv. 8, where ·l· stands for 30, ·j· for 60, and ·r· for 100. The number 90 was denoted by a symbol resembling the Greek *koppa*, like the sign for *kw* with the second stroke lengthened; and 900 by a sign resembling a barbed arrow-head, which took the place of the Greek *sampi*.

SOUNDS.

§ 11. VOWELS.

The exact sounds of all the Gothic vowels and diphthongs are not known with absolute certainty; but from observation of the Gothic spelling of Greek and Latin words and by help of comparative philology their approximate values have been sufficiently ascertained. An account of them may be found in Mr. Ellis's Early English Pronunciation, p. 561, which is based upon the researches of Grimm, Rapp, Gabelentz and Löbe, and Weingärtner; but this account does not take into consideration the varying values of *ai* and *au*, as pointed out by Grimm, nor the probable variation in the sounds of *b* and *d*. I have therefore preferred to follow the account in the excellent *Gotische Grammatik* by W. Braune (Halle, Niemeyer, 1880). The following are the most probable values of the Gothic vowels and diphthongs, with examples, and key-words from English, German, and French.

VOWELS.	KEY-WORDS.	EXAMPLES.
a	*as in* man (German)	hana (*a cock*).

Note. This vowel is very common, and is generally *short*. But in a very few cases it is *long*, and has then the full sound of *a* in *father*. The only instances in St. Mark's Gospel which I have noticed are the following: *bráhtedun* (put for *branhtedun**), 11. 7, 12. 4, 15. 1; *gafáhith* (put for *gafanhith**), 9. 18; *faurcháh* (put for *faurahanh**), 15. 38; *spaikulátur*, 6. 27; and the proper name *Peilátus*.

| ai (*long*) | *as* i *in* bite | bait (*I bit*). |
| ai (*short*) | „ e „ there | bairan (*to bear*). |

Note. The usual and normal sound is the *long* sound, sometimes written *ái* to distinguish from the other, though there are no accents in the MSS. The *short* sound occurs in the *first* syllable of reduplicated verbs, as *hai-hald*, I held (*pronounced* hay-hald, with the accent on the second syllable), or is otherwise due to 'breaking,' explained below (§ 13, group 2), and only occurs when the following letter is *r* or *h* (or *hw*). The occurrence of the *r* or *h* is accordingly the simplest test for it, but there are a very few exceptions, only to be explained by etymology. Examples of the long *ai* before *h* occur in *aihtedun*, 12. 23; *haihamma*, 9. 47; and before *r* in *air* (pronounced as E. *ire*), 1. 35.

| au (*long*) | *as* ou *in* house | kaus (*I chose*). |
| au (*short*) | „ o „ fore | faura (*before*). |

Note. The normal sound is the *long* sound, sometimes written *áu*. The short sound is due to 'breaking' (see above) before *r* and *h* (or *hw*). The exceptions in the latter case are very rare; but we may notice the long *au* in *gaurs*, 3. 5, *hauh*, 9. 2 (A.S. *héah*), *bi-tauh*, 6. 6, *us-tauh*, 1. 12.

VOWELS.			KEY-WORDS.	EXAMPLES.
e	*as* ey *in*		they	wesun (*were*).
ei	„ e „		eve	weis (*we*).
i	„ i „		fill [1]	ist (*is*).
iu	{ *as* e *in* eve, *closely followed by* u *in* full; *the stress being on* i. }			niun (*nine*).
o	*as* o *in*		home	fotus (*foot*).
u	„ ou „		full [1]	sunus (*son*).
y	„ i „		fill	Tyra (Tyre).

The last of these is not a true Gothic letter, being only used in Greek words, where it takes the place of Gk. *v. Tyra* occurs in 3. 8.

The following is an *approximate* table of sounds for those who are acquainted only with English pronunciation. The pronunciation given in parentheses is the nearest that can be expressed in English letters as pronounced in Southern English.

a	*as in*		ask (short)	hana (hăhnăh).
ai (*long*)	*as* i	*in*	bite	bait (bite).
ai (*short*)	„ a	„	bare	bairan (bare-ăhn).
au (*long*)	„ ou	„	house	kaus (kouse).
au (*short*)	„ o	„	fore	faura (for-ăh).
e	„ a	„	fate	wesun (way-sŏŏn).
ei	„ e	„	eve	weis (weece).
i	„ i	„	fill	ist (ist).

---

[1] *I* and *u* are usually *short*; in a few cases they are *long*; see § 13 below, pp. xxix. and xxx.

VOWELS.			KEY-WORDS.	EXAMPLES.
iu	*as* chu *in*		Jehu (*nearly*) [1]	niun (nee′-ŏŏn).
o	„ o „		home	fotus (foa-tŏŏs).
u	„ u „		full	sunus (sŏŏ-nŏŏs)
y	„ i „		fill	Tyra (Tirrăh).

Stress. The stress or accent falls upon the vowel or diphthong of the syllable which contains the root of the word. In the opening verses of St. Mark's Gospel we may notice *anastódcins, gamélith, insándja, meínana, wópjandins, usíddjedun.*

§ 12. CONSONANTS.

b at the beginning of a word, or when occurring as the latter of two consonants, has the sound of Eng. *b*, as in *beitan*, to bite, *arbi*, heritage. But when it occurs after a vowel (especially if between two vowels) it most likely had the sound of *v*. For example, the pl. of *hlaifs*, a loaf, is *hlaibos* ; cf. E. *loaves* as the pl. of *loaf*. Other examples occur in the weak adj. *liuba*, dear (allied to E. *lief*, comp. *lievcr*), *graban*, to dig (E. *grave*), *haban*, to have, *liban*, to live, *biraubon*, to bereave, *sibun*, seven, *skaban*, to shave ; so also *gebum*, we gave, pl. of *gaf*, I gave.

ch is a foreign (Greek) letter, only occurring in the word *Christus*, Christ. We may pronounce it with the *k*-sound, as in English.

d at the beginning of a word, or when occurring as the latter of two consonants, has the sound of the Eng. *d*, as in *daur*, door, *hund*, hound. But when it occurs after a vowel (especially if between two vowels), it most likely had the sound of Eng. voiced *th* in *thou*. For example, the gen. of

---

[1] Rather as *Jé-u*, without any sound of *h* or *y* between the two vowels. The sound of *ew* in *dew* would put the stress on the wrong vowel.

haubiths, head, is *haubidis*; where the voiced *th*-sound in the genitive answers to the voiceless *th*-sound in the nominative.

g is hard as in *gate* ; never soft as in *gem*.

gg is written, after the Greek fashion, for *ng*; thus *laggs*, long, is to be pronounced *langs* (with *a* as in Ger. *lang*).

gk (for which *ggk* is sometimes written) is similarly put for *nk* ; as in *drigkan* or *driggkan*, to drink, which is to be pronounced *drinkan*.

h, when initial, is like E. *h* in *he*, when fully aspirated ; it must also be sounded in the combinations *hl, hn, hr*. But in words like *bráhta*, he brought, the *h* has a strong guttural sound, like that of *ch* in Ger. *dach* or the Scotch *loch*.

hw is like the South Welsh *chw*, or as *wh* is sounded in Scotland and the North of England.

j is the Eng. *y* in *yet*.

kw is the Eng. *qu* in *queen* ; like the A. S. *cw*.

r is the Eng. *r* in *ray*, and should be trilled.

s is generally said to be voiceless as in *sin* ; never voiced, as in Eng. *as, is, rise*; and this is doubtless true in most instances. But there are obvious exceptions in such words as *dags, gards, liubs*, where it can more easily be pronounced as *z*. It readily passes into *z* between two vowels, the genitive of *dius*, a wild beast, being written *diuzis*. Compare also such spellings as *hwazuh* (compounded of *hwas* and *uh*) ; *thizos*, fem. of *this*, gen. of the def. article. So also in *huzds*, a hoard, *azgo*, ashes, *mizdo*, meed, *s* readily becomes *z* before *d* and *g*.

th is (probably) the Eng. voiceless *th* in *thin* in all cases, and is a very common letter, especially in the termination -*ths*, where the *s* is voiceless, and the voiced sound of *th* (as in E. *thou*) would be difficult. Moreover, it never occurs in combination with any of the voiced consonants *b, d,* or *g*.

In instances where the voiced sound might be expected, we find the word spelt with *d*; see remarks upon *d* above.

The remaining consonants, viz. *f, k, l, m, n, p, t, w,* and *z* present no difficulty, being pronounced as in modern English. In the combinations *wl, wr,* the *w* is to be sounded.

PHONOLOGY.

§ 13. VOWELS.

General Remarks. The general relation to each other of the Gothic vowels may be to some extent exhibited in the following scheme.

Original vowels . .	*a*	*i*	*u*
Lengthenings . .	*o, e*	*ei* (*í*)	*iu* (*ú*)
Diphthongs . .		*ai*	*au*

The vowels *i* and *u* are not always original, and in such a case they are weakened forms of the vowel *a*. This appears from the conjugation of such verbs as *bindan,* the past tense of which is *band* in the first and third person singular, whilst the plural is *bundum, bunduth,* or *bundun* according to the person. That the most original form of the stem [1] is BAND, is ascertained by comparative philology ; compare, for example, the Sanskrit form *bandh.* It follows from this, that the stems *bind-* and *bund-* are weakened forms of *band-*.

The most convenient order for considering the vowel-symbols is to discuss each of the above columns separately, viz. (1) *a, o, e*; (2) *i, ei, ai*; and (3) *u, iu, au.*

Group 1. The vowels *a, o, e.*

a. This vowel, which in Gothic is usually *short,* may be considered as an original vowel, and it occurs with much

---

[1] By the 'stem' I meant the part of the word which is left when divested of the suffixes *-an, -um,* &c.

greater frequency than either *i* or *u*. It is extremely common in the pt. t. singular of strong verbs, as in *brak*, I broke, *gaf*, I gave, *draggk*, I drank, belonging to the conjugations numbered 3, 4, and 5 respectively; see the account of Strong Verbs in § 34, p. lviii.

The long sound of *a* is simply due to the loss of a succeeding nasal sound, as in *hāhan* (for *hanhan**, E. *hang*), to suspend; or else the word is foreign, as *spaikulātur*.

o. This vowel, in Gothic, is *always long*, and may be considered as the usual lengthened form of *a*, and derived from it. The pt. t. of *drag-an*, to draw (from a base DRAG), is *drog*; see Strong Verbs, Conj. 2, in § 34. *Fidur-dogs*, on the fourth day, is a derivative from *fidwor*, four, and *dags*, a day. *Gibos* is the genitive of *giba*, a gift. As to the length of *o*, compare Goth. *brothar*, brother, with Lat. *frāter*, Skt. *bhrátar*. For further examples, &c., the reader may consult Helfenstein's Comparative Grammar of the Teutonic languages.

We sometimes find *u* (long) written for *o*, as in *uhtedun* for *ohtedun* (11. 32). Also, *o* is closely allied to *au*; see *au*, in **Group 3**, p. xxxi.

e. This vowel, in Gothic, is *always long*, like *o*, and it appears, in like manner, as a lengthened form of *a*, from which it is derived. Thus the plural of *ik brak*, I broke, is *weis brekum*, we broke; and of *ik gaf*, I gave, is *weis gebum*, we gave; see Strong Verbs, Conj. 3 and 4, in § 34, p. lviii. The close relationship between *o* and *e* appears again in the reduplicating verb *tek-an*, to touch, of which the pt. t. is *tai-tok*; and in other similar instances. See § 33, p. liv.

e is also closely related to Goth. *ei*, as appears from *weisum*, occurring as an occasional spelling of *wesum*, we were; &c. See *ei* in **Group 2**, p. xxix. And in at least one instance it appears as a variant of *ai*, viz. in *taihun-tehund*, written for *taihun-taihund*, a hundred.

Group 2. i. This vowel is commonly *short*, but occasionally *long*; it occurs both as an original vowel and as a weakened form of *a*. As an original (short) vowel, it is less common than *a*, but commoner than *u*. It is original in *fisks*, a fish; cf. Lat. *piscis*. Also in strong verbs belonging to Conj. 6, in which it is the fundamental vowel. As a weakened form of *a*, the short *i* is common, as in *giban*, to give, of which the pt. t. is *gaf*; and a singular instance appears in Goth. *im*, I am, as compared with E. *am*.

i is sometimes written for *ei* or *e*, in which cases it is *long*. Thus *deigan*, to knead, is once written *digan*. Again, *azitizo* occurs for *azetizo* (10. 25). Finally, *i* is the vocalised form of *j*, as in *hari*, acc. of *harjis*, an army; see Strong Nouns (A-form), p. xxxviii.

ei. This is the usual form of long *i*, and may be considered as equivalent to *í*. This appears in *dreiban*, to drive, pt. t. pl. *drib-um*, pp. *drib-ans*, from the base DRIB; see Strong Verbs, Conj. 6, in § 34, p. lviii. Thus it often corresponds etymologically with E. long *i*, as in *dreiban*, to drive, *meins*, mine, *reisan*, to rise, *eisarn*, iron. In some cases, *ei* appears as equivalent to *ji*; compare *lag-jith*, he lies, with *sok-eith*, he seeks; see Weak Verbs, Class 1 (Exception), in § 35, p. lix. Here *ei = í = ii = ji*. We find *e* written for *ei* in *wehsa* (8. 26); *ize* (9. 1).

ai. This diphthong is of common occurrence, and has two distinct values, long (which may be marked *ái*), and short.[1] The long *ai* (*ái*) usually arises from an original *i*, as in *draib*, I drove, pt. t. of *dreiban*, to drive, from the stem DRIB, which is retained in the pt. t. pl. *drib-um* and the pp. *drib-ans*; see Strong Verbs, Conj. 6, in § 34, p. lviii. Other

---

[1] Some German writers express the true diphthongs by *ái* and *áu*, and those which arise from 'breaking' by *ai* and *au*, or simply *ai* and *au*.

examples occur in *hlaifs*, loaf, *skaidan*, to part, *maitan*, to cut, *hails*, whole, *dails*, a part, *laisjan*, to teach, &c. (The A. S. *á* generally corresponds to this diphthong, as in A. S. *stán*, a stone, Goth. *stains*; *dráf*, I drove, Goth. *draib*, as above.)

When *ái* occurs before a vowel, it passes into *aj*; thus from *bai*, both, is formed *baj-oths*, both, and from *aiws*, time, comes *ajukduths*, an age.

Breaking. The German term *brechung* (breaking) has been employed to express the fact, that when the consonants *h*, *hw*, or *r* directly succeed the *short* vowel *i* or *u*, they affect the purity of the pronunciation in such a manner as to draw the sound of *i* or *u* nearer to that of *a*, thus producing a kind of *e* or *o*. In this manner we obtain a new kind of *ai*, essentially *short*, and distinct in its origin from the true diphthong *ái*. The clearest examples occur in the conjugation of Strong Verbs (§ 34), where the vowel of the infinitive is properly *i* (as in Conj. 3, 4, 5). Thus, in Conj. 3, we have *ai* for *i* in *bair-an*, to bear, *ga-tair-an*, to tear, whilst at the same time *au* appears for *u* in the pp. *baur-ans*, *ga-taur-ans*. In Conj. 4, we have *ai* for *i* in *saihw-an*, to see, pp. *saihw-ans*. In Conj. 5, we have *ai* for *i*, and *au* for *u*, in *bairg-an*, to keep, protect, pp. *baurg-ans*; *bi-gaird-an*, to begird, pp. *bi-gaurd-ans*; *wairp-an*, to throw, pp. *waurp-ans*; *wairth-an*, to become, pp. *waurth-ans*. Compare also Goth. *wair*, a man, with Lat. *uir*. (The corresponding A. S. letter is commonly *e*, as in *beran*, to bear, *teran*, to tear, *séon*, to see, *wer*, a man; also *eo*, as in *beorgan*, to protect, *weorpan*, to throw, *weorðan*, to become.)

Group 3. u. This vowel is usually *short*, but occurs as *long* in a few instances. It is frequently a weakening of *a*, as in *bund-um*, we bound, pl. of *band*, I bound. It is less common as an original vowel than either *a* or *i*, but appears in *sunus*, a son, Sanskrit *súnu*; and it is the fundamental vowel of Strong Verbs of Conj. 7, appearing in the pt. t. pl. · and the pp. of such verbs. Examples are: *biug-an*, to bend, pp. *bug-ans*, Sanskrit *bhuj*, to bend; *giut-an*, to pour, pp. *gut-ans*, Lat. *fund-ere* (pt. t. *fud-i*), to pour. The *u* is long in *fuls*, foul (A. S. *fúl*); *hus*, house (A. S. *hús*); *rums*, a room (A. S. *rúm*); *runa*, a mystery (A. S. *rún*); *ut*, out (A. S. *út*). Also in *skura*, a shower, storm (4. 37; A. S. *scúr*).

iu. This diphthong takes, etymologically, the place of long *u*; thus *biug-an* = A. S. *búgan*, to bend, from the base BUG; see above.[1] It also occurs for *iw*, the *w* being vocalised to *u*; as in *kniu*, knee, gen. *kniw-is*, base KNIWA.

au. This diphthong (like *ai*) is both long and short; and the long form or true diphthong may be denoted by *áu*. The long *au* or *áu* commonly arises from an original *u*, as in *kaus*, I chose, pt. t. of *kius-an*, to choose, from the base KUS, which is retained in the pt. t. pl. *kus-um* and the pp. *kus-ans*; see Strong Verbs, Conj. 7, in § 34, p. lviii. (It answers to A. S. *éa*, as in *céas*, I chose, pt. t. of *céosan*, to choose.)

It becomes *aw* before the vowel *i*, as in *mawi*, a maiden, gen. *mau-jos*, base MAU-JO; *taw-ida*, pt. t. of *tau-jan*, to do.

In a very few cases it interchanges with *o*, as in *tojis*, gen. of *taui*, a deed; *stojan*, to judge, pt. t. *stauida*.

Breaking. The short diphthong *au*, when occurring before *h*, *hw*, or *r*, is commonly due to 'breaking'; see this explained under *ai*, in **Group 2.** Thus *dauhtar*, daughter, stands for *duh-tar**;[2] cf. Gk. θυγ-άτηρ. The occurrence of *h* or *r* after *au* is not an invariable test; for there are a few instances where *au* is then long, as in *hauhs*, high (A. S. *héah*).

---

[1] But corresponding A. S. words are much more commonly written with *éo*, as *céosan* (Goth. *kiusan*), *béodan* (Goth. *biudan*), &c.

[2] It is usual to mark with an asterisk all *theoretical* forms, such as *duhtar**.

Elision. We find occasional elisions, as in *thatist = that'ist*, short for *thata ist*, that is to say (7. 2); *nist = n'ist*, for *ni ist*, is not; *niba = n'iba*, for *ni iba*, if not, unless (3. 27). So, in the declension of the pronouns *sah* (= *sa'h = sa uh*) and *saei*, numerous elisions occur, as in the neut. *thatuh* for *thata uh*, *thatei* for *thata ei*.

Hiatus. This is not uncommon, as in *gaarman*, to pity, i. e. *ga-arman*, the vowels belonging to separate syllables (5. 19). So too *gaidreigou*, to repent (Luke 10. 13); where *ai = a-i*, two separate vowels, not a diphthong. The prefix *ga-* is so common, that no difficulty need hence arise.

§ 14. CONSONANTS.

The Gothic consonants are as follows.

Labials: *b, p, f*; *w*; *m*.

Dentals: *d, t, th*; *s, z*; *n*.

Linguals: *r, l*.

Palatal: *j*.

Gutturals: *g, k, h*; *kw, hw*; and the nasalised gutturals *gg* and *gk* (also written *ggk*).

According to the laws of sound-shifting usually called 'Grimm's Law,' the Aryan letters in row 1 below should correspond to the Gothic letters in row 2.

	LABIAL.	DENTAL.	GUTTURAL.
1. Aryan.	b p bh	d t dh	g k gh
2. Gothic.	p f b	t th d	k h g

To this law there are some exceptions, as below :—

Labials. p. There is no clear example of Aryan *b* = Goth. *p*. Gothic words beginning with *p* are very few, and of these most are borrowed from Greek. The etymology of the rest is doubtful.

f. Instead of Gothic *f*, we sometimes find *b*, as in *sibun*, seven; cf. Lat. *septem*. Gothic is sometimes uncertain in its use of *f* and *b*; thus *ik gaf*, I gave, is from *giban*, to give. The word for 'loaf' is both *hlaifs* and *hlaibs*. The pl. of *laufs*, a leaf, is *laubos* (11. 13; 13. 28). See p. xxv.

w. This letter is sometimes vocalised; *aw, iw,* inter-change with *au, iu.*

Dentals. d. A Gothic *d* sometimes appears where *th* might be expected, as in *fadar,* with which compare E. *father,* Lat. *pater.* There is some fluctuation in the use of *d* and *th*; thus *daupiths,* pp. of *daupjan,* to baptise, makes the pl. *daupidai,* not *daupithai*; and the gen. of *manaseths,* the world (14. 9) is *manasedais* (John, 8. 12); see p. xxv.

t. The Aryan *t* is unchanged in the combination *st*; compare Goth. *ist,* he is, with Lat. *est.* The suffix *-ta* replaces *-da* (for ease in pronunciation) in *brah-tedun,* brought (9. 17), *thaurf-ta,* was in need (2. 25); the same substitution is common in English, as in *brough-t, laugh-t.*

th. The interchange of *th* with *d* is noted above. An-other example occurs in *kun-tha,* pt. t. of *kunn-an,* to know; put for *kunn-da,** Middle Eng. *coude.*

s. This sibilant sometimes supplies the place of a dental. Thus *ana-bus-ns,* a commandment (7. 8) is from *ana-biud-an,* to command. The past tense of *wait,* I know, is *wissa* (9. 6); a curious form which has resulted from *wit-da**, changed to *wit-ta** and *wista**, and finally reduced to the form *wissa* by assimilation. Lastly, *s* appears for *th* in *kwast,* thou sayest (12. 32), put for *kwath-t.*

z. We find *z* substituted for *s* between two vowels; as in *ize,* of them, gen. pl. of *is,* he. The comparative suffix of adjectives is written *-iza,* put for *-isa.* It also appears occasionally in place of *s* at the end of a word, as in *aiz* (6. 8); and before *l* in *ga-sai-zlep* (John, 11. 11).

Palatal. The 'semi-vowel' *j,* as it is sometimes called, is often interchanged with *i*; and *ji* with *ei* (the lengthened form of *i*) ; see p. xxix. At the end of a word, *i* is put for *j* without exception.

Gutturals. g, k, h. Both *g* and *k* become *h* before a *t* following, in derivative words. Thus from *mag-an*, to be able, comes *mah-ts*, might; and from the strong verb *siuk-an*, to be sick (pt. t. *sauk*) comes the sb. *sauh-ts*, disease (1. 34).

kw, hw. These represent secondary sounds, due to labialised forms of *k* and *h*, so that they correspond, etymologically, to Aryan *g* and *k̟* respectively. Thus *kwiman*, to come, pt. t. *kwam* (from *kam**) corresponds to Sanskrit *gam*, to go; and *hwas*, who (from *has**) to Skt. *kas*, who.

gg, gk, ggk. These symbols are imitated from the Greek γγ, γκ, so that the first *g* is to be sounded as *n*. Goth. *laggs*=A.S. *lang*=E. *long*; Goth. *drigkan* or *driggkan*=A.S. *drincan*=E. *drink*; Goth. *figgrs*=E. *finger* (7. 33). It is remarkable that derivatives from these nasalised sounds are written with a simple *h*, which takes the place of *nh* by a change similar to that which puts *h* for *g* (see remarks on *g* above). Thus the pt. t. of *brigg-an*, to bring, is *brah-ta* (for *branh-ta**).

Assimilation. Assimilation is the substitution of a double consonant for two dissimilar consonants; as in the Italian *ammirare* (with *mm*) from Lat. *admirare* (with *dm*). It is not very common in Gothic, but we invariably find the prefix *us-* changed to *ur-* when an *r* follows, as in *ur-rann* (for *us-rann*) in Mark, 4. 3. The most remarkable instance of assimilation is in the case of final *h*, which before a word beginning with *th* is changed to *th*. Thus *wasuth-than* (1. 6) stands for *was-uh than*, i. e. 'and then was'; where *-uh* is an enclitic particle used like the Latin *-que*.

§ 15. SUBSTANTIVES.

Gender. There are three genders, masculine, feminine, and neuter. The gender is partly natural, as when the names of male beings are considered masculine; partly grammatical, as when *fotus*, foot, is masculine, and *handus*, hand, is feminine.

In some cases the termination is a guide to the gender;

thus nouns in -*a*, if *strong*, are feminine, if *weak*, are masculine. Nouns such as *waurd* (word) which are destitute of an inflection in the nominative, and nouns in -*u*, as *faih-u* (fee), are neuter. Nouns in -*is* or -*eis* are masculine. Nouns in -*ei* are feminine. Nouns in -*o* are mostly feminine; but there are notable exceptions, the principal being *hairt-o* (heart), *aug-o* (eye), *aus-o* (ear), *kaurn-o* (corn), *nam-o* (name), *wat-o* (water), all neuter. See the forms of declension.

Number. There are only two numbers, singular and plural. *Dual* forms appear among the pronouns only.

Case. There are, practically, only four cases, viz. nominative, genitive, dative, and accusative. Some *vocative* forms are found, but they are merely due to the loss of the nominative suffix -*s*, in such words as have that suffix ; moreover, they only appear in the singular number. In all other instances, the vocative is the same as the nominative. Examples of an *instrumental* case appear among the pronouns only.

Strong and Weak. Weak nouns are those which form their inflections with *n*, such as *han-a* (cock), gen. *han-ins*, pl. nom. *han-ans*. All others are strong.

Base. The *base* or *crude form*[1] of a substantive is the supposed original form of it, divested of the case-ending. To this base the case-ending has been added, after which the case has frequently suffered degradation, and appears in a weakened form. Thus the base FISKA signifies ' fish,' whence was formed the nom. *fiska-s*, afterwards contracted to *fisks*. The form of the base of a Gothic *strong* substan-

---

[1] Called *theme* in Helfenstein, Comparative Grammar of the Teutonic Languages. Some call it the *stem*, but it is convenient to restrict the word *stem* to the *first syllable* of a base, such as *fisk-*, to which the case-endings *appear* to be added in the paradigms of the declensions. A specific name for this first syllable is often required, and *stem* is the most convenient term for it ; see the definition of ' stem ' at p. xxvii.

tive can usually be determined by dropping the suffixed -*m* of the dative plural; that of a *weak* substantive by dropping the suffixed -*e* or -*o* of the genitive plural. The form of the base is important, because it is to the variation in the last letter of the base that the apparent differences of declension arise. Thus the difference between the accusative plurals *fisk-ans* and *balg-ins* is really due to the difference in the bases. The former may be considered as equivalent to *fiska-ns*, and the latter to *balgi-ns*, in which case the suffix -*ns* is really common to both. The bases of the various substantives are given below, and are printed in capital letters.

General Remarks. The following facts are worth observing.

1. Neuter substantives have the accusative and nominative alike, as in Latin and Greek, both in the singular and plural.

2. The genitive singular ends in -*s*, preceded by a vowel, a diphthong, *n*, or *r*.

3. The genitive plural ends in -*e* (-*iwe*, -*ane*, -*ne*) or in -*o* (-*ono*, -*eino*).

4. The dative plural ends in -*m*, suffixed to the base; but the final *n* of the base is dropped in weak nouns.

DECLENSIONS.

§ 16. I. Strong Declension.

There are three forms of declension, according as the base ends in -A, -I, or -U.

Note. There are some exceptional forms, which are best observed by practice. The following paradigms only exhibit the declensions of such words as are declined regularly.

(1) A-form.

Thus are declined masc. *fisks*, a fish (base FISKA); fem. *giba*, a gift (base GIBÂ, for which Gothic substitutes GIBO); and neut. *waurd*, a word (base WAURDA).

SINGULAR.		PLURAL.	
Nom.	fisk-*s*	*N. V.*	fisk-*os*
Gen.	fisk-*is*	*Gen.*	fisk-*e*
Dat.	fisk-*a*	*Dat.*	fisk-*am*
Acc.	fisk	*Acc.*	fisk-*ans*
Voc.	fisk		

So also *dags*, day, *fugls*, bird (fowl), *hlaifs*, loaf. *hunds*, hound, *laufs*, leaf, *stains*, stone, *wigs*, way, *wulfs*, wolf. *Hlaifs*, loaf, *laufs*, leaf, make the pl. *hlaibos, laubos* ; *thius*, servant, makes the pl. *thiwos*.

	SINGULAR.	PLURAL.		SINGULAR.	PLURAL.
N.A.V.	gib-*a*	gib-*os*	*N.A.V.*	waurd	waurd-*a*
Gen.	gib-*os*	gib-*o*	*Gen.*	waurd-*is*	waurd-*e*
Dat.	gib-*ai*	gib-*om*	*Dat.*	waurd-*a*	waurd-*am*

So also fem. *airtha*, earth, *hairda*, herd, *halba*, half, *saiwala*, soul ; neut. *agis*, awe, *ahs*, ear of corn, *akran*, fruit, *barn*, child, *bloth*, blood, *daur*, door, *gulth*, gold, *haurn*, horn, *jer*, year, *juk*, yoke, &c.

Remarks. Masculine bases in -SA form the nom. sing. by merely dropping the final vowel of the base. Thus the base HALSA, neck, has the nom. sing. *hals* (not *halsas*); so also nom. sing. *ans*, a beam (not *ansas*).

Similarly, masc. bases in -RA merely drop the final vowel of the base ; as in *wair*, a man. from the base WAIRA ; *stiur*, a steer, from the base STIURA But if another consonant precedes -*r*, the formation is regular, as in *akrs*, an acre or field, from the base AKRA.

Some masculines have a stem ending in -JA. The nom. sing. is formed by adding -*s* to the weakened stem -JI, whilst the acc. and vocative singular have the final -*j* vocalised to -*i*. Moreover, the nom. sing. suffix -*jis* is altered to -*eis* when a long syllable or more than one syllable precedes it. The plural is regular. Examples are *harjis*, an army, base HARJA, and *hairdeis*, a herd, shepherd, base HAIRDJA ; which are thus declined.

	SINGULAR.		PLURAL.	
Nom.	harj-*is*	haird-*eis*	harj-*os*	hairdj-*os*
Gen.	harj-*is*	haird-*eis*	harj-*e*	hairdj-*e*
Dat.	harj-*a*	hairdj-*a*	harj-*am*	hairdj-*am*
Acc.	hari	haird	harj-*ans*	hairdj-*ans*
Voc.	hari	haird	(as nom.)	(as nom.)

Neuter bases in -JA have a similar declension, but observe the rule of making the nom. like the accusative. Hence *kuni*, kin, base KUNJA, and *andbahti*, service, base ANDBAHTJA, make the nom. and acc. sing. *kuni, andbahti*; gen. *kunj-is, andbaht-eis*, dat. *kunj-a, andbahtj-a*.

So also *badi*, bed ; *nati*, net, &c.

The fem. stem THIUJÂ, a maiden, gives the nom. sing. *thiwi*. Here *thiwi = thiuj-*, the suffix -*â* (*o*) being dropped.

Similarly, when stems end in -WA, the *w* is vocalised to *u*. From the masc. stem THIWA, a servant, are formed nom. *thiu-s*, acc. voc. *thiu*, the gen. *thiw-is* and dat. *thiw-a* being regular. From the neut. stem KNIWA, knee, are formed nom. acc. *kniu*, gen. *kniw-is*, dat. *kniw-a*. But if a diphthong or a long vowel precedes *w*, the *w* remains ; as in masc. *saiws*, sea, acc. *saiw*, from the base SAIWA.

§ 17. I-form.

Thus are declined masc. *balgs*, bag, base BALGI ; fem. *ansts*, grace, base ANSTI. (There are no neuters.)

	SINGULAR.	PLURAL.	SINGULAR.	PLURAL.
Nom.	balg-*s*	balg-*eis*	anst-*s*	anst-*eis*
Gen.	balg-*is*	balg-*e*	anst-*ais*	anst-*e*
Dat.	balg-*a*	balg-*im*	anst-*ai*	anst-*im*
Acc.	balg	balg-*ins*	anst	anst-*ins*
Voc.	balg		anst	

So also masc. *arms*, arm, *barms*, bosom, *gards*, house (yard), *bruth-faths*, bridegroom ; fem. *mahts*, might, *kwens*, woman, *taikns*, token, &c. As before, stems in -SI and -RI form the nom. sing. by merely dropping the final vowel of the base. Exx. fem. *garuns*, a market-place, base GARUNSI ; masc. *baur*, a child, base BAURI.

The fem. *haims*, a village, base HAIMI, forms its plural as if it belonged to the A-form. Hence the pl. *haim-os* (6. 56).[1]

Other exceptional forms appear in fem. *baurgs*, a town, gen. *baurg-s*, dat. acc. *baurg*; pl. nom. acc. *baurg*, gen. *baurg-e*, dat. *baurg-im*. Observe also fem. *mitaths*, a measure, dat. *mitath* (4. 24), not *mitath-ai*; fem. *alhs*, a temple, gen. *alhs* (15. 38), dat. *alh* (12. 35); fem. *nahts*. night, dat. *naht* (4. 27), dat. pl. *nahtam* (5. 5).

§ 18.   U-form.

Thus are declined masc. *sunus*, son, base SUNU ; fem. *hand-us*, hand, base HANDU ; neut. *faihu*, property (fee), base FAIHU.   The feminine sbs. are declined precisely like the masculine ; and the neuter sbs. only differ in the nom. and acc. singular.   The plural form of neuters of this declension is not found; hence only the singular is given.

	SINGULAR.	PLURAL.	SINGULAR.
Nom.	sun-*us*	sun-*jus*	faih-*u*
Gen.	sun-*aus*	sun-*iwe*	faih-*aus*
Dat.	sun-*au*	sun-*um*	faih-*au*
Acc.	sun-*u*	sun-*uns*	faih-*u*
Voc.	sun-*u*		

So also masc. *airus*, messenger, *skadus*, shadow, *wintrus*, winter, *fotus*, foot, &c. An exceptional form appears in the acc. *handau* (7. 32), as this is really the dat. form.

§ 19.   Bases in -ar.

Brothar, brother, *fadar*, father, *dauhtar*, daughter, *swistar*, sister, are declined according to the following scheme. (The Gothic for ' mother ' is *aithei*.)

---

[1] References such as this, between marks of parenthesis, are to the chapter and verse of *St. Mark's Gospel*, unless some other book of the Bible is distinctly mentioned.

	SINGULAR.	PLURAL.
Nom.	brothar	brothr-*jus*
Gen.	brothr-*s*	brothr-*e*
Dat.	brothr	brothr-*um*
Acc.	brothar	brothr-*uns*

§ 20. Bases in -nda.

From some verbs are formed substantives, which were originally present participles. Thus *gibands*, a giver, base GIBANDA, is obviously the pres. part. of *giban*, to give. A few are formed from weak verbs in *-on*, of which the most remarkable is *frijonds*, friend, originally the pres. part. of *frijon*, to love. Such sbs. are declined according to the following scheme.

Nom.	giband-*s*	giband-*s*
Gen.	giband-*is*	giband-*e*
Dat.	giband	giband-*am*
Acc.	giband	giband-*s*

So also *daupjands*, baptist, *fijands*, enemy, &c.

§ 21. II. Weak or Consonantal Declension.

In this declension, the base invariably ends in *-n*. The vocative has no peculiar form, but resembles the nominative. Typical examples are those of masc. *hana*, a cock, base HANAN; fem. *tuggo* (pronounced *tungo*), tongue, base TUGGON, and *managei*, multitude, base MANAGEIN; neut. *hairto*, heart, base HAIRTAN, and *wato*, water, base WATAN.

A. Masculine.

Nom.	han-*a*	han-*ans*
Gen.	han-*ins*	han-*ane*
Dat.	han-*in*	han-*am*
Acc.	han-*an*	han-*ans*

So also *guma*, man, *mena*, moon, *sunna*, sun, &c.

B. Feminine.

	SINGULAR.	PLURAL.
Nom.	tugg-*o*	tugg-*ons*
Gen.	tugg-*ons*	tugg-*ono*
Dat.	tugg-*on*	tugg-*om*
Acc.	tugg-*on*	tugg-*ons*
Nom.	manag-*ei*	manag-*eins*
Gen.	manag-*eins*	manag-*eino*
Dat.	manag-*ein*	manag-*eim*
Acc.	manag-*ein*	manag-*eins*

So also *gatwo*, street, *stairno*, star, &c. ; *aithei*, mother, *marei*, sea, &c.

C. Neuter.

Nom. Acc.	hairt-*o*	hairt-*ona*
Gen.	hairt-*ins*	hairt-*ane*
Dat.	hairt-*in*	hairt-*am*
Nom. Acc.	wat-*o*	wat-*na*
Gen.	wat-*ins*	wat-*ne*
Dat.	wat-*in*	wat-*nam*

Like *hairto* are declined *augo*, eye, *auso*, ear, *kaurno*, grain, &c.

Remarks. Weak substantives may generally be known by the ending of the nom. sing. in -*a*, -*o*, or -*ei*. The only exception is in the case of strong *feminine* substantives of the A-form, such as *giba*, gift ; and even these may be distinguished by observing the *gender*; since all weak substantives in -*a* are masculine.

The dat. pl. *watnam* (short for *watan-am*) preserves the *n* of the base, which is lost in *hairt-am*, dat. pl. of *hairto*. There is only one other neuter sb. which is declined like *wato*, viz. *namo*, name, stem NAMAN; dat. pl. *nam-nam*. We also find dat. pl. *ab-nam*, from the *masculine* sb. *aba*, man.

The declension of weak substantives is, in general, very regular. The only examples of irregularity occur in the two following words. Masc. *manna*, man, bases MAN and MANNAN, is thus declined.

	SINGULAR.	PLURAL.
Nom.	mann-*a*	mann-*ans*, man-*s*
Gen.	man-*s*	mann-*e*
Dat.	mann ·	mann-*am*
Acc.	mann-*an*	mann-*ans*, man-*s*

Neut. *fon*, fire, is only found in the singular (9. 22). *Nom. and acc.* fon ; *gen.* fun-*ins* ; *dat.* fun-*in* (9. 47, 49).

§ 22. ADJECTIVES.

Adjectives have three genders and two numbers, like substantives ; and have also a double form of declension, strong and weak. It is important to know under what circumstances these are used.

1. The *strong* declension is employed when the adjective is used either without the definite article, or alone. So also are declined the possessive pronouns, and nearly all demonstrative pronouns, except *sama*, same, *silba*, self ; all cardinal numbers ; the ordinal *anthar*, second ; and the words following, viz. *alls*, all, *fulls*, full, *ganohs*, enough, *halbs*, half, *midjis*, middle, *sums*, some, *swaleiks*, such.

2. The *weak* declension is used whenever the definite article is used (with or without a substantive) ; also for some adjectives used almost with the force of substantives, such as *unkarja*, a careless person (4. 15), *usfilma*, an amazed man (1. 22). So also the pronouns *sama*, same, *silba*, self ; all ordinals, except *anthar*, second (which is strong), and *frumists*, first (both strong and weak); a few *old* superlatives, such as *aftuma*, last (10. 31), *fruma*, first (15. 42), *iftuma*, next, the morrow (11. 12) ; *hleiduma*, left (10. 37). So also all present participles, with the exception of the nom. sing., which often has the strong form.

§ 23. I. STRONG DECLENSION.

A-form.

Blind-s, blind, base BLINDA, is thus declined.

SINGULAR.

	Masc.	*Fem.*	*Neut.*
Nom.	blind-*s*	blind-*a*	blind, blind-*ata*
Gen.	blind-*is*	blind-*aizos*	blind-*is*
Dat.	blind-*amma*	blind-*ai*	blind-*amma*
Acc.	blind-*ana*	blind-*a*	blind, blind-*ata*

PLURAL.

	Masc.	*Fem.*	*Neut.*
Nom.	blind-*ai*	blind-*os*	blind-*a*
Gen.	blind-*aize*	blind-*aizo*	blind-*aize*
Dat.	blind-*aim*	blind-*aim*	blind-*aim*
Acc.	blind-*ans*	blind-*os*	blind-*a*

Bases in -JA show similar forms; Exx. *midj-aim*, dat. pl. (9. 36); *unsibj-aim*, dat. pl. (15. 28); *airzj-ai*, nom. pl. (12. 24). So also bases in -WA, as *faw-aim*, dat. pl. (6. 5); *kwiw-aize*, gen. pl. (12. 27), from the nom. sing. masc. *kwius-s*, where the *w* is vocalised to *u*. *Th* and *f* pass into *d* and *b*; thus the gen. of *froths*, wise, is *frod-is*; and that of *liufs*, dear, is *liub-is*.

§ 24. I-form.

There are but slight traces of bases in -I, but we may notice *gamainj-aim*, dat. pl. (7. 2) from the base GAMAINI; *authj-ana*, acc. sing. masc. (1. 35), from the base AUTHI. Here, as usual, *i* becomes *j* before another vowel.

§ 25. U-form.

Hardu-s, hard, base HARDU, is thus declined.

SINGULAR.

	Masc.	*Fem.*	*Neut.*
Nom.	hard-*us*	hard-*us*	hard-*u*, hardj-*ata*
Gen.	hardj-*is*	hardj-*aizos*	hardj-*is*
Dat.	hardj-*amma*	hardj-*ai*	hardj-*amma*
Acc.	hardj-*ana*	hardj-*a*	hard-*u*, hardj-*ata*

The plural is hardj-*ai̇́, -os, -a*; &c.

This resembles *blinds* except in the nominative, in the acc. neuter, and in the introduction of the *j*.

Not many adjectives are of this form; we may note *aglu*, nom. sing. neut. (10. 24); *thlakwus*, nom. sing. masc. (13. 28); *manwjata*, acc. sing. neut. (14. 15).

§ 26. II. WEAK DECLENSION.

This declension agrees with that of the three substantives *hana* (masc.), *luggo* (fem.), and *hairto* (neut); see § 21, p. xl. Hence it is as follows. *Sa blinda*, the blind; used with the article.

SINGULAR.

	Masc.	Fem.	Neut.
Nom.	blind-*a*	blind-*o*	blind-*o*
Gen.	blind-*ins*	blind-*ons*	blind-*ins*
Dat.	blind-*in*	blind-*on*	blind-*in*
Acc.	blind-*an*	blind-*on*	blind-*o*

PLURAL.

	Masc.	Fem.	Neut.
Nom.	blind-*ans*	blind-*ons*	blind-*ona*
Gen.	blind-*ane*	blind-*ono*	blind-*ane*
Dat.	blind-*am*	blind-*om*	blind-*am*
Acc.	blind-*ans*	blind-*ons*	blind-*ona*

We may note a trace of the U-form in the weak declension in the introduction of the *j* in *laushandjan*, acc. sing. masc. (12. 3), as if from a base LAUS-HANDU.

Note.—But adjectives in the comparative degree, and present participles (which, as observed above, are usually strong in the nom. sing. masc.) form their feminines in -*ei*, following the declension of *managei*, not of *luggo*; see p. xli.

§ 27. Degrees of Comparison.

The comparative degree is formed by adding -*iza*, or occasionally -*oza* (Eng. -*er*) to the stem. Comparatives follow the weak declension, but have their feminines in *-ei*, not *-o*. Examples are *hard-iza*, hard-er, *blind-oza*, blind-er; *sut-izo*, nom. neut. sing. (6. 11). The corresponding adverbial suffixes are *-is*, *-os*, see § 39.

The superlative degree is formed by adding the suffix *-ist* (really a double suffix *-is-ta*) to the stem; and follows both declensions. Examples are *blind-ists*, blind-est, *sa blind-ista*, the blind-est; *this hauh-ist-ins*, of the highest (5. 7). The strong neuter ends in *-ist*, not *-istata*, which is too long.

The following are irregular in their comparison :—

gods, batiza, batists	good, better, best.
ubils, wairsiza, (wairsists ?)	evil, worse, worst.
mikils, maiza, maists	mickle, more, most.
leitils, minniza, minnists	little (less, least).
{ sineigs, altheis, } aldiza, sinista	old, older (oldest).
juggs, juhiza, ...	young, younger, ...

A few old superlatives exhibit the Aryan suffix -MA; cf. Lat. *pri-mus*, first. Examples are *fru-ma*, first, *innu-ma*, inmost. A few others exhibit the Aryan suffix -TA-MA; cf. Lat. *op ti-mus*, best. This is weakened in Gothic to *-tuma* or *-duma*, and the superlative sense is sometimes lost. Examples are *af-tuma*, last, *if-tuma*, next, *hin-duma*, hindmost, *hlei-duma*, left (most on the left). The loss of the superlative sense gave rise to the further addition of *-ist*, as in *af-tum-ists*, last, *fru-m-ists*, first, *auhu-m-ists* highest, *hin-dum-ists*, hindmost. Here *af-tumists* really exhibits a quadruple suffix, composed of the Aryan -TA, -MA, -AS, and -TA. The English words *foremost, hindmost*, are, similarly, double superlatives, being corruptions of *fore-m-est*, *hind-m-est* due to confusion with *most*.

§ 28. Participles.

Present participles can be used as equivalent either to a substantive or an adjective. In the former case, the declension has been already exhibited under bases in -NDA, p. xl. In the latter case, it has already been explained that the nom. sing. masc. may be either strong or weak, and that otherwise they are declined (like comparatives) like the words *hana, managei,* and *hairto,* i. e. according to the weak declension; see p. xliv.

Past participles follow both declensions. Past participles of weak verbs, which terminate in -*iths,* change the *th* into *d* whenever a syllable is added; hence from *daup-iths,* pp. of *daupjan,* we have the nom. pl. masc. *daup-idai* (1. 5).

§ 29. Proper Names and Foreign words.

These are frequently undeclined; hence we find acc. *Kafarnaum* (2. 1); dat. *sabbato* (2. 28). Yet we find dat. pl. *sabbatim* (2. 24, 3. 4), gen. pl. *sabbate* (16. 1). Greek words frequently follow the Greek declension; hence gen. sing. *Galileias* (1. 9); acc. sing. *Andraian* (1. 16); *synagogen* (1. 21). Yet *synagogen* is also used as a dative (1. 29). We also find Gothic suffixes, as in *Satan-in* (1. 13). There is a good deal of uncertainty here in the author's method; as might be expected.

§ 30. NUMERALS.

Cardinals. The cardinal numbers are as follows:—

1. *ains.* 2. *twai.* 3. *threis.* 4. *fidwor.* 5. *fimf, fif.* 6. *saihs.* 7. *sibun.* 8. *ahtau.* 9. *niun.* 10. *taihun.* 11. *ainlif.* 12. *twalif.* 14. *fidwor-taihun.* 15. *fimf-taihun.* 20. *twai tigjus.* 30. *threis tigjus.* 40. *fidwor tigjus.* 50. *fimf tigjus.* 60. *saihs tigjus.* 70. *sibun-tehund.* 80. *ahtau-tehund.* 90. *niun-tehund.* 100. *taihun-tehund,* or *taihun-taihund.* 200. *twa hunda.* 300. *thrija hunda.* 500. *fimf hunda.* 900. *niun hunda.* 1000. *thusundi.*

Most of these are undeclined, except 1, 2, and 3. The declensions are as follows.

1. *ains* is declined in the singular as a strong adjective,

but when it means 'alone,' is weak. In the plural, it is declined strong, with the signification 'only' (Gk. μόνοι); hence dat. pl. *ainaim* (2. 26).

2. *Twai* is necessarily plural. It takes the following forms: nom. *twai, twos, twa*; gen. *twaddje*; dat. *twaim*; acc. *twans, twos, twa*.

3. *Threis* only occurs in the nom. in the neut. *thrija*. The gen. is *thrije*; dat. *thrim*; acc. masc. *thrins*, neut. *thrija*.

4. The dat. *fidworim* occurs (2. 3).

9. The gen. is *niune*.

11. The dat. is *ainlibim*.

12. The dat. is *twalibim* (4. 10), or *twalif*; gen. *twalibe* (5. 42). We may also note acc. *fidwor-tiguns* (1. 13); nom. *twos thusundjos* (5. 13); *fidwor-thusundjos* (8. 9), dat. *fidwor-thusundjom* (8. 20); &c.

Ordinals. Of these only the following occur:—

1st. *fruma*. 2nd. *anthar* (E. *other*); formed with a comparative suffix from a pronominal base ANA. 3rd. *thridja*. 6th. *saihsta*. 8th. *aihtada*. 9th. *niunda*. 10th. *taihunda*. 15th. *fimfta-taihunda*. All these follow the weak declension, with the exception of *anthar*.

Other numeral adjectives. 'Both' is expressed by masc. *bai*, dat. *baim*, acc. *bans*; neuter, nom. and acc. *ba*. Also by *bajoths* (Luke, 5. 38). The only distributive form is *tweihnai*, two apiece (Luke, 9. 3). Multiplicative forms are neut. *ain-falth*, one-fold, single; *fidur-falth*, fourfold; *managfalth*, many-fold; *taihun-taihund-falth*, a hundred-fold.

§ 31. PRONOUNS.

Personal. The personal pronouns of the first and second person are *ik*, I; *thu*, thou. Of these, dual forms are found, viz. *wit*, we two; *jut* (?), ye two. They are thus declined:—

	SINGULAR.	DUAL.	PLURAL.
Nom.	ik	wit	weis
Gen.	meina	ugkara	unsara
Dat.	mis	ugkis	unsis, uns
Acc.	mik	ugkis, ugk	unsis, uns

	SINGULAR.	DUAL.	PLURAL.
Nom.	thu	(jut?)	jus
Gen.	theina	igkwara	izwara
Dat.	thus	igkwis, iggkwis	izwis
Acc.	thuk	igkwis, iggkwis	izwis

A reflexive form of the third personal pronoun is used for all genders, in the oblique cases only. *Gen.* seina, *dat.* sis, *acc.* sik.

The third personal pronoun is *is, si, ita*, he, she, it. It is made up from two other pronouns, originally demonstrative; the Aryan base SYA being used for the nom. fem. sing. only, and the base ɪ for the rest. It is thus declined :—

	SINGULAR.	PLURAL.
Nom.	is, si, ita	eis, ijos, ija
Gen.	is, izos, is	ize, izo, ize
Dat.	imma, izai, imma	im, im, im
Acc.	ina, ija, ita	ins, ijos, ija

Possessive Pronouns. These are *meins*, mine, *theins*, thine, *seins*, his (reflexive); declined like strong adjectives. So also *unsar*, our, *izwar*, your, *seins*, their (reflexive).

There is one example of the dual form in Matt. 9. 29: 'bi galaubeinai *iggkwarai* wairthai iggkwis,' according to the faith of you two be it done unto you two.

Demonstrative Pronouns. The simple demonstrative pronoun is *sa, so, thata*, this, that ; also used as the definite article, and therefore in very frequent use. Cf. the A. S. article *se, séo, ðæt.*

SINGULAR.

	Masc.	Fem.	Neut.
Nom.	sa	so	thata
Gen.	this	thizos	this
Dat.	thamma	thizai	thamma
Acc.	thana	tho	thata
Inst.	the	the	the

PLURAL.

	Masc.	Fem.	Neut.
Nom.	thai	thos	tho
Gen.	thize	thizo	thize
Dat.	thaim	thaim	thaim
Acc.	thans	thos	tho

The instrumental case *the* occurs in the compounds *du-the* or *duth-the*, therefore, *bi-the*, whilst, *jath-the*, whether. Cf. A. S. ðȳ.

Sa is often followed by the enclitic particle *uh*, and is then contracted to *sah*. This is so common that the declension of *sah* is here given in full.

SINGULAR.

	Masc.	Fem.	Neut.
Nom.	sah	soh	thatuh
Gen.	thizuh	thizozuh	thizuh
Dat.	thammuh	thizaih	thammuh
Acc.	thanuh	thoh	thatuh

PLURAL.

	Masc.	Fem.	Neut.
Nom.	thaih	thozuh	thoh
Gen.	thizeh	thizoh	thizeh
Dat.	thaimuh	thaimuh	thaimuh
Acc.	thanzuh	thozuh	thoh.

From the demonstrative stem III, this, are formed the dat. sing. masc. and neut. *himma*, the accus. masc. *hina*, and the acc. neut. *hita*. These occur chiefly in such phrases as *himma*

d

daga, on this day, *und hina dag*, till this day, *und hita*, till now, *fram himma*, henceforth. Cf. E. *him, it* (A. S. *hit*).

Another demonstrative pronoun is *jains*, that (E. *yon*), declined like strong adjectives; the neut. sing. is *jain-ata*.

Sama, same, *silba*, self, are declined like weak adjectives.

Swaleiks, such, *swelauds*, such, are declined like strong adjectives.

Relative Pronouns. Relatives are formed by the addition of the particle *ei*, that, which is freely added to various pronouns. Hence we find *ik-ei*, I who, I that, *thu-ei*, thou who, thou that, *thuk-ei*, thee who, whom, *juz-ei*, ye who; &c. Ex. *in thuzei waila galeikaida*, in whom (lit. thee that) I am well pleased (1. 11).

From the pronoun *is*, he, is formed the relative *iz-ei*, who, which is *indeclinable*, so that we find it used in the plural, and even in the contracted form *ize*. Moreover, the demonstrative force of *is* in this compound was so entirely lost, that a second demonstrative was prefixed; hence *thai ize* = who (lit. they they who; 9. 1).

The particle *ei* is often added to *sa*, giving *sa-ei*, used as a relative. It is thus declined :—

SINGULAR.

	Masc.	*Fem.*	*Neut.*
Nom.	sa-ei	so-ei	that-ei
Gen.	thiz-ei	thizoz-ei	thiz-ei
Dat.	thamm-ei	thizai-ei	thamm-ei
Acc.	than-ei	tho-ei	that-ei

PLURAL.

	Masc.	*Fem.*	*Neut.*
Nom.	thai-ei	thoz-ei	tho-ei
Gen.	thize-ei	thizo-ei	thize-ei
Dat.	thaim-ei	thaim-ei	thaim-ei
Acc.	thanz-ei	thoz-ei	tho-ei

Interrogative Pronouns. *Hwas,* who, fem. *hwo,* neut. *hwa,* what, only occurs in the singular.

Nom.	hwas	hwo	hwa
Gen.	hwis	hwizos	hwis
Dat.	hwamma	hwizai	hwamma
Acc.	hwana	hwo	hwa
Inst.	hwe	hwe	hwe

The instrumental case appears in *du-hwe,* wherefore (2.18); also in *hwe-lauds,* what sort of, *hwe-leiks,* what sort of (4. 30), which are declined like strong adjectives.

Hwathar, which of two (E. *whether*), occurs in the nom. masc. and neut. only (2. 9), and in the dat. masc. sing. *hwatharamma.*

Hwarjis, which (of more than two) is declined like a strong adjective (9. 34, 12. 23). The neut. is *hwarjata.*

Hwileiks, hweleiks, what sort of, is similarly declined ; but the neut. is *hwileik* or *hweleik.*

Indefinite Pronouns. The following are the indefinite forms.

Sums, some; of the strong declension. It also occurs with the addition of the particle *uh,* as in the acc. pl. masc. *sumanz-uh,* and some (12. 5).

From the sb. *manna,* a man, with the suffix *-hun,* when preceded by the negative *ni,* we obtain the indefinite pronoun *ni manna-hun,* no one; gen. *ni mans-hun* ; dat. *ni mann-hun* ; acc. *ni mannan-hun;* only in the singular. The numeral *ains,* one, with the suffix *-hun,* and preceded by *ni,* gives *ni ains-hun,* none. Only the following singular forms occur. Masculine; nom. *ains-hun,* gen. *ainis-hun,* dat. *ainumme-hun,* acc. *ainno-hun, aino-hun.* Feminine; nom. *aino-hun,* dat. *ainai-hun,* acc. *ainno-hun, aino-hun.* Neuter; nom. and acc. *ain-hun.*

Ni hwas-hun, no one, only occurs in the nom. sing. masc. (10. 18, 29).

Hwas, who, with the suffix *-uh*, gives *hwaz-uh*, every
(9. 49). The dat. *hwamma-uh* is contracted to *hwammeh*
(14. 49); and the acc. masc. *hwana-uh* to *hwanoh*. The
phrase *twans hwanz-uh* (acc. pl. masc.) means 'two and two'
(6. 7). From *hwazuh* are deduced the phrases *sahwazuh
saei*, whosoever (9. 37); dat. *this-hwammeh saei*, to whomsoever (4. 25); *this-hwazuh ei*, whosoever (11. 23); gen.
this-hwizuh thei, whatsoever (6. 22); *this-hwah thei*, whatsoever (6. 23).

Hwarjis, which, with the suffix. *-uh*, gives the indef.
hwarjiz-uh, each, every; acc. fem. *hwarjo-h* (for *hwarja-uh*,
15. 6). Cf. *hwarjizuh hwa nemi*, who should take what (τίς
τί ἄρῃ, 15. 24).

It must also be observed that the word *hwas*, properly an
interrogative pronoun (see p. li.), is frequently used indefinitely with the sense of 'any one' or 'any' (8. 4). Hence
nih hwa = nothing (4. 22); *ei hwas*, that any one (9. 30);
jabai hwas, if any one, whosoever (4. 23).

§ 32. VERBS.

Of Verbs in general. Verbs have three forms or Voices,
Active, Passive, and Middle. The Passive voice has a
special form for the present tense only, being otherwise
made up of a past participle used with *wairthan*, to become,
or *wisan*, to be.

Besides the Infinitive, there are three Moods; Indicative,
Subjunctive, and Imperative.

There are but two Tenses; the Present, also used as a
Future; and the Past tense, used generally to express
imperfect, perfect, aorist, &c.

There are three Numbers; Singular, Dual, and Plural.
Dual forms are scarce.

There are two Participles; the Present, with an active sense, and the Past, with a passive sense.

The forms of conjugation are distinguished as *strong* and *weak*. Strong verbs form the past tense by vowel-change, as *giban*, to give, *ik gaf*, I gave; or else by reduplication, as *haldan*, to hold, *ik haihald*, I held. Weak verbs form the past tense with the suffix *-da* (*-i-da, -ai-da, -o-da*) or *-ta*.

§ 33. Active Voice; Reduplicating Verbs.

A. Simple form. As a good example, take the verb *haldan*, to hold; where *hald-an* is the infinitive mood, *hald-* being the stem, and *-an* the suffix.

For the scheme of conjugation, see that of the verb *rinn-an*, to run, on p. liv.

The peculiarity of the verb is in the mode of formation of the past tense. The reduplication consists in repeating the first letter of the stem before the diphthong *ai*; thus from *haldan* is formed the past tense *hai-hald*. If the stem begins with a combination of consonants, both consonants are repeated in the case of verbs beginning with *st, sk, hl, hw,* but not otherwise. Hence the past tenses of *staggan, skaidan, hlaupan, hwopan*, are, respectively, *stai-stagg, skai-skaid, hlai-hlaup,* and *hwai-hwop*. But the past tense of *fraisan* is *fai-frais*. That of *slepan* is both *sai-slep* and *sai-zlep* (with *z* for *s*). If the first letter be a vowel, the prefix is simply *ai-*, as in *althan*, pt. t. *ai-alth*.

B. Form with vowel-change. In all verbs (with the exception of *slepan*, pt. t. *saizlep*, noted above) which contain the vowel *e* in the stem, the pt. t. has *o*. Thus the pt. t. of *flek-an* is *fai-flok*. When the stem ends in *ai-*, the pt. t. likewise has *o*; thus the pt. t. of *wai-an* is *wai-wo*.

It is probable that some verbs belong to this class, of which the past tense does not happen to occur. In many cases, the pt. t. is only found in a compound of the verb. The following are examples:—

A-form. *aikan,* to say, whence *af-ai-aik,* denied (14. 68); *aukan,* to increase, whence *ana-ai-auk* (Luke, 3. 20); *fahan,* to catch, pt. t. *fai-fah* ; *falthan,* to fold, pt. t. *fai-falth* (Luke, 4. 20) ; *fraisan,* to tempt, pt. t. *fai-frais* ; *hahan,* to suspend, whence *us-hai-hah* (Matt. 27. 5); *haitan,* to call, pt. t. *hai-hait* ; *haldan,* to hold, pt. t. *hai-hald* ; *hwopan,* to boast, pt. t. *hwai-hwop* ; *laikan,* to skip, pt. t. *lai-laik* ; *maitan,* to cut, pt. t. *mai-mait* (11. 8); *skaidan,* to sever, whence *af-skai-skaid* (Gal. 2. 12); *slepan,* to sleep, whence *ga-sai-zlep* (Joh. 11. 11); *staldan,* to win, whence *ga-stai-staldjau* (1 Cor. 9. 19).

B-form. *flekan,* to lament, pt. t. *fai-flok* (Luke, 8. 52); *gretan,* to weep, pt. t. *gai-grot* (ibid.); *laian,* to revile, pt. t. *lai-lo* ; *letan,* to let, pt. t. *lai-lot* (5. 19); *redan,* to provide for, whence *faura-ga-rai-roth* (Eph. 1. 5); *saian,* to sow, pt. t. *sai-so* (4. 4); *tekan,* to touch, pt. t. *tai-tok* (5. 30); *waian,* to blow, pt. t. *wai-wo* (Matt. 7. 25).[1]

The past participle of a reduplicating verb is formed by merely adding *s* to the infinitive mood. Thus from *haldan,* to hold, is formed the pp. *haldans,* holden, held.

§ 34. Active Voice; Strong Verbs, with vowel-change.

The general form of a strong verb may be exemplified by the following conjugation of *rinnan,* to run.

INDICATIVE MOOD.

	Present Tense.	*Past Tense.*
Sing. 1.	rinn-*a*	rann
2.	-*is*	rann-*t*
3.	-*ith*	rann

---

[1] Several others are given by German grammarians; but whoever attempts to *verify* them will meet with much difficulty, and will certainly fail in most cases, the results given being merely theoretical.

Indicative Mood.

		Present Tense.	Past Tense.
Dual	1.	rinn-*os*	runn-*u*
	2.	-*ats*	runn-*uts*
Plu.	1.	-*am*	runn-*um*
	2.	-*ith*	runn-*uth*
	3.	-*and*	runn-*un*

Subjunctive Mood.

Sing.	1.	rinn-*au*	runn-*jau*
	2.	-*ais*	-*eis*
	3.	-*ai*	-*i*
Dual	1.	-*aiwa*	-*eiwa*
	2.	-*aits*	-*eits*
Plu.	1.	-*aima*	-*eima*
	2.	-*aith*	-*eith*
	3.	-*aina*	-*eina*

Imperative Mood.

Sing. 2. rinn.   *Dual* 2. rinn-*ats*.   *Plu.* 1. rinn-*am*.
2. rinn-*ith*.

Pres. Part. Act. rinn-*ands*.   *Past Part. Pass.* runn-*ans*.

It will here be observed that the stem-form, which in the present is *rinn-*, becomes *rann-* in the past tense singular, and *runn-* in the past tense dual and plural and in the past participle. Vowel-changes of this character prevail throughout all strong verbs; but the vowels vary. In some verbs the vowel of the past participle is *different* from that of the past tense plural. In others, again, the vowel remains unchanged throughout the past tense.

Instead of adhering to the order of conjugations in Gabelentz and Löbe, I here rearrange them so as to agree with the order of Early English Verbs in Morris's Specimens of English, Part I. (The mere *order* is not material.)

The first conjugation of Strong verbs (Morris, p. lxvi) answers to that of the Gothic reduplicating verbs, discussed above.

The simplest way of exhibiting the conjugations is to name them after English verbs which resemble them. There are thus seven conjugations, viz.—1. *hold.* 2. *draw.* 3. *break.* 4. *give.* 5. *drink.* 6. *drive.* 7. *choose.*[1]

The 'principal parts' of the verb, on which the conjugations depend, are the infinitive mood, the first person singular of the past tense, the first person plural of the past tense, and the past participle. These are frequently given in the Glossary within a parenthesis, as : bindan (band, bundum, bundans).

The above representative verbs have the following 'principal parts' in Gothic.

INFIN.	PT. T. 1 P. SING.	PT. T. 1 P. PL.	PAST PART.
1. haldan	haihald	haihaldum	haldans
2. dragan	drog	drogum	dragans
3. brikan	brak	brekum	brukans
4. giban	gaf	gebum	gibans
5. driggkan	draggk	druggkum	druggkans
6. dreiban	draib	dribum	dribans
7. kiusan	kaus	kusum	kusans

It must here be noted that *bairan*, to bear, and some others having *ai* for *i* in the infinitive, belong to conj. 3 or conj. 5, and put *au* for *u*. Hence for such verbs the scheme is *bairan, bar, berum, baurans* ; *wairpan, warp, waurpum, waurpans.* So also *saihwan*, to see, in conj. 4.

---

[1] These agree with the Early English verbs ; since *hold* and *fall* belong to the same conjugation, and so also *draw* and *shake,* &c. For the last four conjugations, the very same repres.ntative words have been chosen.

A list of a few representative verbs of each conjugation is here added.

1. See above ; p. liv.

2. Faran (for, forum, farans), *fare, go* ; graban (grob, grob-um, grabans), *grave, dig* ; slahan (sloh, slohum, slahans), *slay, strike* ; standan (stoth, stothum, stothans¹), *stand* ; swaran, *swear* ; wakan, *watch*.

3. Niman (nam, nemum, numans) *take* ; kwiman (kwam, kwemum, kwumans), *come* ; stilan, *steal*.

4. Itan (at, etum, itans), *eat* ; kwithan (kwath, kwethum, kwithans), *say* (cf. E. *quoth*) ; ligan, *lie* ; sitan, *sit* ; saihwan² (sahw, sehwum, saihwans), *see*. Bidjan (bath *or* bad, bedum, bidans), *ask*, has a weak form for its infinitive. The pt. t. of fra-itan, *devour*, is contracted to fret (=fra-at).

Note.—In all verbs of this conjugation the vowel *i* or diphthong *ai* occurs before a *single* consonant (*th, hw* being single letters).

5. Bindan, *bind* ; brinnan, *burn* ; duginnan, *begin* ; finthan, *find* ; hilpan, *help* ; rinnan, *run* ; siggwan, *sing*. So also bairgan (barg, baurgum, baurgans), *keep* ; wairpan (warp, waurpum, waurpans), *throw* ; wairthan (warth, waurthum, waurthans), *become*. Here again *ai* : *au* :: *i* : *u*.

Note.—In all verbs of this conjugation the vowel *i* or diphthong *ai* is followed by *two* consonants or a *doubled* consonant.

6. Beidan, *bide* ; beitan, *bite* ; leithan, *go, travel* ; skeinan, *shine* ; steigan, *climb* ; urreisan, *arise*.

---

¹ The pt. t. *stoth* is for *stond**, the *n* being dropped; but the pp. *stothans* is irregular. Some verbs belonging to this conjugation have a *weak* form (in *-jan*) for the infinitive mood; as *skath-jan* (*skoth, skothum, skathans*), to injure.

² The vowel (*ai*) of the infin. reappears in the pp. ; as in all other verbs of this conjugation.

7. Biudan, *bid*, pt. t. bauth; biugan, *bow*; driusan, *fall*; giutan, *pour*; liugan, *tell lies*; skiuban, *shove*; sliupan, *slip.* Also (with breaking) tiuhan (tauh, tauhum, tauhans), *draw.*

The vowel-scheme of strong verbs is therefore as follows.

	INFIN.	PT. T. I P. SING.	PT. T. PL.	PAST PART.
1. (*hold*)	a, ai, &c.	(*redup.*)	(*redup.*)	a, ai, &c.
2. (*draw*)	a	o	o	a
3. (*break*)	i (ai)[1]	a	e	u (au)[1]
4. (*give*)	i (ai)[1]	a	e	i (ai)[1]
5. (*drink*)	i (ai)[1]	a	u (au)[1]	u (au)[1]
6. (*drive*)	ei	ai	i (ai)[1]	i (ai)[1]
7. (*choose*)	iu	au	u (au)[1]	u (au)[1]

In conj. 1 and 2, the stem remains the same throughout the past tense. Conj. 3 and 4 have the same vowels in the pt. tense. In conj. 4 the vowel of the pp. is that of the infinitive. In conj. 5, 6, and 7 the vowel of the pp. is that of the pt. t. plural.

We learn, from comparative philology, that the root-vowel or fundamental vowel is A in conj. 1–5, I in conj. 6, and U in conj. 7.

§ 35. Active Voice; Weak Verbs.

There are three classes of weak verbs (1) those in which the pt. t. ends in *-ida*, and the pp. in *-iths*; (2) those in which it ends in *-aida*, and the pp. in *-aiths*; (3) those in which it ends in *-oda*, and the pp. in *-oths*.

Class 1. To this class belong most verbs with the infin. in *-jan*, as *lagjan*, to lay. The pt. t. *lag-ida = lagj-da*, the *i* being due to the *-j-* of the base. *Lagjan* is thus conjugated.

---

[1] The diphthongs *ai, au* occur when the succeeding consonant is *h, hw,* or *r.* See the notes on 'breaking'; pp. xxx. and xxxi.

INDICATIVE.

		Present Tense.	*Past Tense.*
Sing.	1.	lag-*ja*	lag-*ida*
	2.	-*jis*	-*ides*
	3.	-*jith*	-*ida.*
Dual.	1.	-*jos*	-*idedu*
	2.	-*jats*	-*idceduts*
Plu.	1.	-*jam*	-*idedum*
	2.	-*jith*	-*ideduth*
	3.	-*jand*	-*idedun*

SUBJUNCTIVE.

Sing.	1.	lag-*jau*	lag-*idedjau*
	2.	-*jais*	-*idedeis*
	3.	-*jai*	-*idedi*
Dual.	1.	-*jaiwa*	-*idedeiwa*
	2.	-*jaits*	-*idedeits*
Plu.	1.	-*jaima*	-*idedeima*
	2.	-*jaith*	-*idedeith*
	3.	-*jaina*	-*idedeina*

IMPERATIVE.

Sing. 2. lag-*ei*.　　*Dual.* 2. lag-*jats*.　　*Plu.* 1. lag-*jam*.

2. -*jith*.

Pres. Part. Act. lag-*jands*.　　*Past Part. Pass.* lag-*iths*.

Exception. Some verbs, like *sok-jan* (to seek) depart from the above form, in substituting *ei* for *ji* wherever it occurs, viz. in the 2nd and 3rd p. sing. and the 2nd p. pl. of the pres. indic. and in the 2nd p. pl. imperative. Thus for *sok-jis*, *sok-jith* we find *sok-eis*, *sok-eith*.

Hence the 1st class of weak verbs is subdivided into two classes: (A) like *lagjan* ; (B) like *sokjan*.

(A). Like *lagjan* are conjugated verbs with a *short* stem-syllable, or in which the stem-syllable ends in a *vowel* or *diphthong*. Examples are: hramjan, *crucify*; nasjan, *save*; satjan, *set*; waljan, *choose*; wrakjan, *persecute*. Also: stojan, *judge* (pt. t. stauida); straujan, *strew* (pt. t. strawida); taujan, *do* (pt. t. tawida). Also: afdaujan, *vex*; ananiujan, *renew*; gakwiujan, *quicken*; siujan, *sew*.

(B). Like *sokjan* are conjugated verbs with *long* vowels *within* the stem-syllable, or in which the stem-syllable ends with *two* consonants or a *double* consonant. Examples are: domjan, *deem*; draibjan, *drive*; gaskeirjan, *explain*; hausjan, *hear*; meljan, *write*; merjan, *proclaim*. Also airzjan, *err*; balthjan, *be bold, dare*; fulljan, *fill*; sandjan, *send*. So also verbs with stems of more than one syllable, as: audagjan, *bless*; glitmunjan, *glisten*; mikiljan, *magnify*; swogatjan, *sigh*; &c.

Class 2. *Haban*, to have, is thus conjugated.

INDICATIVE.

		Present Tense.	*Past Tense.*
Sing.	1.	hab-*a*	hab-*aida*
	2.	-*ais*	-*aides*
	3.	-*aith*	-*aida*
Dual.	1.	-*os*	-*aidedu*
	2.	-*ats*	-*aideduts*
Plu.	1.	-*am*	-*aidedum*
	2.	-*aith*	-*aideduth*
	3.	-*and*	-*aidedun*

SUBJUNCTIVE.

Sing.	1.	hab-*au*	hab-*aidedjau*
	2.	-*ais*	-*aidedeis*
	3.	-*ai*	-*aidedi*
Dual.	1.	-*aiwa*	-*aidedeiwa*
	2.	-*aits*	-*aidedeits*
Plu.	1.	-*aima*	-*aidedeima*
	2.	-*aith*	-*aidedeith*
	3.	-*aina*	-*aidedeina*

IMPERATIVE.

Sing. 2. hab-*ai.*　　*Dual.* 2. hab-*ats.*　　*Plu.* 1. hab-*am.*

　　　　　　　　　　　　　　　　　　　　　　　　　2.　　-*aith.*

Pres. Part. hab-*ands.*　　*Past Part. Pass.* hab-*aiths.*

Some of the principal verbs of this class are: arman, *pity*; bauan, *build*; fastan, *fast*; fijan, *hate*; hlifan, *steal*; leikan, *please*; liban, *live*; liugan, *marry*; munan, *consider*; skaman, *be ashamed of*; slawan, *be silent*; sweran, *honour*; thahan, *be silent*; thulan, *suffer*; trauan, *trow, trust.*

Class 3. To this class belong all infinitives in -*on*, and the conjugation is like that of Class 2, but with *o* throughout in place of *ai* (or *a*, or *o*). Thus the pres. indic. of *spill-on* (to tell) is: spill-*o*, -*os*, -*oth*; -*os*, -*ots*; -*om*, -*oth*, -*ond*. The pt. t. is: spill-*oda*, -*odes*, &c. *Subj. pres.* spill-*o*, -*os*, -*o*, &c.

Note.—When we compare the three classes of strong verbs, it becomes obvious that the pt. t. is really formed by subjoining to the base of the verb a suffix which is thus conjugated: -*da*, -*des*, -*da*; -*dedu*, -*deduts*; -*dedum*, -*dedut*, -*dedun*.

This suffix originated in a reduplicated past tense from the base DA, to do, which is still preserved in the mod. E. *did* (A. S. *dy-de*). Thus *habai-dedun = have-did*, now abbreviated to *had*. We hence learn that the -*ed* in mod. E. *lov-ed* is nothing but a much mutilated remnant of the same reduplicated past tense. It is remarkable that the verb *to do*, after being thus turned into an auxiliary suffix, was otherwise entirely lost in Gothic, though preserved in Anglo-Saxon and English.

§ 36. Verbs ending in -nan.

Verbs ending in -*nan* have a passive signification, as *fullnan*, to be filled or to become full, *gahailnan*, to be healed, to become whole, *gawaknan*, to become awake. They are *weak* verbs, regularly conjugated like *lagjan* (writing *n* for *j*) in the present indicative and subjunctive, and like *spillon* (Class 3) in the past tense. Thus the present of *fullnan* is *full-na*, -*nis*, -*nith*, &c.; and the past is *fulln-oda*, -*odes*, -*oda*, &c. The second person sing. imperative is *fulln.*

The *n* is due to the strong pp. suffix; thus *us-gutn-an*, to be poured out, gush out, is derived from *us*, out, and *gutan-s*, pp. of *giutan*, to pour; though several of these verbs must have been formed by analogy merely.

§ 37. Passive Voice.

There is a special form for the passive voice in the present tense only, which is easily recognised, in general, by the suffix -*da* (subj. -*dau*). The past tense is formed by using the pp. in conjunction with *wisan*, to be, or *wairthan*, to become. Moreover, this passive form only occurs in a limited number of verbs.

The same form serves for verbs of all conjugations, and may be exemplified in the verb *hailan*, to call, passive *ik hailada*, I am called, which is thus conjugated.

INDICATIVE.

Sing. hait-*ada*, -*aza*, -*ada*.   *Plu.* 1. 2. 3. hait-*anda*.

SUBJUNCTIVE.

Sing. hait-*aidau*, -*aizau*, -*aidau*.   *Plu.* 1. 2. 3. hait-*aindau*.

Verbs in -*on* preserve the *o* throughout. Thus the indic. is spill-*oda*, -*oza*, -*oda*, pl. -*onda*; and the subj. is spill-*odau*, &c.

The following examples occur in St. Mark's Gospel.

(A). *Strong verbs.* Afletanda (2. 5); afnimada (2. 20); saiada (4. 15); saltada (9. 49).

(B.) *Weak verbs.* Gadailjada (3. 24); satjaidau (4. 21); gabairht-jaidau (4. 22); daupjada, daupjaindau (10. 38); gawagjanda (13. 25); merjada, rodjada (14. 9); galewjada (14. 41).

Middle Voice.

The form is the same as for the passive. The traces of a middle voice are very slight. In St. Mark's Gospel there is one instance in the word *atsteigadau*, let him come down (15. 32).

§ 38.   Anomalous and Auxiliary Verbs.

The verbs 1–13 below use as a present tense an old *strong* preterite form, from which new *weak* preterites were afterwards formed. Many of them are very imperfect, and some of their forms are conjectural[1]; but some are of common occurrence and of considerable importance. Compare Sweet, A.S. Primer, p. 34.

1. Aigan, aihan, *own, have. Pr. sing.* aih, *pl.* aigum; *pt. t.* aihta. (Cf. E. *ought.*)

2. Dugan*, *avail, be worth. Pr. sing.* daug. (Cf. A.S. *dúgan,* whence E. *doughty.*) This verb is used impersonally.

3. Ga-daursan, *dare. Pr. sing.* gadars, *pl.* gadaursum; *pt. t.* gadaursta. (E. *dare, durst.*)

4. Ga-motan*, *find place. Pr. sing.* gamot, *pl.* gamotum*; *pt. t.* gamosta. (E. *must.*)

5. Kunnan, *know. Pr. sing.* kann, *pl.* kunnum; *pt. t.* kuntha, *pp.* kunths. (E. *can, could, un-couth.*)

6. Leisan*, *learn.* Only in the *pr. s.* lais = I have learnt, I know (Phil. 4. 12).

7. Magan, *may. Pr. s.* mag, *pl.* magum; *pt. t.* mahta; *pp.* mahts (*possible*). (E. *may, might.*)

8. Munan, *think, suppose. Pr. s.* man, *pl.* munum; *pt. t.* munda. The form ga-munan also occurs; *pr. s.* gaman, *pl.* gamunum; *pt. t.* gamunda. (A.S. *geman,* I remember.)

9. Nahan*, *suffice.* Only impersonally, in the compounds *bi-nah, ga-nah,* it suffices. The pp. *bi-nauhts,* sufficient, occurs in 1 Cor. 10. 23. (E. *e-nough.*)

10. Ogan*, *fear. Pr. s.* og, *pl.* ogum*; *pt. t.* ohta.

11. Skulan* (*be obliged to do*). *Pr. s.* skal, *pl.* skulum; *pt. t.* skulda; *pp.* skulds. (E. *shall, should.*)

---

[1] The unauthorised forms are marked *.

12. Thaurban*, *need.* *Pr. s.* tharf, *pl.* thaurbum; *pt. t.*
thaurfta; *pp.* thaurfts (*necessary*). (A. S. þearf.)

13. Witan*, *see, know.* *Pr. s.* wait, *pl.* witum; *pt. t.* wissa.
(E. *wit, wot, wist.*)

Note 1. The above verbs *kunnan, munan,* and *witan,* are distinct
from the allied verbs *gakunnan,* to know (pt. t. *gakunnaida*), *munan,*
to intend (pt. t. *munaida*), and *witan,* to observe (pt. t. *witaida,* 3. 2).

Note 2. The above verbs are conjugated in the present tense like
the preterites of strong verbs; thus the pres. t. of *kunnan* is *kann,
kann-t, kann;* pl. *kunnum,* &c. The past tense follows the analogy of
the preterites of weak verbs; thus the pt. t. is *kunth-a, kunth-es, kunth-a;*
pl. *kunth-edum, kunth-eduth, kunth-edun.* This abbreviated form is
due to the great antiquity of such formations and their consequent
corruption.

14. Wiljan, *will, wish.* This verb only appears (in the
present) in an *optative* form, which in Gothic is the same
as the subjunctive. This peculiar use is due to the peculiar
sense. It is thus conjugated. *Sing.* wil-*jau, -eis, -i;* *dual,*
wil-*eiwa, -eits;* *pl.* wil-*eima, -eith, -eina.* The pt. t. is *wilda.*
(E. *will, would.*)

15. Wisan, *be.* This verb is made up from two separate
Aryan roots ᴀs and wᴀs. In Gothic the dual and plural of
the present have inflections resembling those of a past tense.
It is thus conjugated.

INDICATIVE.

		Present Tense.	*Past Tense.*
Sing.	1.	im	was
	2.	is	wast
	3.	ist	was
Dual.	1.	siju	wesu
	2.	sijuts	wesuts
Plu.	1.	sijum	wesum
	2.	sijuth	wesuth
	3.	sind	wesun

SUBJUNCTIVE.

		Present Tense.	Past Tense.
Sing.	1.	sijau	wesjau
	2.	sijais	weseis
	3.	sijai	wesi
Dual.	1.	sijaiwa	weseiwa
	2.	sijaits	weseits
Plu.	1.	sijaima	weseima
	2.	sijaith	weseith
	3.	sijaina	weseina

Used with past participles, *wisan* helps to form passive verbs; as, *swa gamelith ist,* as it is written (1. 2); *daupidai wesun,* were baptized (1. 5).

Wisan also occurs in the sense 'to continue, remain'; cf. *wesun* (8. 2).

16. Gaggan, *go.* The pt. t. is properly *gaggida* (Luke, 19. 12), but this only occurs once. The pt. t. *iddja,* went, is commonly used, though it is from a different root. (Cf. A. S. *éode,* went, used as pt. t. of *gán,* to go.) The pp. is *gaggans* (see 7. 30).

17. The following weak verbs also have a peculiar formation of the pt. tense and pp.

a. Briggan, *bring.* *Pt. t.* brahta (*brought,* 9. 17).

b. Brukjan, *make use of.* *Pt. t.* bruhta.

c. Bugjan, *buy.* *Pt. t.* bauhta (*bought*); *pp.* bauhts.

d. Thagkjan, *think.* *Pt. t.* thahta (*thought,* 8. 16); *pp.* thahts.

e. Thugkjan, *seem.* *Pt. t.* thuhta; *pp.* thuhts.

f. Waurkjan, *work.* *Pt. t.* waurhta; *pp.* waurhts.

These past tenses are conjugated like *kuntha*; see no. 13 above, note 2.

Note. Haban, *have,* is conjugated above, on p. lx. So also wairthan, *become,* which belongs to conj. 5; see p. lvii.

The usual ending of adverbs formed from adjectives is
-aba (also *-iba*, *-uba*). The variation of vowel depends upon
the original final vowel of the base. Exx. *baitr-aba*, bitterly,
from *baitrs* (base BAITRA), bitter : *analaugn-iba*, secretly,
from *analaugns*, secret, pointing to a base ANALAUGNI : *hard-
uba* (but also *hard-aba*), hardly, from *hardus* (base HARDU),
hard.

Another common suffix is *-o*; as *uhteigo*, seasonably, from
uhteigs, seasonable.

Comparison. The comparative suffix is properly *-is*, as
in *ma-is*, more, *fram-is*, further (1. 19); but also *-s*, as in
wair-s, worse. The superlative suffix is *-ist*, as in *frum-ist*,
first (4. 28).

Some of the more important adverbs are the following.

1. **Of time.** Aftra *again*, air *early*, anaks *suddenly*, bithe
whilst, hwan *when*, ni hwanhun *never*, hweilohun *awhile*,
ju *already*, juthan *already*, nauh *still*, *yet*, ni nauhthan *not yet*,
nu *now*, seithu *late*, simle *once*, sinteino *always*, suman *once on
a time*, suns *soon*, sunsaiw *straightway*, than *then*, thanuh *then*,
ufta *often*.

2. **Of place.** Faur *forth*, inn *in* (verbal prefix), nehw
nigh, ut *out*. With suffix *-a*: afta *behind*, dalatha *below*,
fairra *far*, faura *before*, inna *in* (verbal prefix), iupa *above*,
nehwa *nigh*, uta *out*. With suffix *-ar* (*-er*): aljar *elsewhere*,
her *here*, hindar *beyond*, away (also a verbal prefix), hwar
where, jainar *there*, thar *there*, ufar *beyond*. With suffix *-aro*:
aftaro *behind*, ufaro *thereon*. With suffix *-ana*: aftana *behind*,
innana *within*, iupana *again*, utana *without*. With suffix
-ath: aljath *away*, dalath *down*, hwath *whither*. With suffix
-dre: hidre *hither*, hwadre *whither*, jaindre *there* (*yonder*).
With suffix *-thro*: aljathro *by another way*, fairrathro *from*

afar, hwathro *whence*, innathro *from within*, iupathro *from above*, jainthro *thence*, thathro *thence*, utathro *from without*. Compounded with *ei*: thadei *whither*, tharei *where*, thathroei *whence*. With enclitic *uh*: tharuh *there*. Also: bisunjane *round about*, sundro *separately*.

3. **Of manner.** Here belong adverbs in *-aba, -iba, -uba, -o, -leiko* (E. *-ly*).

Other adverbs are: allis *wholly*, duhwe *wherefore*, duthe *therefore*, filu *much*, hwe *how*, hweh *only*, ja, jai *yes*, ne *no*, ni, nih *nor*, niu *not*, sunja *verily*, swa *so*, sware *in vain*, thatainei *only*, thishun *especially*, waila *well*, wainei *if only*, waitei *perhaps*, &c.

§ 40. PREPOSITIONS.

1. With the dative: af *from*, alja *except*, faura *before*, fram *from*, mith *with*, undaro *under*, us *out*.

2. With the accusative: and *along, at*, faur *for, before*, inuh *without*, thairh *through*, undar *under*, withra *against*.

3. With both dative and accusative: afar *after*, ana *on*, at *at*, bi *by*, du *to*, hindar *behind*, uf *under*, ufar *over*, und *unto*. Of these, *du* takes the accusative once only (Col. 4. 10).

4. With genitive, dative, and accusative: in *in, on account of*. With the sense 'on account of' it takes the genitive. *Bi* and *du* also occur with the instrumental, as in *bi-the*, *du-the*. *Faur* takes the genitive in *faurthis*, beforehand.

§ 41. CONJUNCTIONS.

These are (1) Copulative, as: jah *and*, -uh *and* (used as an enclitic, and often abbreviated to *-h*), nih *and not*. So also in the phrases: nih thatainei—ak jah, *not only—but also*, nih—ak jah, *not only—but also*. (2) Disjunctive, as: aiththau *or*, andizuh—aiththau, *either—or*, jabai—aiththau, *either—or*, jaththe—jaththe, *whether—or*. (3) Denoting opposition, as: ak *but*, akei *however*, aththan *but*, ith *but*, than *but*. (4) Causal, as: allis *for*, auk *for*, raihtis *for*, unte *because*. (5) Expressing a conclusion, as: eithan *therefore*, nu *now*, thannu *therefore*, thanuh *therefore*, tharuh *therefore*. (6) Conditional, as: jabai *if*, niba, nibai *if not, except*. (7) Expressing concession, as: thauhjabai *though*, jah jabai *even if*, swethauh *however*. (8) Final, as: ci *that*, thatei *that*, theei *that*, unte *in order that*, swe *so that*, swaei *so that*, swaswe *so as that*. (9) Of comparison, as: hwaiwa *how?* swe *so*, swaswe *so as*, *as*; and in the phrases: swe—jah, *as—so*, swe—swah, *as—so*, swaswe—swa, *as—so*. (10) Of time, as: afar thatei *after that*, bithe *while*, faurthizei *before that*, miththanei *whilst*, sunsei *as soon as*, swe *just as*, than *when*, thande *when, as long as*, unte *until*, und thatei *until that*.

§ 42. INTERJECTIONS.

These are: O *oh!* sai *see!* wai *woe!* We also find an old imperative used interjectionally: hiri *come thou hither!* hirjats *come here, you two!* hirjith *come ye hither!*

§ 43. PREFIXES.

The following are the most important prefixes:—

af-, originally 'from,' 'away,' or 'off'; also used intensively. (E. *of, off*.)

afar-, 'after.'

ana-, 'on' or 'upon'; also used intensively, or with the notion of addition. (E. *on*.)

anda-, 'in return,' like Gk. ἀντί; also 'against.'

and-, orig. the same as the above; also used as a verbal prefix with the notion of reversing an action, answering to E. verbal *un-*. Ex. *bindan*, to bind, *and-bindan*, to unbind.[1]

---

[1] We thus learn that the E. verbal prefix in *un-bind* is of totally different origin from *un-* as a negative prefix (= Goth. *un-*).

at-, 'at,' 'before,' 'near'; hence 'to' or 'towards,' 'upon.'

bi-, originally 'by' or 'around'; sometimes used to specialise the meaning of a verb. Cf. E. *be-*; thus Goth. *bi-thaggkjan* = E. *be-think.*

dis-, originally 'apart' or 'in twain,' used as an intensive prefix; as in *dis-tairan,* to tear asunder.

du-, originally 'to' or 'towards.'

faur-, faura-, originally 'before'; the former also occurs in the sense 'forth,' or 'by,' or intensively. (E. *fore-.*)

fra-, rarely **fair-,** an intensive prefix answering to E. *for-* in *for-bear* (Goth. *fra-bairan*). It often implies 'loss' or 'destruction,' as in *fra-lusts,* destruction (G. *ver-lust*). We can explain E. *fr-et* as = *for-eat* (Goth. *fra-itan*).

ga-, originally 'together,' or expressive of 'completion.' But its sense is very weak, and it frequently seems to add no force to the word. It is extremely common. (A. S. *ge-.*)

id-, originally 'back' or 'again,' like Lat. *re-.* Occurs in *id-weit,* reproach, *id-weitjan,* to reproach. (A. S. *ed-.*)

in-, inn-, inna-, 'in' or 'on'; hence 'into' or 'upon.' (E. *in.*)

missa-, answering to E. *mis-* in *mis-deed.*

mith-, 'with'; merely the preposition. (A. S. *mid.*)

n-, negative prefix; as in *n-i,* not, *n-e,* nay.

sama-, Eng. *same*; as in *sama-kuns,* of the same kin.

thairh-, 'through'; the preposition.

tus-, orig. 'apart.' Only in *tuz-werjan,* to doubt. Probably the same as, or allied to, the following.

twis-, orig. 'in twain' or 'apart'; as in *twis-stass,* sedition, lit. a standing apart.

uf-, 'under' or 'up.'

ufar-, 'over' or 'above.' (E. *over.*)

un-, negative prefix; common. (E. *un-*, except before verbs; see p. lxviii., note 1.)

us- (which before *r* becomes **ur-**), orig. 'out'; used also as an intensive prefix, like A. S. *á-*, E. *a-* in *a-rise* (Goth. *ur-reisan*). Cf. also A. S. *or-*, E. *or-* in *or-deal*.

ut-, 'out.' (A. S. *út*, E. *out.*)

withra-, against; the preposition.

§ 44. SYNTAX.

So far as concerns the translation, the syntax presents but little difficulty ; for the more minute points, the reader should consult the Notes at p. 41, or Stamm's edition. The following hints may prove useful.

Article. The definite article *sa, so, thata* is declined on p. xlix. It agrees with its sb. in gender and case. As it was originally a demonstrative pronoun, we find it used (when joined with *ei*) even as a relative, as in: *thata badi, ana thammei lag sa uslitha*, the bed on which the paralytic man lay (2. 4). Observe also *Johannis sa daupjands*, John the Baptist (6. 14); *hwo so laiseino so niujo*, of what sort is this doctrine, new as it is (1. 27). It is sometimes followed by the genitive, as: *Jakobau thamma Zaibaidaiaus* James the (son) of Zebedee (3. 17); cf. 16. 1.

§ 45. Adjectives.

The circumstances under which these take the strong or weak declension are given in § 22. An example of the use of the weak declension where there is no definite article is: *at fairgunja alewjin*, at the Mount of Olives, lit. Olive Mountain (11. 1). Sometimes the comparative is formed by help of *mais*, more, instead of with a suffix, as : *goth ist imma mais*, it is more good for him (9. 42).

§ 46. Numerals.

These sometimes govern a genitive, as: *twans siponje seinaize*, two of his disciples (11. 1).

§ 47. Pronouns.

Pronouns are frequently omitted, where the person is sufficiently indicated by the suffix of the verb. The insertion of them renders them more emphatic, as: *si*, she (6. 24). *Sama* without the def. article means ' one and the same ' (10. 8).

A curious use of the relative occurs in: *hwa nu wileith, ei taujau thammei kwithith thiudan Iudaie*, what now do ye wish that I shall do to the man whom ye call the king of the Jews? (15. 12.) Here *thammei* = *thamma thanei*, i. e. to the man, whom that; the fact being that *thamma* is the dative after *taujau*, whilst *ei*, the indeclinable relative, is the accusative governed by *kwithith*. *Thai ize*, those who (9. 1), stands for *thai eiz-ei*, lit. they those who.

Hwas, the interrogative pronoun, is also used in the sense of ' any one ' or ' one '; see 8. 4.

Alls can be used without a sb., as: *aftra gaboteith alla*, will restore all things (9. 12). It can even govern a genitive, as: *allata thata frawaurhte*, lit. the every one of transgressions (3. 28).

§ 48. Verbs.

Verbs agree with their nominatives in number and person; but we find a plural verb with a noun of multitude, as: *setun bi ina managei*, the multitude sat about him (3. 32).

The future is expressed by the present, as: *gasaihwith thana suna mans*, they shall see the Son of man (14. 62).

Examples of the subjunctive are: *ni haband hwa matjaina* lit. they have not what they may eat (8. 2); *andrunnun, hwarjis maists wesi,* lit. they disputed, which might be the greatest (9. 34).

It is very common after *ei* (that), as: *jah ni wilda ei hwas wissedi,* and he would not that any one should know it (9. 30).

The latter of two verbs is put in the infinitive, as in Latin, as: *ohtedun ina fraihnan,* they feared to ask him (9. 32). When it is intended to express an intention, the prep. *du* is used before the infinitive, as: *sat du aihtron,* he sat for the purpose of begging (10. 46).

The passive infinitive is variously expressed. Sometimes the phrase *maht wisan* or *skuld wisan* is employed, as: *maht wesi frabugjan,* lit. it were possible to sell, i. e. it might have been sold (14. 5). Sometimes the infinitive active is awkwardly employed for the passive, as: *gawairpan* = to be cast (9. 45).

The present participle can be used with *wisan* or *wairthan* to express past time, as: *was Iohannes daupjands,* John was baptizing (1. 4). This is not only an English idiom, but occurs in the original Greek (ἐγένετο βαπτίζων).

Similarly the past participle can be used to express the passive, as: *was Iohannes gawasiths,* John was clothed (1. 6).

The rather common use of the **dative absolute** should here be noticed. A curious instance is: *jah wisandin Paitrau in rohsnai dalatha jah atiddja aina thiujo,* and Peter being in the hall below, there came also a maid-servant (14. 66). The occurrence of the second *jah* is here quite superfluous and exceptional. We even find a *nominative absolute,* as: *waurthans dags gatils,* a convenient day being come (6. 21); but this is quite unusual.

§ 49. Government of Verbs.

Accusative after Verbs. Most verbs govern an accusative case. We also find a *double* accusative after verbs of calling, naming, considering, taking, giving. Ex.: *Daweid kwithith ina fraujan*, David calls him Lord (12. 37); and see 10. 45. The construction of 'the accusative before the infinitive' is not uncommon, as: *hwa wileits taujan mik igkwis*, what will ye that I shall do for you two? (10. 36). Compare: *baudans gataujith gahausjan*, he makes the deaf to hear (7. 37).

Genitive after Verbs. Some verbs govern the genitive, chiefly such as express freeing, filling full of or taking away from, using, asking, &c. The verb *wisan*, to be, is often followed by a genitive. Ex.: *ainis thus wan ist*, there is lack of one thing to thee (10. 21); *hwis ist sa manleika*, whose is the image? (12. 16); *Christaus sijuth*, ye are Christ's (9. 41)· The occurrence of a genitive is sometimes due to ellipsis, as: *ei nemi akranis*, that he might receive (some) of the fruit (12. 2).

Dative after Verbs. This is most common in conjunction with an accusative. The accusative is understood in: *gif tharbam*, give (it) to the poor (10. 21). Compare: *andbahtos lofam slohun ina*, the servants struck him with the palms of their hands (14. 65).

Some verbs take the dative instead of an accusative, as: *galaistans waurthun imma*, they followed him (1. 36); *wairp thus*, cast thyself (11. 23).

§ 50.   EPITOME OF THE PRINCIPAL INFLECTIONS.

The following brief epitome, shewing the inflections, etc., which are of *most frequent occurrence,* may be of some help to the beginner.

Definite Article.

N. sa	so	thata	*Pl.* thai	thos	tho
G. this	thizos	this	thize	thizo	thize
D. thamma	thizai	thamma	thaim	thaim	thaim
A. thana	tho	thata	thans	thos	tho

Instrumental, the.   *Sa* is often followed by the enclitic *uh* or *h* ; as *sa-h, so-h, that-uh,* etc.

Strong Substantives.

The cases are given in the order *nom. gen. dat. acc.*   The vocative is omitted.

1. *Masc.* Fisk-*s, -is, -a,* — *; -os, -e, -am, -ans.   Fem.* Gib-*a, -os, -ai, -a : -os, -o, -om, -os.   Neut.* Waurd, *-is, -a,* — *; -a, -e, -am, -a.*

2. *Masc.* Balg-*s, -is, -a,* — *; -eis, -e, -im, -ins.   Fem.* Anst-*s, -ais, -ai,* — *; -eis, -e, -im, -ins.*

3. *Masc.* Sun-*us, -aus, -au, -u ; -jus, -iwe, -um, -uns.*   So also *Fem.* Hand-*us.   Neut.* Faih-*u, -aus, -au, -u.*

4. Broth-*ar, -rs, -r, -ar ;* brothr-*jus, -e, -um, -uns.*

5. Giband-*s, -is,* —, — *; -s, -e, -am, -s.*

Weak Substantives.

1. *Masc.* Han-*a, -ins, -in, -an ; -ans, -ane, -am, -ans.*

2. *Fem.* Tuggo (Managei), *-ns, -n, -n ; -ns, -no, -m, -ns.*

3. *Neut.* Hairt-*o, -ins, -in, -o ; -ona, -ane, -am, -ona.*

Strong Adjectives.

1. *Masc.* Blind-*s, -is, -amma, -ana ; -ai, -aize, -aim, -ans.*
   Fem. Blind-*a, -aizos, -ai, -a ; -os, -aizo, -aim, -os.*
   Neut. Blind(*ata*), *-is, -amma, -(ata) ; -a, -aize, -aim, -a.*

2. *Masc.* Hard-*us,* hardj-*is, -amma, -ana ;* hardj-*ai,* etc.
   Fem. Hard-*us,* hardj-*aizos, -ai, -a ;* hardj-*os,* etc.
   Neut. Hard-*u* (*-jata*), hardj-*is, -amma,* hard-*u* (*-jata*) ; hardj-*a,* etc.

Weak Adjectives.

Masc. as Hana ;   *Fem. as* Tuggo ;   *Neut. as* Hairto.   *See Weak Sbs.*

Pronouns.

Personal. 1. Ik, meina, mis, mik; *pl.* weis, unsara, unsis (uns), unsis (uns).

2. Thu, theina, thus, thuk ; jus, izwara, izwis, izwis.

3. *Masc.* is, is, imma, ina; eis, ize, im, ins.

   Fem. si, izos, izai, ija ; ijos, izo, im, ijos.

   Neut. ita, is, imma, ita ; ija, ize, im, ija.

Possessive. 1. Meins. 2. Theins. 3. Seins (*as strong adj.*).

So also: 1. Unsar. 2. Izwar. 3. Seins.

Relative. Commonly the def. art., followed by *ei.*

Interrogative (*also indefinite*). Hwas, *fem.* hwo, *neut.* hwa ; (*declined like* sa). *Hwas is often followed by* -uh *or* -hun.

Strong Verbs.

The *principal parts* are (1) *infin.* (2) *pt. t.* 1 *p. s.* (3) *pt. t.* 1 *p. pl.* (4) *pp.*

1. (*hold*). Haldan, haihald, haihaldum, haldans.
2. (*draw*). Dragan, drog, drogum, dragans . . . a, o, o, a.
3. (*break*). Brikan, brak, brekum, brukans . . . i, a, e, u.
4. (*give*). Giban, gaf, gebum, gibans . . . i, a, e, i.
5. (*drink*). Driggkan, draggk, druggkum, druggkans . . . i, a, u, u.
6. *drive*). Dreiban, draib, dribum, dribans . . . ei, ai, i, i.
7. (*choose*). Kiusan, kaus, kusum, kusans . . . iu, au, u, u.

Weak Verbs.

1. (*lay*). Lagjan, *pt. t.* lagida, *pp.* lagiths.
2. (*have*). Haban, *pt. t.* habaida, *pp.* habaiths.
3. (*tell*). Spillon, *pt. t.* spilloda, *pp.* spilloths.

General Scheme of endings (*strong verbs have also vowel-change*).

Indic. Pres. -*a* (-*o*), -*s*, -*th* ; -*os*, -*ts* ; -*m*, -*th*, -*nd.*

Past Tense (strong). —, -*t*, — ; -*u*, -*uts* ; -*um*, -*uth*, -*un.*

Past Tense (weak). -*da*, -*des*, -*da* ; -*dedu*, -*deduts* ; -*dedum*, -*deduth.* -*dedun.*

Subjunct. Pres. -*au* (-*o*), -*s*, -*ai* (-*o*) ; -*wa*, -*ts* ; -*ma*, -*th*, -*na.*

Past Tense (strong). -*jau*, -*eis*, -*i* ; . . ., -*eits* ; -*eima*, -*eith*, -*eina.*

Past Tense (weak). -*dedjau*, -*dedeis*, -*dedi* ; . . ., -*dedeits* ; -*dedeima*, -*dedeith*, -*dedeina.*

Imperative. *Dual.* 2. -*ts* ; *pl.* 1. -*m* ; 2. -*th.*

Infinitive (strong). -*an* ; (weak) -*jan*, -*an*, -*on.*

Pres. Part. (strong). -*ands* ; (weak) -*jands*, -*ands*, -*onds.*

Past. Part. (strong). -*ans* ; (weak) -*iths*, -*aiths*, -*oths.*

For anomalous verbs, see § 38, pp. lxiii-lxv.

ERRATA.

P. 12, ch. v, verse 22. *For* Jaeirus *read* Iaeirus.

P. 52, note to ch. ix, verse 1. *For* those of them who *read* lit. 'they-they-who'; see § 47, line 11.

AIWAGGELJO THAIRH MARKU

ANASTODEITH.

CHAPTER I.

1 Anastodeins aiwaggeljons Iesuis Christaus sunaus guths.

2 Swe gamelith ist in Esaïin praufetau:
Sai, ik insandja aggilu meinana faura thus,
saei gamanweith wig theinana faura thus.

3 Stibna wopjandins in authidai:
Manweith wig fraujins,
raihtos waurkeith staigos guths unsaris.

4 Was Iohannes daupjands in authidai jah merjands daupein
5 idreigos du aflageinai frawaurhte. Jah usiddjedun du imma
all Iudaialand jah Iairusaulymeis, jah daupidai wesun allai in
Iaurdane ahwai fram imma, andhaitandans frawaurhtim sein-
6 aim. Wasuth-than Iohannes gawasiths taglam ulbandaus
jah gairda filleina bi hup seinana, jah matida thramsteins jah
7 milith haithiwisk; Jah merida kwithands: kwimith swinthoza
mis sa afar mis, thizei ik ni im wairths anahneiwands and-
8 bindan skaudaraip skohe is. Aththan ik daupja izwis in
watin, ith is daupeith izwis in ahmin weihamma.

9 Jah warth in jainaim dagam, kwam Iesus fram Nazaraith
Galeilaias, jah daupiths was fram Iohanne in Iaurdane.
10 Jah suns usgaggands us thamma watin gasahw usluknans
11 himinans, jah ahman swe ahak atgaggandan ana ina. Jah

---

10. MS. usluknans; U. usluknandans.

stibna kwam us himinam: thu is sunus meins sa liuba, in thuzei waila galeikaida.

12,13 Jah suns sai, ahma ina ustauh in authida. Jah was in thizai authidai dage fidwor tiguns fraisans fram Satanin, jah was mith diuzam; jah aggileis andbahtidedun imma.

14 Ith afar thatei atgibans warth Iohannes, kwam Iesus in
15 Galeilaia merjands aiwaggeljon thiudangardjos guths, Kwithands, thatei usfullnoda thata mel jah atnehwida sik thiudangardi guths: idreigoth jah galaubeith in aiwaggeljon.

16 Jah hwarbonds faur marein Galeilaias gasahw Seimonu jah Andraian brothar is, this Seimonis, wairpandans nati in mar-
17 ein; wesun auk fiskjans. Jah kwath im Iesus: hirjats afar
18 mis, jah gatauja igkwis wairthan nutans manne. Jah suns
19 afletandans tho natja seina laistidedun afar imma. Jah jainthro inn gaggands framis leitil gasahw Iakobu thana Zaibaidaiaus jah Iohanne brothar is, jah thans in skipa
20 manwjandans natja. Jah suns haihait ins. Jah afletandans attan seinana Zaibaidaiu in thamma skipa mith asnjam, galithun afar imma.

21 Jah galithun in Kafarnaum; jah suns sabbato daga ga-
22 leithands in synagogen laisida ins. Jah usfilmans waurthun ana thizai laiseinai is: unte was laisjands ins swe waldufni
23 habands jah ni swaswe thai bokarjos. Jah was in thizai synagogen ize manna in unhrainjamma ahmin, jah ufhropida,
24 Kwithands: fralet, hwa uns jah thus, Iesu Nazorenai, kwamt frakwistjan uns? Kann thuk, hwas thu is, sa weiha guths.
25 Jah andbait ina Iesus kwithands: thahai, jah usgagg ut us
26 thamma, ahma unhrainja. Jah tahida ina ahma sa unhrainja,
27 jah hropjands stibnai mikilai usiddja us imma. Jah afslauthnodedun allai sildaleikjandans, swaei sokidedun mith sis misso kwithandans: hwa sijai thata? hwo so laiseino so

---

niujo, ei mith waldufnja jah ahmam thaim unhrainjam
28 anabiudith jah ufhausjand imma? Usiddja than meritha is
suns and allans bisitands Galeilaias.

29 Jah suns us thizai synagogen usgaggandans kwemun in
garda Seimonis jah Andraiins mith Iakobau jah Iohannen.
30 Ith swaihro Seimonis lag in brinnon; jah suns kwethun
31 imma bi ija. Jah duatgaggands urraisida tho undgreipands
handu izos, jah aflailot tho so brinno suns, jah andbahtida
im.

32 Andanahtja than waurthanamma, than gasaggkw sauil,
berun du imma allans thans ubil habandans jah unhulthons
33 habandans. Jah so baurgs alla garunnana was at daura.
34 Jah gahailida managans ubil habandans missaleikaim sauh-
tim, jah unhulthons managos uswarp, jah ni fralailot rodjan
thos unhulthons, unte kunthedun ina.

35 Jah air uhtwon usstandands usiddja, jah galaith ana auth-
36 jana stath, jah jainar bath. Jah galaistans waurthun imma
37 Seimon jah thai mith imma. Jah bigitandans ina kwethun
38 du imma, thatei allai thuk sokjand. Jah kwath du im:
gaggam du thaim bisunjane haimom jah baurgim, ei jah
39 jainar merjau, unte duthe kwam. Jah was merjands in
synagogim ize and alla Galeilaian jah unhulthons uswairpands.

40 Jah kwam at imma thrutsfill habands, bidjands ina jah
kniwam knussjands jah kwithands du imma, thatei jabai
41 wileis, magt mik gahrainjan. Ith Iesus infeinands, ufrak-
jands handu seina attaitok imma, jah kwath imma: wiljau,
42 wairth hrains. Jah bithe kwath thata Iesus, suns thata thruts-
43 fill aflaith af imma, jah hrains warth. Jah gahwotjands
44 imma, suns ussandida ina, Jah kwath du imma: saihw ei
mannhun ni kwithais waiht; ak gagg thuk silban ataugjan

---

38. MS. haimon.

B 2

gudjin, jah atbair fram gahraineinai theinai thatei anabauth
45 Moses, du weitwodithai im.   Ith is usgaggands dugann
merjan filu jah uskwithan thata waurd, swaswe is juthan
ni mahta andaugjo in baurg galeithan, ak uta ana authjaim
stadim was; jah iddjedun du imma allathro.

CHAPTER II.

1   Jah galaith aftra in Kafarnaum afar dagans, jah gafrehun
2 thatei in garda ist.   Jah suns gakwemun managai, swaswe
juthan ni gamostedun nih at daura, jah rodida im waurd.
3 Jah kwemun at imma uslithan bairandans, hafanana fram
4 fidworim.   Jah ni magandans nehwa kwiman imma faura
manageim, andhulidedun hrot tharei was Iesus; jah usgrab-
andans insailidedun thata badi jah fralailotun, ana thammei
5 lag sa uslitha.   Gasaihwands than Iesus galaubein ize kwath
du thamma uslithin: barnilo, afletanda thus frawaurhteis
6 theinos.   Wesunuh than sumai thize bokarje jainar sitandans
7 jah thagkjandans sis in hairtam seinaim : Hwa sa swa rodeith
naiteinins? hwas mag afletan frawaurhtins, niba ains guth?
8 Jah suns ufkunnands Iesus ahmin seinamma thatei swa thai
mitodedun sis, kwath du im: duhwe mitoth thata in hairtam
9 izwaraim?   Hwathar ist azetizo du kwithan thamma uslithin:
afletanda thus frawaurhteis theinos, thau kwithan: urreis jah
10 nim thata badi theinata jah gagg?   Aththan ei witeith thatei
waldufni habaith sunus mans ana airthai afletan frawaurhtins,
11 kwath du thamma uslithin: Thus kwitha: urreis, nimuh thata
12 badi thein jah gagg du garda theinamma.   Jah urrais suns
jah ushafjands badi usiddja faura andwairthja allaize, swaswe
usgeisnodedun allai jah hauhidedun mikiljandans guth, kwithandans thatei aiw swa ni gasehwun.

---

3. MS. fidworin.   9. MS. aflethanda.   12. M. gasehwum.

13 Jah galaith aftra faur marein, jah all manageins iddjedun
14 du imma, jah laisida ins.   Jah hwarbonds gasahw Laiwwi
thana Alfaiaus sitandan at motai jah kwath du imma : gagg
15 afar mis; jah usstandands iddja afar imma.   Jah warth,
bithe is anakumbida in garda is, jah managai motarjos jah
frawaurhtai mith anakumbidedun Iesua jah siponjam is ;
16 wesun auk managai jah iddjedun afar imma.   Jah thai
bokarjos jah Farcisaieis gasaihwandans ina matjandan mith
thaim motarjam jah frawaurhtaim, kwethun du thaim siponjam
is : hwa ist [thatei mith motarjam jah] frawaurhtaim matjith
17 jah driggkith?   Jah gahausjands Iesus kwath du im: ni
thaurbun swinthai lekeis, ak thai ubilaba habandans ; ni
kwam lathon uswaurhtans, ak frawaurhtans.
18 Jah wesun siponjos Iohannis jah Fareisaieis fastandans ;
jah atiddjedun jah kwethun du imma: duhwe siponjos
Iohannis jah Fareisaieis fastand, ith thai theinai siponjos ni
19 fastand?   Jah kwath im Iesus: ibai magun sunjus bruth-
fadis, und thatei mith im ist bruthfaths, fastan? swa lagga
hweila swe mith sis haband bruthfad, ni magun fastan.
20 Aththan atgaggand dagos than afnimada af im sa bruthfaths,
21 jah than fastand in jainamma daga.   Ni manna plat fanins
niujis siujith ana snagan fairnjana ; ibai afnimai fullon af
thamma sa niuja thamma fairnjin, jah wairsiza gataura wairth-
22 ith.   Ni manna giutith wein juggata in balgins fairnjans ;
ibai aufto distairai wein thata niujo thans balgins, jah wein
usgutnith jah thai balgeis frakwistnand ; ak wein juggata in
balgins niujans giutand.
23 Jah warth thairhgaggan imma sabbato daga thairh atisk,
24 jah dugunnun siponjos is skewjandans raupjan ahsa.   Jah
Fareisaieis kwethun du imma: sai, hwa taujand siponjos

_____

16. MS. *omits* thatei mith motarjam jah ; *and for* frawaurhtaim *has*
fraᵃurhtaim.   18. *For the second* Iohannis *the* MS. *has* Iohannes.

25 theinai sabbatim thatei ni skuld ist? Jah is kwath du im:
niu ussuggwuth aiw hwa gatawida Daweid, than thaurfta jah
26 gredags was, is jah thai mith imma? Hwaiwa galaith in gard
guths uf Abiathara gudjin jah hlaibans faurlageinais matida,
thanzei ni skuld ist matjan niba ainaim gudjam, jah gaf jah
27 thaim mith sis wisandam? Jah kwath im: sabbato in mans
28 warth gaskapans, ni manna in sabbato dagis; Swaei frauja
ist sa sunus mans jah thamma sabbato.

CHAPTER III.

1　　Jah galaith aftra in synagogen, jah was jainar manna ga-
2 thaursana habands handu. Jah witaidedun imma hailidediu
3 sabbato daga, ei wrohidedeina ina. Jah kwath du thamma
mann thamma gathaursana habandin handu: urreis in
4 midumai. Jah kwath du im: skuldu ist in sabbatim thiuth
taujan aiththau unthiuth taujan, saiwala nasjan aiththau
5 uskwistjan? Ith eis thahaidedun. Jah ussaihwands ins mith
moda, gaurs in daubithos hairtins ize, kwath du thamma
mann: ufrakei tho handu theina! Jah ufrakida, jah gastoth
6 aftra so handus is. Jah gaggandans than Fareisaieis sunsaiw
mith thaim Herodianum garuni gatawidedun bi ina, ei imma
uskwemeina.
7　　Jah Iesus aflaith mith siponjam seinaim du marein, jah
filu manageins us Galeilaia laistidedun afar imma, jah us
8 Iudaia, Jah us Iairusaulymim, jah us Idumaia, jah hindana
Iaurdanaus; jah thai bi Tyra jah Seidona, manageins filu,
9 gahausjandans hwan filu is tawida, kwemun at imma. Jah
kwath thaim siponjam seinaim ei skip habaith wesi at imma
10 in thizos manageins, ei ni thraiheina ina. Managans auk
gahailida, swaswe drusun ana ina ei imma attaitokeina, jah

---

2. M. hailidedi.　　　　　　　7. MS. Galeilaian.

11 swa managai swe habaidedun wundufnjos jah ahmans unhrainjans, thaih than ina gasehwun, drusun du imma jah
12 hropidedun kwithandans, thatei thu is sunus guths. Jah filu
andbait ins ei ina ni gaswikunthidedeina.
13 Jah usstaig in fairguni jah athaihait thanzei wilda is, jah
14 galithun du imma. Jah gawaurhta twalif du wisan mith sis,
15 jah ei insandidedi ins merjan, Jah haban waldufni du hailjan
16 sauhtins jah uswairpan unhulthons. Jah gasatida Seimona
17 namo Paitrus; Jah Iakobau thamma Zaibaidaiaus, jah Iohanne
brothr Iakobaus, jah gasatida im namna Bauanairgais, thatei
18 ist: sunjus theihwons; Jah Andraian jah Filippu jah Bar-
thaulaumaiu jah Matthaiu jah Thoman jah Iakobu thana
19 Alfaiaus, jah Thaddaiu jah Seimona thana Kananeiten, Jah
Iudan Iskarioten, saei jah galewida ina.
20 Jah atiddjedun in gard, jah gaïddja sik managei, swaswe
21 ni mahtedun nih hlaif matjan. Jah hausjandans fram imma
bokarjos jah antharai usiddjedun gahaban ina: kwethun auk,
22 thatei usgaisiths ist. Jah bokarjos thai af Iairusaulymai
kwimandans kwethun thatei Baiailzaibul habaith, jah thatei
in thamma reikistin unhulthono uswairpith thaim unhulthom.
23 Jah athaitands ins in gajukom kwath du im: hwaiwa mag
24 Satanas Satanan uswairpan? Jah jabai thiudangardi withra
25 sik gadailjada, ni mag standan so thiudangardi jaina. Jah
jabai gards withra sik gadailjada, ni mag standan sa gards
26 jains. Jah jabai Satana usstoth ana sik silban jah gadailiths
27 warth, ni mag gastandan, ak andi habaith. Ni manna mag
kasa swinthis galeithands in gard is wilwan, niba faurthis
thana swinthan gabindith; ja [than] thana gard is diswilwai.
28 Amen, kwitha izwis, thatei allata afletada thata frawaurhte
sunum manne, jah naiteinos swa managos swaswe wajamer-
29 jand; Aththan saei wajamereith ahman weihana ni habaith

30 fralet aiw, ak skula ist aiweinaizos frawaurhtais.   Unte
kwethun : ahman unhrainjana habaith.

31   Jah kwemun than aithei is jah brothrjus is, jah uta standand-
32 ona insandidedun du imma, haitandona ina.   Jah setun bi
ina managei ; kwethun than du imma : sai, aithei theina jah
brothrjus theinai jah swistrjus theinos uta sokjand thuk.

33 Jah andhof im kwithands : hwo ist so aithei meina aiththau
34 thai brothrjus meinai ?   Jah bisaihwands bisunjane thans bi
sik sitandans kwath : sai, aithei meina jah thai brothrjus
35 meinai.   Saei allis waurkeith wiljan guths, sa jah brothar
meins jah swistar jah aithei ist.

CHAPTER IV.

1   Jah aftra Iesus dugann laisjan at marein, jah galesun sik
du imma manageins filu, swaswe ina galeitha[nda]n in skip
gasitan in marein ; jah alla so managei withra marein ana
2 statha was.   Jah laisida ins in gajukom manag, jah kwath
3 im in laiseinai seinai : Hauseith !   Sai, urrann sa saiands du
4 saian fraiwa seinamma.   Jah warth, miththanei saiso, sum
raihtis gadraus faur wig, jah kwemun fuglos jah fretun thata.
5 Antharuth-than gadraus ana stainahamma, tharei ni habaida
airtha managa, jah suns urrann, in thizei ni habaida diupai-
6 zos airthos ; At sunnin than urrinnandin ufbrann, jah unte ni
7 habaida waurtins, gathaursnoda.   Jah sum gadraus in thaurnuns ; jah ufarstigun thai thaurnjus jah afhwapidedun thata,
8 jah akran ni gaf.   Jah sum gadraus in airtha goda, jah gaf
akran urrinnando jah wahsjando ; jah bar ain ·l· jah ain ·j·
9 jah ain ·r·   Jah kwath : saei habai ausona hausjandona,
gahausjai.

10   Ith bithe warth sundro, frehun ina thai bi ina mith thaim

---

iv. 1. MS. galeithan.

11 twalibim thizos gajukons. Jah kwath im: izwis atgiban ist
kunnan runa thiudangardjos guths, ith jainaim thaim uta in
12 gajukom allata wairthith, Ei saihwandans saihwaina jah ni
gaumjaina, jah hausjandans hausjaina jah ni frathjaina, nibai
13 hwan gawandjaina sik jah afletaindau im frawaurhteis. Jah
kwath du im: ni wituth tho gajukon, jah hwaiwa allos thos
14, 15 gajukons kunneith? Sa saijands waurd saijith. Aththan
thai withra wig sind, tharei saiada thata waurd, jah than
gahausjand unkarjans, suns kwimith Satanas jah usnimith
16 waurd thata insaiano in hairtam ize. Jah sind samaleiko
thai ana stainahamma saianans, thaiei than hausjand thata
17 waurd, suns mith fahedai nimand ita, Jah ni haband waurtins
in sis, ak hweilahwairbai sind; thathroh, bithe kwimith aglo
18 aiththau wrakja in this waurdis, suns gamarzjanda. Jah thai
sind thai in thaurnuns saianans, thai waurd hausjandans,
19 Jah saurgos thizos libainais jah afmarzeins gabeins jah thai
bi thata anthar lustjus inn atgaggandans afhwapjand thata
20 waurd, jah akranalaus wairthith. Jah thai sind thai ana
airthai thizai godon saianans, thaiei hausjand thata waurd
jah andnimand jah akran bairand, ain ·l· jah ain ·j· jah
ain ·r·
21 Jah kwath du im: ibai lukarn kwimith duthe ei uf melan
satjaidau aiththau undar ligr? niu ei ana lukarnastathan
22 satjaidau? Nih allis ist hwa fulginis thatei ni gabairhtjaidau;
23 nih warth analaugn, ak ei swikunth wairthai. Jabai hwas
24 habai ausona hausjandona, gahausjai. Jah kwath du im:
saihwith, hwa hauseith! In thizaiei mitath mitith, mitada
25 izwis, jah biaukada izwis thaim galaubjandam. Unte this-
hwammeh saei habaith, gibada imma; jah saei ni habaith,
jah thatei habaith afnimada imma.
26 Jah kwath: swa ist thiudangardi guths, swaswe jabai

---

11. MS. gajukon; *see verse* 33.

27 manna wairpith fraiwa ana airtha. Jah slepith jah urreisith
naht jah daga, jah thata fraiw keinith jah liudith swe ni wait
28 is. Silbo auk airtha akran bairith: frumist gras, thathroh
29 ahs, thathroh fulleith kaurnis in thamma ahsa. Thanuh
bithe atgibada akran, suns insandeith giltha, unte atist
asans.

30   Jah kwath: hwe galeikom thiudangardja guths, aiththau
31 in hwileikai gajukon gabairam tho? Swe kaurno sinapis,
thatei than saiada ana airtha, minnist allaize fraiwe ist thize
32 ana airthai; Jah than saiada, urrinnith jah wairthith allaize
grase maist, jah gataujith astans mikilans, swaswe magun uf
skadau is fuglos himinis gabauan.

33   Jah swaleikaim managaim gajukom rodida du im thata
34 waurd, swaswe mahtedun hausjon. Ith inuh gajukon ni
rodida im, ith sundro siponjam seinaim andband allata.

35   Jah kwath du im in jainamma daga, at andanahtja than
36 waurthanamma: usleitham jainis stadis. Jah afletandans
tho managein andnemun ina swe was in skipa; jah than
37 anthara skipa wesun mith imma. Jah warth skura windis
mikila jah wegos waltidedun in skip, swaswe ita juthan
38 gafullnoda. Jah was is ana notin ana waggarja slepands,
jah urraisidedun ina jah kwethun du imma: laisari, niu kara
39 thuk thizei frakwistnam? Jah urreisands gasok winda jah
kwath du marein: gaslawai, afdumbn! Jah anasilaida sa
40 winds jah warth wis mikil. Jah kwath du im: duhwe
faurhtai sijuth swa? hwaiwa ni nauh habaith galaubein?
41 Jah ohtedun sis agis mikil jah kwethun du sis misso: hwas
thannu sa sijai, unte jah winds jah marei ufhausjand imma?

CHAPTER V.

1, 2 Jah kwemun hindar marein in landa Gaddarene. Jah
usgaggandin imma us skipa, suns gamotida imma manna us

3 aurahjom in ahmin unhrainjamma, Saei bauain habaida in
aurahjom : jah ni naudibandjom eisarncinaim manna mahta
4 ina gabindan.   Unte is ufta eisarnam bi fotuns gabuganaim
jah naudibandjom eisarneinaim gabundans was, jah galausida
af sis thos naudibandjos jah tho ana fotum eisarna gabrak,
5 jah manna ni mahta ina gatamjan.   Jah sinteino nahtam jah
dagam in aurahjom jah in fairgunjam was hropjands jah
6 bliggwands sik stainam.   Gasaihwands than Iesu fairrathro
7 rann jah inwait ina, Jah hropjands stibnai mikilai kwath : hwa
mis jah thus, Iesu, sunau guths this hauhistins? biswara
8 thuk bi gutha, ni balwjais mis! Unte kwath imma : usgagg,
9 ahma unhrainja, us thamma mann! Jah frah ina : hwa
namo thein? Jah kwath du imma : namo mein Laigaion,
10 unte managai sijum.   Jah bath ina filu ei ni usdrebi im us
11 landa.   Wasuh than jainar hairda sweine haldana at thamma
12 fairgunja.   Jah bedun ina allos thos unhulthons kwithan-
deins : insandei unsis in tho sweina, ei in tho galeithaima.
13 Jah uslaubida im Iesus suns.   Jah usgaggandans ahmans
thai unhrainjans galithun in tho sweina, jah rann so hairda
and driuson in marein ; wesunuth-than swe twos thusundjos,
14 jah afhwapnodedun in marein.   Jah thai haldandans tho
sweina gathlauhun, jah gataihun in baurg jah in haimom, jah
15 kwemun saihwan hwa wesi thata waurthano.   Jah atiddjedun du Iesua, jah gasaihwand thana wodan sitandan jah
gawasidana jah frathjandan thana saei habaida laigaion, jah
16 ohtedun. . Jah spillodedun im thaiei gasehwun, hwaiwa
17 warth bi thana wodan jah bi tho sweina. Jah dugunnun
18 bidjan ina galeithan hindar markos seinos. Jah inn gaggand-
an ina in skip bath ina, saei was wods, ei mith imma wesi.
19 Jah ni lailot ina, ak kwath du imma : gagg du garda thein-

---

6. MS. gasaisaihwands ; *obviously an error.*
10. MS. usdrebi ; *but read* usdribi.

amma du theinaim, jah gateih im, hwan filu thus frauja
20 gatawida jah gaarmaida thuk. Jah galaith jah dugann merjan
in Daikapaulein, hwan filu gatawida imma Iesus ; jah allai
sildaleikidedun.
21   Jah usleithandin Iesua in skipa aftra hindar marein, gakwemun sik manageins filu du imma, jah was faura marein.
22 Jah sai, kwimith ains thize synagogafade namin Jaeirus ; jah
23 saihwands ina gadraus du fotum Iesuis, Jah bath ina filu,
kwithands, thatei dauhtar meina aftumist habaith, ei kwimands
24 lagjais ana tho handuns, ei ganisai jah libai. Jah galaith
mith imma ; jah iddjedun afar imma manageins filu jah
thraihun ina.
25   Jah kwinono suma wisandei in runa blothis jera twalif,
26 Jah manag gathulandei fram managaim lekjam jah frakwim-
andei allamma seinamma jah ni waihtai botida, ak mais
27 wairs habaida, Gahausjandei bi Iesu, atgaggandei in mana-
28 gein aftana attaitok wastjai is. Unte kwath, thatei jabai
29 wastjom is atteka, ganisa. Jah sunsaiw gathaursnoda sa
brunna blothis izos, jah ufkuntha ana leika thatei gahailnoda
30 af thamma slaha. Jah sunsaiw Iesus ufkuntha in sis silbin
tho us sis maht usgaggandein ; gawandjands sik in managein
31 kwath : hwas mis taitok wastjom ? Jah kwethun du imma
siponjos is : saihwis tho managein threihandein thuk, jah
32 kwithis : hwas mis taitok. Jah wlaitoda saihwan tho thata
33 taujandein. Ith so kwino ogandei jah reirandei, witandei
thatei warth bi ija, kwam jah draus du imma, jah kwath imma
34 alla'tho sunja. Ith is kwath du izai : dauhtar, galaubeins
theina ganasida thuk ; gagg in gawairthi, jah sijais haila af
thamma slaha theinamma.
35   Nauhthanuh imma rodjandin, kwemun fram thamma syn-
agogafada, kwithandans, thatei dauhtar theina gaswalt ; hwa
36 thanamais draibeis thana laisari ? Ith Iesus sunsaiw gahausjands thata waurd rodith, kwath du thamma synagogafáda :

37 ni faurhtei; thatainei galaubei.   Jah ni fralailot ainohun ize
mith sis afargaggan, nibai Paitru jah Iakobu jah Iohannen
38 brothar Iakobis.   Jah galaith in gard this synagogafadis, jah
gasahw auhjodu jah gretandans jah waifairhwjandans filu.
39 Jah inn atgaggands kwath du im : hwa auhjoth jah gretith?
40 thata barn ni gadauthnoda, ak slepith.   Jah bihlohun ina.
Ith is uswairpands allaim ganimith attan this barnis jah
aithein jah thans mith sis, jah galaith inn tharei was thata
41 barn ligando.   Jah fairgraip bi handau thata barn kwathuh
du izai : taleitha kumei, thatei ist gaskeirith : mawilo, du thus
42 kwitha : urreis.   Jah suns urrais so mawi jah iddja; was
43 auk jere twalibe; jah usgeisnodedun faurhtein mikilai.   Jah
anabauth im filu ei manna ni funthi thata; jah haihait izai
giban matjan.

CHAPTER VI.

1   Jah usstoth jainthro jah kwam in landa seinamma, jah
2 laistidedun afar imma siponjos is.   Jah bithe warth sabbato,
dugann in synagoge laisjan, jah managai hausjandans sildaleikidedun kwithandans : hwathro thamma thata, jah hwo so
handugeino so gibano imma, ei mahteis swaleikos thairh
3 handuns is wairthand?   Niu thata ist sa timrja, sa sunus
Marjins, ith brothar Iakoba jah Iuse jah Iudins jah Seimonis?
jah niu sind swistrjus is her at unsins?   Jah gamarzidai
4 waurthun in thamma.   Kwath than im Iesus thatei nist
praufetus unswers, niba in gabaurthai seinai jah in ganithjam
5 jah in garda seinamma.   Jah ni mahta jainar ainohun mahte
gataujan, niba fawaim siukam handuns galagjands gahailida.
6 Jah sildaleikida in ungalaubeinais ize, jah bitauh weihsa
bisunjane, laisjands.

---

37. *Perhaps* ainnohun ; *but see* ix. 8.

7 Jah athaihait thans twalif jah dugann ins insandjan twans
8 hwanzuh, jah gaf im waldufni ahmane unhrainjaize. Jah
   faurbauth im ei waiht ni nemeina in wig, niba hrugga aina,
9 nih matibalg nih hlaif nih in gairdos aiz, Ak gaskohai suljom:
10 jah ni wasjaith twaim paidom. Jah kwath du im: thishwaduh
   thei gaggaith in gard, thar saljaith, unte usgaggaith jainthro.
11 Jah swa managai swe ni andnimaina izwis, nih hausjaina izwis,
   usgaggandans jainthro ushrisjaith mulda tho undaro fotum
   izwaraim du weitwodithai im. Amen, kwitha izwis: sutizo
   ist Saudaumjam aiththau Gaumaurjam in daga stauos thau
12 thizai baurg ja[i]nai. Jah usgaggandans meridedun ei
13 idreigodedeina. Jah unhulthons managos usdribun, jah
   gasalbodedun alewa managans siukans, jah gahailidedun.
14   Jah gahausida thiudans Herodes, swikunth allis warth
   namo is, jah kwath thatei Iohannis sa daupjands us dauthaim urrais, duththe waurkjand thos mahteis in imma.
15 Antharai than kwethun thatei Helias ist; antharai than
16 kwethun thatei praufetes ist swe ains thize praufete. Gahausjands than Herodes kwath, thatei thammei ik haubith afmai-
17 mait Iohanne, sa ist: sah urrais us dauthaim. Sa auk raihtis
   Herodes insandjands gahabaida Iohannen jah gaband ina in
   karkarai in Hairodiadins kwenais Filippaus brothrs seinis,
18 unte tho galiugaida. Kwath auk Iohannes du Heroda, thatei
19 ni skuld ist thus haban kwen brothrs theinis. Ith so Herodia
20 naiw imma jah wilda imma uskwiman, jah ni mahta; Unte
   Herodis ohta sis Iohannen, kunnands ina wair garaihtana
   jah weihana, jah witaida imma jah hausjands imma manag
21 gatawida jah gabaurjaba imma andhausida. Jah waurthans
   dags gatils, than Herodis mela gebaurthais seinaizos nahta-

---

10. MS. usgaggaggaith.   11. MS. nihausjaina. MS. janai.
19. *For* naiw *the* MS. *has* naiswor, *but, according to* Uppström, *it is
corrected to* naiw *by the scribe.*

mat waurhta thaim maistam seinaize jah thusundifadim jah
22 thaim frumistam Galeilaias, Jah atgaggandein inn dauhtr
Herodiadins jah plinsjandein jah galeikandein Heroda jah
thaim mith anakumbjandam, kwath thiudans du thizai maujai :
23 bidei mik thishwizuh thei wileis, jah giba thus. Jah swor
izai, thatei thishwah thei bidjais mik, giba thus, und halba
24 thiudangardja meina. Ith si usgaggandei kwath du aithein
seinai : hwis bidjau ? Ith si kwath : haubidis Iohannis this
25 daupjandins. Jah atgaggandei sunsaiw sniumundo du thamma thiudana bath kwithandei : wiljau ei mis gibais ana mesa
26 haubith Iohannis this daupjandins. Jah gaurs waurthans sa
thiudans in thize aithe jah in thize mith anakumbjandane ni
27 wilda izai ufbrikan. Jah suns insandjands sa thiudans
spaikulatur, anabauth briggan haubith is. Ith is galeithands
28 afmaimait imma haubith in karkarai. Jah atbar thata haubith
is ana mesa, jah atgaf ita thizai maujai, jah so mawi atgaf ita
29 aithein seinai. Jah gahausjandans siponjos is kwemun jah
usnemun leik is jah galagidedun ita in hlaiwa.
30 Jah gaïddjedun apaustauleis du Iesua jah gataihun imma
allata jah swa filu swe gatawide[dun] — —
53, 54 — — jah duatsniwun. Jah usgaggandam im us skipa,
55 sunsaiw ufkunnandans ina, Birinnandans all thata gawi dugunnun ana badjam thans ubil habandans bairan, thadei
56 hausidedun ei is wesi. Jah thishwaduh thadei iddja in
haimos aiththau baurgs aiththau in weihsa, ana gagga lagide-
dun siukans jah bedun ina ei thau skauta wastjos is attaitokeina ; jah swa managai swe attaitokun imma, ganesun.

CHAPTER VII.

1 Jah gakwemun sik du imma Fareisaieis jah sumai thize
2 bokarje, kwimandans us Iairusaulymim. Jah gasaihwandans

---

sumans thize siponje is gamainjaim handum, that-ist un-
3 thwahanaim, matjandans hlaibans; Ith Fareisaieis jah allai
Iudaieis, niba ufta thwahand handuns, ni matjand, habandans
4 anafilh thize sinistane, Jah af mathla niba daupjand ni matjand, jah anthar 'ist manag thatei andnemun du haban,
5 daupeinins stikle jah aurkje jah katile jah ligre; Thathroh than
frehun ina thai Fareisaieis jah thai bokarjos : duhwe thai
siponjos theinai ni gaggand bi thammei anafulhun thai sinist-
6 ans, ak unthwahanaim handum matjand hlaif? Ith is andhafjands kwath du im, thatei waila praufetida Esaïas bi izwis
thans liutans, swe gamelith ist :
So managei wairilom mik sweraith,
ith hairto ize fairra habaith sik mis.
7   Ith sware mik blotand,
laisjandans laiseinins, anabusnins manne ;
8 Afletandans raihtis anabusn guths habaith thatei anafulhun
mannans, daupeinins aurkje jah stikle, jah anthar galeik
9 swaleikata manag taujith.   Jah kwath du im : waila inwidith
10 anabusn guths, ei thata anafulhano izwar fastaith. Moses auk
raihtis kwath : swerai attan theinana jah aithein theina ; jah
saei ubil kwithai attin seinamma aiththau aithein seinai,
11 dauthau afdauthjaidau. Ith jus kwithith: jabai kwithai manna
attin seinamma aiththau aithein : kaurban, thatei is maithms,
12 thishwah thatei us mis gabatnis, Jah ni fraletith ina ni waiht
13 taujan attin seinamma aiththau aithein seinai, Blauthjandans
waurd guths thizai anabusnai izwarai, thoei anafulhuth ; jah
14 galeik swaleikata manag taujith.   Jah athaitands alla tho
15 managein kwath im : hauseith mis allai jah frathjaith.   Ni
waihts ist utathro mans inn gaggando in ina thatei magi ina
gamainjan ; ak thata ut gaggando us mann thata ist thata
16 gamainjando mannan.   Jabai hwas habai ausona hausjand-
17 ona, gahausjai.   Jah than galaith in gard us thizai mana-
18 gein, frehun ina siponjos is bi tho gajukon, Jah kwath du

im: swa jah jus unwitans sijuth? Ni frathjith thammei all
thata utathro inn gaggando in mannan ni mag ina gamainjan:
19 Unte ni galeithith imma in hairto, ak in wamba, jah in ur-
20 runsa usgaggith, [jah] gahraineith allans matins. Kwathuth-
than thatei thata us mann usgaggando thata gamaincith
21 mannan. Innathro auk us hairtin manne mitoneis ubilos
22 usgaggand: kalkinassjus, horinassjus, maurthra, Thiubja, faihu-
frikeins, unseleins, liutei, aglaitei, augo unsel, wajamereins,
23 hauhhairtei, unwiti. Tho alla ubilona innathro usgaggand
jah gagamainjand mannan.
24 Jah jainthro usstandands galaith in markos Tyre jah Seidone, jah galeithands in gard ni wilda witan mannan jah ni
25 mahta galaugnjan. Gahausjandei raihtis kwino bi ina, thizozei
habaida dauhtar ahman unhrainjana, kwimandei draus du
26 fotum is. Wasuth-than so kwino haithno, Saurini-fynikiska
gabaurthai, jah bath ina ei tho unhulthon uswaurpi us dauhtr
27 izos. Ith Iesus kwath du izai: let faurthis sada wairthan
barna, unte ni goth ist niman hlaib barne jah wairpan hund-
28 am. Ith si andhof imma jah kwath du imma: jai, frauja;
jah auk hundos undaro biuda matjand af drauhsnom barne.
29 Jah kwath du izai: in this waurdis gagg; usiddja unhultho
30 us dauhtr theinai. Jah galeithandei du garda seinamma
bigat unhulthon usgaggana jah tho dauhtar ligandein ana
ligra.
31 Jah aftra galeithands af markom Tyre jah Seidone kwam
at marein Galeilaie mith tweihnaim markom Daikapaulaios.
32 Jah berun du imma baudana stammana, jah bedun ina ei
33 lagidedi imma handau. Jah afnimands ina af managein
sundro, lagida figgrans seinans in ausona imma jah spewands
34 attaitok tuggon is, Jah ussaihwands du himina gaswogida, jah
35 kwath du imma: aiffatha, thatei ist, uslukn. Jah sunsaiw

---

20. MS. *omits* jah.   33. M. speiwands.

usluknodedun imma hliumans jah andbundnoda bandi tugg-
36 ons is jah rodida raihtaba.   Jah anabauth im ei mann ni
kwetheina.   Hwan filu is im anabauth, mais thamma eis
37 meridedun, Jah ufarassau sildaleikidedun kwithandans : waila
allata gatawida, jah baudans gataujith gahausjan jah unrod-
jandans rodjan.

CHAPTER VIII.

1   In jainaim than dagam aftra at filu managai managein
wisandein jah ni habandam hwa matidedeina, athaitands
2 siponjans kwathuh du im : Infeinoda du thizai managein,
unte ju dagans thrins mith mis wesun, jah ni haband hwa
3 matjaina; Jah jabai fraleta ins lauskwithrans du garda ize,
4 ufligand ana wiga ; sumai raihtis ize fairrathro kwemun. Jah
andhofun imma siponjos is : hwathro thans mag hwas
5 gasothjan hlaibam ana authidai? Jah frah ins : hwan mana-
6 gans habaith hlaibans? Ith eis kwethun : sibun. Jah anabauth thizai managein anakumbjan ana airthai ; jah nimands
thans sibun hlaibans jah awiliudonds gabrak jah atgaf siponjam seinaim, ei atlagidedeina faur ; jah atlagidedun faur tho
7 managein. Jah habaidedun fiskans fawans, jah thans ga-
8 thiuthjands kwath ei atlagidedeina jah thans. Gamatidedun
than jah sadai waurthun ; jah usnemun laibos gabruko sibun
9 spyreidans. Wesunuth-than thai matjandans swe fidwor
10 thusundjos ; jah fralailot ins. Jah galaith sunsaiw in skip
mith siponjam seinaim jah kwam ana fera Magdalan.

11   Jah urrunnun Fareisaieis jah dugunnun mithsokjan imma
12 sokjandans du imma taikn us himina, fraisandans ina. Jah
ufswogjands ahmin seinamma kwath : hwa thata kuni taikn
sokeith? Amen, kwitha izwis : jabai gibaidau kunja thamma
13 taikne. Jah afletands ins, galeithands aftra in skip uslaith
hindar marein.

14 Jah ufarmunnodedun niman hlaibans jah niba ainana hlaif
15 ni habaidedun mith sis in skipa. Jah anabauth im kwithands:
saihwith ei atsaihwith izwis this beistis Fareisaie jah beistis
16 Ierodis. Jah thahtedun mith sis misso kwithandans : unte
17 hlaibans ni habam. Jah frathjands Iesus kwath du im : hwa
thaggkeith, unte hlaibans ni habaith? ni nauh frathjith nih
18 wituth, unte daubata habaith hairto izwar. Augona habandans
ni gasaihwith, jah ausona habandans ni gahauseith, jah ni
19 gamunuth. Than thans fimf hlaibans gabrak fimf thusundjom,
hwan managos tainjons fullos gabruko usnemuth? Kwethun
20 du imma : twalif. Aththan than thans sibun hlaibans fidwor
thusundjom, hwan managans spyreidans fullans gabruko
21 usnemuth? Ith eis kwethun : sibun. Jah kwath du im:
hwaiwa ni nauh frathjith?
22 Jah kwemun in Bethaniin jah berun du imma blindan, jah
23 bedun ina ei imma attaitoki. Jah fairgreipands handu this
blindins ustauh ina utana weihsis jah speiwands in augona is,
24 atlagjands ana handuns seinos frah ina gau-hwa-sehwi? Jah
ussaihwands kwath : gasaihwa mans, thatei swe bagmans
25 gasaihwa gaggandans. Thathroh aftra galagida handuns ana
tho augona is jah gatawida ina ussaihwan ; jah aftra gasatiths
26 warth jah gasahw bairhtaba allans. Jah insandida ina du
garda is kwithands : ni in thata weihs gaggais, ni mannhun
kwithais in thamma wehsa.
27 Jah usiddja Iesus jah siponjos is in wehsa Kaisarias thizos
Filippaus ; jah ana wiga frah siponjans seinans, kwithands du
28 im : hwana mik kwithand mans wisan? Ith eis andhofun :
Iohannen thana daupjand, jah antharai Helian ; sumaih than
29 ainana praufete. Jah is kwath du im : aththan jus, hwana
mik kwithith wisan? Andhafjands than Paitrus kwath du
30 imma : thu is Christus. Jah faurbauth im ei mannhun ni
31 kwetheina bi ina. Jah dugann laisjan ins thatei skal sunus
mans filu winnan, jah uskiusan skulds ist fram thaim sinistam

jah thaim auhumistam gudjam jah bokarjam, jah uskwiman
32 jah afar thrins dagans usstandan. Jah swikunthaba thata
waurd rodida ; jah aftiuhands ina Paitrus dugann andbeitan
33 ina ; Ith is gawandjands sik jah gasaihwands thans siponjans
seinans andbait Paitru kwithands : gagg hindar mik, Satana ;
34 unte ni frathjis thaim guths, ak thaim manne. Jah athaitands
tho managein mith siponjam seinaim kwath du im : saei wili
afar mis laistjan, inwidai sik silban jah nimai g algan seinana
35 jah laistjai mik. Saei allis wili saiwala seina ganasjan,
frakwisteith izai ; ith saei frakwisteith saiwalai seinai in meina
36 jah in thizos aiwaggeljons, ganasjith tho. Hwa auk boteith
mannan, jabai gageigaith thana fairhwu allana jah gasleitheith
37 sik saiwalai seinai ? Aiththau hwa gibith manna inmaidein
38 saiwalos seinaizos ? Unte saei skamaith sik meina jah waurde
meinaize in gabaurthai thizai horinondein jah frawaurhton,
jah sunus mans skamaith sik is, than kwimith in wulthau
attins seinis mith aggilum thaim weiham.

CHAPTER IX.

1   Jah kwath du im : amen, kwitha izwis thatei sind sumai
thize her standandane, thai ize ni kausjand dauthaus, unte
gasaihwand thiudinassu guths kwumanana in mahtai.
2   Jah afar dagans saihs ganam Iesus Paitru jah Iakobu jah
Iohannen, jah ustauh ins ana fairguni hauh sundro ainans :
3 jah inmaidida sik in andwairthja ize. Jah wastjos is waurthun glitmunjandeins, hweitos swe snaiws, swaleikos swe
4 wullareis ana airthai ni mag gahweitjan. Jah ataugiths
warth im Helias mith Mose ; jah wesun rodjandans mith
5 Iesua. Jah andhafjands Paitrus kwath du Iesua ; Rabbei,
goth ist unsis her wisan, jah gawaurkjam hlijans thrins, thus
6 ainana jah Mose ainana jah ainana Helijin. Ni auk wissa

7 hwa rodidedi ; wesun auk usagidai. Jah warth milhma ufarskadwjands im, jah kwam stibna us thamma milhmin : 8 sa ist sunus meins sa liuba, thamma hausjaith. Jah anaks insaihwandans ni thanaseiths ainohun gasehwun, alja Iesu ainana mith sis.

9 Dalath than atgaggandam im af thamma fairgunja, ana- bauth im ei mannhun ni spillodedeina thatei gasehwun, niba 10 bithe sunus mans us dauthaim usstothi. Jah thata waurd habaidedun du sis misso sokjandans : hwa ist thata us 11 dauthaim usstandan? Jah frehun ina kwithandans : unte kwithand thai bokarjos thatei Helias skuli kwiman faurthis? 12 Ith is andhafjands kwath du im : Helias swethauh kwimands faurthis aftra gaboteith alla ; jah hwaiwa gamelith ist bi 13 sunu mans, ei manag winnai jah frakunths wairthai. Akei kwitha izwis thatei ju Helias kwam jah gatawidedun imma, swa filu swe wildedun, swaswe gamelith ist bi ina. 14 Jah kwimands at siponjam gasahw filu manageins bi ins, 15 jah bokarjans sokjandans mith im. Jah sunsaiw alla man- agei gasaihwandans ina usgeisnodedun, jah durinnandans in- 16 witun ina. Jah frah thans bokarjans : hwa sokeith mith thaim? 17 Jah andhafjands ains us thizai managein kwath : laisari, brahta sunu meinana du thus habandan ahman unrodjandan. 18 Jah thishwaruh thei ina gafahith, gawairpith ina, jah hwath- jith jah kriustith tunthuns seinans jah gastaurknith ; jah kwath siponjam theinaim ei usdreibeina ina, jah ni mahtedun. 19 Ith is andhafjands im kwath : o kuni ungalaubjando ! und hwa at izwis sijau? und hwa thulau izwis? Bairith ina du 20 mis. Jah brahtedun ina at imma. Jah gasaihwands ina sunsaiw sa ahma tahida ina ; jah driusands ana airtha 21 walwisoda hwathjands. Jah frah thana attan is : hwan lagg

---

8. *See* v. 37.   12. MS. Heliaswethauh.   15. MS. usdrei- beina ; *for* usdribeina.

mel ist ei thata warth imma?   Ith is kwath : us barniskja.

22 Jah ufta ina jah in fon atwarp jah in wato, ei uskwistidedi imma ; akei jabai mageis, hilp unsara, gableithjands unsis.

23 Ith Iesus kwath du . imma thata jabai mageis galaubjan ;

24 allata mahteig thamma galaubjandin.   Jah sunsaiw ufhropjands sa atta this barnis mith tagram kwath : galaubja ; hilp

25 meinaizos ungalaubeinais !   Gasaihwands than Iesus thatei samath rann managei, gahwotida ahmin thamma unhrainjin, kwithands du imma : thu ahma, thu unrodjands jah bauths, ik thus anabiuda : usgagg us thamma, jah thanaseiths ni galeithais

26 in ina.   Jah hropjands jah filu tahjands ina usiddja ; jah warth

27 swe dauths, swaswe managai kwethun thatei gaswalt.   Ith Iesus undgreipands ina bi handau urraisida ina ; jah usstoth.

28 Jah galeithandan ina in gard, siponjos is frehun ina sundro :

29 duhwe weis ni mahtedum usdreiban thana?   Jah kwath du im : thata kuni in waihtai ni mag usgaggan, niba in bidai jah fastubnja.

30   Jah jainthro usgaggandans iddjedun thairh Galeilaian ;

31 jah ni wilda ei hwas wissedi, Unte laisida siponjans seinans, jah kwath du im thatei sunus mans atgibada in handuns manne, jah uskwimand imma, jah uskwistiths thridjin daga

32 usstandith.   Ith eis ni frothun thamma waurda, jah ohtedun ina fraihnan.

33   Jah kwam in Kafarnaum, jah in garda kwumans frah ins :

34 hwa in wiga mith izwis misso mitodeduth?   Ith eis slawaidedun ; du sis misso andrunnun, hwarjis maists wesi.

35 Jah sitands atwopida thans twalif jah kwath du im : jabai hwas wili frumists wisan, sijai allaize aftumists jah allaim

36 andbahts.   Jah nimands barn gasatida ita in midjaim im,

37 jah ana armins nimands ita kwath du im : Saei ain thize swaleikaize barne andnimith ana namin meinamma, mik

---

28. MS. mahtedun.

andnimith; jah sahwazuh saei mik andnimith, ni mik andnimith, ak thana sandjandan mik.

38 Andhof than imma Iohannes kwithands: laisari! sehwum
sumana in theinamma namin usdreibandan unhulthons, saei
ni laisteith unsis, jah waridedum imma, unte ni laisteith
39 unsis. Ith is kwath : ni warjith imma ; ni mannahun auk
ist saei taujith maht in namin meinamma jah magi sprauto
40 ubilwaurdjan mis ; Unte saei nist withra izwis, faur izwis ist.
41 Saei auk allis gadragkjai izwis stikla watins in namin meinamma, unte Christaus sijuth, amen kwitha izwis ei ni
42 frakwisteith mizdon seinai. Jah sahwazuh saei gamarzjai
ainana thize leitilane thize galaubjandane du mis, goth ist
imma mais ei galagjaidau asilukwairnus ana halsaggan is
43 jah frawaurpans wesi in marein. Jah jabai marzjai thuk
handus theina, afmait tho ; goth thus ist hamfamma in libain
galeithan, thau twos handuns habandin galeithan in gaiain-
44 nan, in fon thata unhwapnando, Tharei matha ize ni gaswiltith
45 jah fon ni afhwapnith. Jah jabai fotus theins marzjai thuk,
afmait ina ; goth thus ist galeithan in libain haltamma, thau
twans fotuns habandin gawairpan in gaiainnan, in fon thata
46 unhwapnando, Tharei matha ize ni gaswiltith jah fon ni
47 afhwapnith. Jah jabai augo thein marzjai thuk, uswairp
imma ; goth thus ist haihamma galeithan in thiudangardja
guths, thau twa augona habandin atwairpan in gaiainnan
48 funins, Tharei matha ize ni gadauthnith jah fon ni afhwapnith.
49 Hwazuh auk funin saltada jah hwarjatoh hunsle salta salt-
50 ada. Goth salt; ith jabai salt unsaltan wairthith, hwe
supuda? Habaith in izwis salt, jah gawairtheigai sijaith
mith izwis misso.

---

42. MS. balsaggan.   50. MS. supuda ; *for* supoda.

CHAPTER X.

1   Jah jainthro usstandands kwam in markom Iudaias hindar
Iaurdanau ; jah gakwemun sik aftra manageins du imma,
2 jah, swe biuhts, aftra laisida ins.   Jah duatgaggandans
Fareisaieis frehun ina, skuldu sijai mann kwen afsatjan,
3 fraisandans ina.   Ith is andhafjands kwath : hwa izwis
4 anabauth Moses ?   Ith eis kwethun ; Moses uslaubida unsis
5 bokos afsateinais meljan jah afletan.   Jah andhafjands Iesus
kwath du im : withra harduhairtein izwara gamelida izwis
6 tho anabusn.   Ith af anastodeinai gaskaftais gumein jah
7 kwinein gatawida guth.   Inuh this bileithai manna attin,
8 seinamma jah aithein seinai, Jah sijaina tho twa du leika
9 samin, swaswe thanaseiths ni sind twa, ak leik ain.   Thatei
10 nu guth gawath, manna thamma ni skaidai.   Jah in garda
11 aftra siponjos is bi thata samo frehun ina.   Jah kwath du
im : sahwazuh saei afletith kwen seina jah liugaith anthara,
12 horinoth du thizai.   Jah jabai kwino afletith aban seinana
jah liugada antharamma, horinoth.
13   Thanuh atberun du imma barna, ei attaitoki im ; ith thai
14 siponjos is sokun thaim bairandam du.   Gasaihwands than
Iesus unwerida jah kwath du im : letith tho barna gaggan
du mis jah ni warjith tho, unte thize ist thiudangardi guths.
15 Amen, kwitha izwis : saei ni andnimith thiudangardja guths
16 swe barn, nih thauh kwimith in izai.   Jah gathlaihands im,
lagjands handuns ana tho thiuthida im.
17   Jah usgaggandin imma in wig, duatrinnands ains jah
knussjands bath ina kwithands : laisari thiutheiga, hwa tau-
18 jau ei libainais aiweinons arbja wairthau ?   Ith is kwath du
imma : hwa mik kwithis thiutheigana ? ni hwashun thiuth-
19 eigs, alja ains guth.   Thos anabusnins kant : ni horinos ;

13, 14. L. *reads* bairandam.   Dugasaihwands.

ni maurthrjais; ni hlifais; ni sijais galiugaweitwods; ni
20 anamahtjais; swerai attan theinana jah aithein theina. Tharuh
andhafjands kwath du imma: laisari, tho alla gafastaida us
21 jundai meinai. Ith Iesus insaihwands du imma frijoda ina
jah kwath du imma: ainis thus wan ist; gagg, swa filu swe
habais frabugei jah gif tharbam, jah habais huzd in himinam;
22 jah hiri laistjan mik nimands galgan. Ith is ganipuands in
this waurdis galaith gaurs; was auk habands faihu manag.

23 Jah bisaihwands Iesus kwath siponjam seinaim: sai,
hwaiwa agluba thai faiho gahabandans in thiudangardja
24 guths galeithand. Ith thai siponjos afslauthnodedun in
waurde is. Tharuh Iesus aftra andhafjands kwath im: barn-
ilona, hwaiwa aglu ist thaim hugjandam afar faihau in
25 thiudangardja guths galeithan. Azitizo ist ulbandau thairh
thairko nethlos galeithan, thau gabigamma in thiudangardja
26 guths galeithan. Ith eis mais usgeisnodedun kwithandans
27 du sis misso: jah hwas mag ganisan? Insaihwands du im
Iesus kwath: fram mannam unmahteig ist, akei ni fram
28 gutha; allata auk mahteig ist fram gutha. Dugann than
Paitrus kwithan du imma: sai, weis aflailotum alla jah
29 laistidedum thuk. Andhafjands im Iesus kwath: amen,
kwitha izwis: ni hwashun ist saei aflailoti gard aiththau
brothruns aiththau aithein aiththau attan aiththau kwen aiththau barna aiththau haimothlja in meina jah in thizos aiw-
30 aggeljons, Saei ni andnimai ˑrˑ falth, nu in thamma mela
gardins jah brothruns jah swistruns jah attan jah aithein
jah barna jah haimothlja mith wrakom, jah in aiwa thamma
31 anawairthin libain aiweinon. Aththan managai wairthand
frumans aftumans, jah aftumans frumans.

---

23. MS. faiho; *for* faihu. 24. *In the* MS., hugjandam *is in-*
distinct and uncertain. 25. MS. Azitizo; *for* Azetizo. 27. *In*
the MS., akei *wrongly follows* kwath. 29. MS. aflailailoti. MS.
attin.

32 Wesunuth-than ana wiga gaggandans du Iairusaulymai
jah faurbigaggands ins Iesus, jah sildaleikidedun jah afar-
laistjandans faurhtai waurthun.   Jah andnimands aftra thans
twalif dugann im kwithan thoei habaidedun ina gadaban.
33 Thatei sai, usgaggam in Iairusaulyma jah sunus mans atgibada thaim ufargudjam jah bokarjam, jah gawargjand ina dauth-
34 au, —— Jah bilaikand ina jah bliggwand ina, jah speiwand
ana ina jah uskwimand imma, jah thridjin daga usstandith.
35   Jah athabaidedun sik du imma Iakobus jah Iohannes,
sunjus Zaibaidaiaus, kwithandans: laisari, wileima ei thatei
36 thuk bidjos, taujais uggkis.   Ith Iesus kwath im: hwa
37 wileits taujan mik igkwis?   Ith eis kwethun du imma:
fragif ugkis ei ains af taihswon theinai jah ains af hleidumein
38 theinai sitaiwa in wulthau theinamma.   Ith Iesus kwathuh
du im: ni wituts hwis bidjats; maguts-u driggkan stikl
thanei ik driggka, jah daupeinai thizaiei ik daupjada, ei
39 daupjaindau?   Ith eis kwethun du imma: magu.   Ith Iesus
kwathuh du im: swethauh thana stikl thanei ik driggka,
driggkats, jah thizai daupeinai thizaiei ik daupjada [daup-
40 janda]; Ith thata du sitan af taihswon meinai aiththau af
hleidumein nist mein du giban, alja thaimei manwith was.
41 Jah gahausjandans thai taihun dugunnun unwerjan bi Iakobu
42 jah Iohannen.   Ith is athaitands ins kwath du im: wituth
thatei [thaiei] thuggkjand reikinon thiudom, gafraujinond
43 im, ith thai mikilans ize gawaldand im.   Ith ni swa sijai in
izwis; ak sahwazuh saei wili wairthan mikils in izwis, sijai
44 izwar andbahts; Jah saei wili izwara wairthan frumists, sijai
45 allaim skalks.   Jah auk sunus mans ni kwam at andbahtjam,
ak andbahtjan jah giban saiwala seina faur managans lun.

---

33. *In the* MS., *the verse is unfinished.*   34. MS. ustandith.
38. MS. wituths.   39. MS. *omits* daupjanda.   42. MS. *omits*
thaiei.   44. MS. frumist sijai.

46 Jah kwemun in Iairikon. Jah usgaggandin imma jainthro mith siponjam seinaim jah managein ganohai, sunus
Teimaiaus, Barteimaiaus blinda, sat faur wig du aihtron.
47 Jah gahausjands thatei Iesus sa Nazoraius ist, dugann hrop-
48 jan jah kwithan : sunau Daweidis, Iesu, armai mik ! Jah
hwotidedun imma managai ei gathahaidedi ; ith is filu mais
49 hropida : sunau Daweidis, armai mik ! Jah gastandans Iesus
haihait atwopjan ina. Jah wopidedun thana blindan, kwith-
50 andans du imma : thrafstei thuk ; urreis, wopeith thuk. Ith
is afwairpands wastjai seinai ushlaupands kwam at Iesu.
51 Jah andhafjands kwath du imma Iesus : hwa wileis ei taujau
thus ? Ith sa blinda kwath du imma : Rabbaunei, ei us-
52 saihwau. Ith Iesus kwath du imma : gagg, galaubeins
theina ganasida thuk. Jah sunsaiw ussahw jah laistida in
wiga Iesu.

CHAPTER XI.

1 Jah bithe nehwa wesun Iairusalem, in Bethsfagein jah
Bithaniin at fairgunja alewjin, insandida twans siponje sein-
2 aize, Jah kwath du im : gaggats in haim tho withrawairthon
iggkwis, jah sunsaiw inn gaggandans in tho baurg bigitats
fulan gabundanana, ana thammei nauh ainshun manne ni
3 sat : andbindandans ina attiuhats. Jah jabai hwas iggkwis
kwithai : duhwe thata taujats ? kwithaits : thatei frauja this
4 gairneith ; jah sunsaiw ina insandeith hidre. Galithun than
jah bigetun fulan gabundanana at daura uta ana gagga ; jah
5 andbundun ina. Jah sumai thize jainar standandane kweth-
6 un du im : hwa taujats andbindandans thana fulan ? Ith
eis kwethun du im, swaswe anabauth im Iesus, jah lailotun
7 ins. Jah brahtedun thana fulan at Iesua ; jah galagidedun

---

8 ana wastjos seinos, jah gasat ana ina. Managai than wastjom seinaim strawidedun ana wiga ; sumai astans maimaitun
9 us bagmam jah strawidedun ana wiga.   Jah thai fauragaggandans hropidedun , kwithandans : osanna, thiuthida sa
10 kwimanda in namin fraujins !   Thiuthido so kwimandei
thiudangardi in namin attins unsaris Daweidis, osanna in
hauhistjam !

11   Jah galaith in Iairusaulyma Iesus jah in alh ; jah bisaihwands alla, at andanahtja juthan wisandin hweilai usiddja
in Bethanian mith thaim twalibim.

12   Jah iftumin daga usstandandam im us Bethaniin gredags
13 was.   Jah gasaihwands smakkabagm fairrathro habandan
lauf atiddja, ei aufto bigeti hwa ana imma ; jah kwimands at
imma ni waiht bigat ana imma niba lauf ; ni auk was mel
14 smakkane.   Jah usbairands kwath du imma : ni thanaseiths
us thus aiw manna akran matjai.   Jah gahausidedun thai
siponjos is.

15   Jah iddjedun du Iairusaulymai.   Jah atgaggands Iesus in
alh dugann uswairpan thans frabugjandans jah bugjandans
in alh, jah mesa skattjane jah sitlans thize frabugjandane
16 ahakim uswaltida.   Jah ni lailot ei hwas thairhberi kas thairh
17 tho alh.   Jah laisida kwithands du im: niu gamelith ist
thatei razn mein razn bido haitada allaim thiudom ? ith jus
18 gatawideduth ita du filigrja waidedjane.   Jah gahausidedun
thai bokarjos jah gudjane auhumistans jah sokidedun, hwaiwa
imma uskwistidedeina : ohtedun auk ina, unte alla managei
sildaleikidedun in laiseinais is.

19   Jah bithe andanahti warth, usiddja ut us thizai baurg.

20   Jah in maurgin faurgaggandans gasehwun thana smakka-
21 bagm thaursjana us waurtim.   Jah gamunands Paitrus

---

9. *After* fauragaggandans *we should probably insert* jah thai afargagg-
andans.

kwath du imma : Rabbei, sai, smakkabagms thanei frakwast
22 gathaursnoda. Jah andhafjands Iesus kwath du im : habaith
23 galaubein guths! Amen auk kwitha izwis, thishwazuh ei
kwithai du thamma fairgunja : ushafei thuk jah wairp thus
in marein, jah ni tuzwerjai in hairtin seinamma, ak galaubjai
thata, ei thatei kwithith gagaggith, wairthith imma thishwah
24 thei kwithith. Duththe kwitha izwis, allata thishwah thei
bidjandans sokeith, galaubeith thatei nimith, jah wairthith
25 izwis. Jah than standaith bidjandans, afletaith, jabai hwa
habaith withra hwana, ei jah atta izwar sa in himinam afletai
26 izwis missadedins izwaros. Ith jabai jus ni afletith, ni thau
atta izwar sa in himinam afletith izwis missadedins izwaros.
27 Jah iddjedun aftra du Iairusaulymai. Jah in alh hwarbond-
in imma, atiddjedun du imma thai auhumistans gudjans jah
28 bokarjos jah sinistans. Jah kwethun du imma : in hwamma
waldufnje thata taujis? jah hwas thus thata waldufni atgaf,
29 ei thata taujis? Ith Iesus andhafjands kwath du im : fraihn ı
jah ik izwis ainis waurdis jah andhafjith mis, jah kwitha izwis
30 in hwamma waldufnje thata tauja. Daupeins Iohannis uzuh
31 himina was thau uzuh mannam? andhafjith mis. Jah thahtedun du sis misso kwithandans, jabai kwitham : us himina,
32 kwithith : aththan duhwe ni galaubideduth imma? Ak
kwitham : us mannam, uhtedun tho managein. Allai auk
alakjo habaidedun Iohannen thatei bi sunjai praufetes was.
33 Jah anhafjandans kwethun du Iesua : ni witum. Jah andhafjands Iesus kwath du im : nih ik izwis kwitha in hwamma
waldufnje thata tauja.

CHAPTER XII.

1 Jah dugann im in gajukom kwithan : weinagard ussatida
manna, jah bisatida ina fathom jah usgrof dal uf mesa jah

---

32. *Read* ohtedun.

gatimrida kelikn, jah anafalh ina waurstwjam, jah aflaith
2 aljath.   Jah insandida du thaim waurstwjam at mel skalk, ei
3 at thaim waurstwjam nemi akranis this weinagardis.   Ith eis
nimandans ina usbluggwun jah insandidedun laushandjan.
4 Jah aftra insandida du im antharana skalk; jah thana
stainam wairpandans gaaiwiskodedun jah haubith wundan
5 brahtedun jah insandidedun ganaitidana.   Jah aftra insandida antharana; jah jainana afslohun, jah managans antharans, sumans usbliggwandans, sumanzuh than uskwimand-
6 ans.   Thanuh nauhthanuh ainana sunu aigands, liubana
sis, insandida jah thana du im spedistana, kwithands thatei
7 gaaistand sunu meinana.   Ith jainai thai waurstwjans kwethun
du sis misso thatei sa ist sa arbinumja, hirjith! uskwimam
8 imma, jah unsar wairthith thata arbi.   Jah undgreipandans
ina uskwemun, jah uswaurpun imma ut us thamma weina-
9 garda.   Hwa nuh taujai frauja this weinagardis?   Kwimith
jah uskwisteith thans waurstwjans, jah gibith thana weinagard
10 antharaim.   Nih thata gamelido ussuggwuth:
>   Stains thammei uswaurpun thai timrjans,
>   sah warth du haubida waihstins?
11 >   Fram fraujin warth sa,
>   jah ist sildaleiks in augam unsaraim.
12 Jah sokidedun ina undgreipan, jah ohtedun tho managein;
frothun auk thatei du im tho gajukon kwath.   Jah afletandans ina galithun.
13   Jah insandidedun du imma sumai thize Fareisaie jah Hero-
14 diane, ei ina ganuteina waurda.   Ith eis kwimandans kwethun
du imma: laisari, witum thatei sunjeins is jah ni kara thuk
manshun ni auk saihwis in andwairthja manne, ak bi sunjai
wig guths laiseis: skuldu ist kaisaragild giban kaisara, thau
15 niu gibaima?   Ith Iesus gasaihwands ize liutein kwath du
im: hwa mik fraisith? atbairith mis skatt, ei gasaihwau.
16 Ith eis atberun, jah kwath du im: hwis ist sa manleika jah

17 so ufarmeleins? Ith eis kwethun du imma : Kaisaris. Jah andhafjands Iesus kwath du im: usgibith tho Kaisaris Kaisara jah tho guths gutha. Jah sildaleikidedun ana thamma. ·

18 Jah atiddjedun Saddukaieis du imma thaiei kwithand 19 usstass ni wisan, jah frehun ina kwithandans : Laisari, Moses gamelida unsis thatei jabai hwis brothar gadauthnai, jah bileithai kwenai, jah barne ni bileithai, ei nimai brothar is 20 tho kwen is, jah ussatjai barna brothr seinamma. Sibun brothrahans wesun ; jah sa frumista nam kwen, jah ga- 21 swiltands ni bilaith fraiwa. Jah anthar nam tho ; jah gadauthnoda, jah ni sa bilaith fraiwa. Jah thridja samaleiko. 22 Jah nemun tho samaleiko thai sibun, jah ni bilithun fraiwa. 23 Spedumista allaize gaswalt jah so kwens. In thizai usstassai, than usstandand, hwarjamma ize wairthith kwens ? Thai 24 auk sibun aihtedun tho du kwenai. Jah andhafjands Iesus kwath du im: niu duthe airzjai sijuth, ni kunnandans mela 25 nih maht guths? Allis than usstandand usdauthaim, ni liugand 26 ni liuganda, ak sind swe aggiljus thai in himinam. Aththan bi dauthans, thatei urreisand, niu gakunnaideduth ana bokom Mosezis ana aihwatundjai, hwaiwa imma kwath guth kwith- 27 ands : ik im guth Abrahamis jah guth Isakis jah Iakobis? Nist guth dauthaize, ak kwiwaize. Aththan jus filu airzjai sijuth. 28 Jah duatgaggands ains thize bokarje, gahausjands ins samana sokjandans, gasaihwands thatei waila im andhof, 29 frah ina: hwarja ist allaizo anabusne frumista? Ith Iesus andhof imma thatei frumista allaizo anabusns : hausei Israel, 30 frauja guth unsar frauja ains ist. Jah frijos fraujan guth theinana us allamma hairtin theinamma jah us allai saiwalai theinai jah us allai gahugdai theinai jah us allai mahtai 31 theinai. So frumista anabusns. Jah anthara galeika thizai : frijos nehwundjan theinana swe thuk silban. Maizei thaim 32 anthara anabusns nist. Jah kwath du imma sa bokareis : waila, laisari, bi sunjai kwast thatei ains ist, jah nist anthar

33 alja imma; Jah thata du frijon ina us allamma hairtin jah us
allamma frathja jah us allai saiwalai jah us allai mahtai, jah
thata du frijon nehwundjan swe sik silban, managizo ist
34 allaim thaim alabrunstim jah saudim. Jah Iesus gasaihwands
ina thatei frodaba andhof, kwath du imma: ni fairra is
thiudangardjai guths. Jah ainshun thanaseiths ni gadaursta
ina fraihnan.

35 Jah andhafjands Iesus kwath laisjands in alh: hwaiwa
kwithand thai bokarjos thatei Christus sunus ist Daweidis?
36 Silba auk Daweid kwath in ahmin weihamma:
Kwithith frauja du fraujin meinamma,
Sit af taihswon meinai,
unte ik galagja fijands theinans fotubaurd fotiwe theinaize.
37 Silba raihtis Daweid kwithith ina fraujan, jah hwathro imma
sunus ist? Jah alla so managei hausidedun imma gabaurjaba.

38 Jah kwath du im in laiseinai seinai: saihwith faura bo-
[karjam] — —

CHAPTER XIII.

16, 17 — — wastja seina. Aththan wai thaim kwithuhaftom
18 jah daddjandeim in jainaim dagam. Aththan bidjaith ei ni
19 wairthai sa thlauhs izwar wintrau. Wairthand auk thai dagos
jainai aglo swaleika, swe ni was swaleika fram anastodeinai
20 gaskaftais thoci gaskop guth, und hita, jah ni wairthith. Jah
ni frauja gamaurgidedi thans dagans, ni thauh ganesi ainhun
leike; akei in thize gawalidane thanzei gawalida, gamaurgida
21 thans dagans. Jah than jabai hwas izwis kwithai: sai, her
22 Christus, aiththau sai, jainar, ni galaubjaith; Unte urreisand
galiugachristjus jah galiugapraufeteis, jah giband taiknins jah
fauratanja du afairzjan, jabai mahteig sijai, jah thans gawal-
23 idans. Ith jus saihwith, sai, fauragataih izwis allata.

---

24 Akei in jainans dagans afar tho aglon jaina sauil rikwizeith
25 jah mena ni gibith liuhath sein. Jah stairnons himinis
   wairthand driusandeins jah mahteis thos in himinam ga-
26 wagjanda. Jah than gasaihwand sunu mans kwimandan in
27 milhmam mith mahtai managai jah wulthau. Jah than
   insandeith aggiluns seinans jah galisith thans gawalidans
   seinans af fidwor windam fram andjam airthos und andi
   himinis.
28   Aththan af smakkabagma ganimith tho gajukon. Than
   this juthan asts thlakwus wairthith jah uskeinand laubos,
29 kunnuth thatei nehwa ist asans. Swah jah jus, than gasaihwith thata wairthan, kunneith thatei nehwa sijuth at — —

CHAPTER XIV.

4,5   — — [frakwis]teins this balsanis warth? Maht wesi auk
   thata balsan frabugjan in managizo thau thrija hunda skatte
6 jah giban unledaim. Jah andstaurraidedun tho. Ith Iesus
   kwath : letith tho! duhwe izai usthriutith? thannu goth
7 waurstw waurhta bi mis. Sinteino auk thans unledans
   habaith mith izwis, jah than wileith, maguth im waila taujan ;
8 ith mik ni sinteino habaith. Thatei habaida so gatawida ;
9 faursnau salbon mein leik du usfilha. Amen, kwitha izwis :
   thishwaruh thei merjada so aiwaggeljo and alla manaseth,
   jah thatei gatawida so rodjada du gamundai izos.
10   Jah Iudas Iskarioteis, ains thize twalibe, galaith du thaim
11 gudjam, ei galewidedi ina im. Ith eis gahausjandans fagi-
   nodedun jah gahaihaitun imma faihu giban ; jah sokida
   hwaiwa gatilaba ina galewidedi.
12   Jah thamma frumistin daga azyme, than paska salidedun,
   kwethun du imma thai siponjos is : hwar wileis ei galeith-

---

13 andans manwjaima, ei matjais paska? Jah insandida twans
siponje seinaize kwathuh du im: gaggats in tho baurg, jah
gamoteith igkwis manna kas watins bairands: gaggats afar
14 thamma, Jah thadei inn galeithai, kwithaits thamma heiwa-
fraujin thatei laisareis kwithith: hwar sind salithwos tharei
15 paska mith siponjam meinaim matjau? Jah sa izwis taikneith
kelikn mikilata, gastrawith, manwjata; jah jainar manwjaith
16,41 unsis. Jah usiddjedun thai sipon[jos] — — sai, galewjada
42 sunus mans in handuns frawaurhtaize. Urreisith, gaggam!
Sai, sa lewjands mik atnehwida.

43   Jah sunsaiw nauhthanuh at imma rodjandin kwam Iudas,
sums thize twalibe, jah mith imma managei mith hairum jah
triwam fram thaim auhumistam gudjam jah bokarjam jah
44 sinistam. Atuh-than-gaf sa lewjands im bandwon kwithands:
thammei kukjau, sa ist: greipith thana jah tiuhith arniba.
45 Jah kwimands sunsaiw, atgaggands du imma kwath: Rabbei,
46 Rabbei! jah kukida imma. Ith eis uslagidedun handuns ana
47 ina jah undgripun ina. Ith ains sums thize atstandandane
imma uslukands hairu sloh skalk auhumistins gudjins jah
48 afsloh imma auso thata taihswo. Jah andhafjands Iesus
kwath du im: swe du waidedjin urrunnuth mith hairum jah
49 triwam greipan mik. Daga hwammeh was at izwis in alh
laisjands jah ni griputh mik: ak ei usfullnodedeina bokos.
50 Jah afletandans ina gathlauhun allai.
51   Jah ains sums juggalauths laistida afar imma biwaibiths
52 leina ana nakwadana; jah gripun is thai juggalaudeis. Ith
is bileithands thamma leina nakwaths gathlauh faura im.
53   Jah gatauhun Iesu du auhumistin gudjin; jah garunnun
mith imma auhumistans gudjans allai jah thai sinistans jah
54 bokarjos. Jah Paitrus fairrathro laistida afar imma, unte
kwam in garda this auhumistins gudjins; jah was sitands

---

13. *For the second* gaggats, MS. *has* gaggast.   16–41. *A gap in the* MS.

55 mith andbahtam jah warmjands sik at liuhada.   Ith thai
auhumistans gudjans jah alla so gafaurds sokidedun ana
56 Iesu weitwoditha du afdauthjan ina ; jah ni bigetun.   Managai auk galiug weitwodidedun ana ina, jah samaleikos thos
57 weitwodithos ni wesun.   Jah sumai usstandandans galiug
58 weitwodidedun ana ina kwithandans : Thatei weis gahausi-
dedum kwithandan ina thatei ik gataira alh tho handu-
waurhton, jah bi thrins dagans anthara unhanduwaurhta
59 gatimrja.   Jah ni swa samaleika was weitwoditha ize.
60 Jah usstandands sa auhumista gudja in midjaim frah Iesu
kwithands: niu andhafjis waiht, hwa thai ana thuk weit-
61 wodjand?   Ith is thahaida, jah waiht ni andhof.   Aftra sa
auhumista gudja frah ina jah kwath du imma : thu is Christus
62 sa sunus this thiutheigins?   Ith is kwathuh: ik im ; jah
gasaihwith thana sunu mans af taihswon sitandan mahtais,
63 jah kwimandan mith milhmam himinis.   Ith sa auhumista
gudja disskreitands wastjos seinos kwath : hwa thanamais
64 thaurbum weis weitwode?   Hausideduth tho wajamerein is :
hwa izwis thugkeith?   Tharuh eis allai gadomidedun ina
65 skulan wisan dauthau.   Jah dugunnun sumai speiwan ana
wlit is jah huljan andwairthi is jah kaupatjan ina, jah
kwethun du imma : praufetei ! jah andbahtos gabaurjaba
lofam slohun ina.

66   Jah wisandin Paitrau in rohsnai dalatha jah atiddja aina
67 thiujo this auhumistins gudjins, Jah gasaihwandei Paitru
warmjandan sik, insaihwandei du imma kwath : jah thu mith
68 Iesua thamma Nazoreinau wast.   Ith is afaiaik kwithands :
ni wait, ni kann hwa thu kwithis.   Jah galaith faur gard, jah
69 hana wopida.   Jah thiwi gasaihwandei ina aftra dugann
70 kwithan thaim faurastandandam, thatei sa thizei ist.   Ith is
aftra laugnida.   Jah afar leitil aftra thai atstandandans

---

69. *Read* thize.

kwethun du Paitrau: bi sunjai, thizei is; jah auk razda
71 theina galeika ist. Ith is dugann afaikan jah swaran thatei
72 ni kann thana mannan thanei kwithith. Jah antharamma
sintha hana wopida, Jah gamunda Paitrus thata waurd,
swe kwath imma Iesus, thatei faurthize hana hrukjai twaim
sintham, inwidis mik thrim sintham. Jah dugann greitan.

CHAPTER XV.

1   Jah sunsaiw in maurgin garuni taujandans thai auhumistans gudjans mith thaim sinistam jah bokarjam, jah alla
so gafaurds gabindandans Iesu brahtedun ina at Peilatau.
2 Jah frah ina Peilatus: thu is thiudans Iudaie? Ith is andhaf-
3 jands kwath du imma: thu kwithis.   Jah wrohidedun ina
4 thai auhumistans gudjans filu.   Ith Peilatus aftra frah ina
kwithands: niu andhafjis ni waiht? sai, hwan filu ana thuk
5 weitwodjand.   Ith Iesus thanamais ni andhof, swaswe sildaleikida Peilatus.
6   Ith and dulth hwarjo[h] fralailot im ainana bandjan thanei
7 bedun.   Wasuh than sa haitana Barabbas mith thaim mith
imma drobjandam gabundans, thaiei in auhjodau maurthr
8 gatawidedun.   Jah usgaggandei alla managei dugunnun
9 bidjan, swaswe sinteino tawida im.   Ith Peilatus andhof im
kwithands: wileidu fralcitan izwis thana thiudan Iudaie?
10 Wissa auk thatei in neithis atgebun ina thai auhumistans
11 gudjans.   Ith thai auhumistans gudjans inwagidedun tho
12 managein ei mais Barabban fralailoti im.   Ith Peilatus aftra
andhafjands kwath du im: hwa nu wileith ei taujau thammei
13 kwithith thiudan Iudaie? Ith eis aftra hropidedun: ushramei
14 ina.   Ith Peilatus kwath du im: hwa allis ubilis gatawida?

---

15 Ith eis mais hropidedun : ushramei ina. Ith Peilatus wiljands thizai managein fullafahjan, fralailot im thana Barabban, ith Iesu atgaf usbliggwands, ei ushramiths wesi.

16 Ith gadrauhteis gatauhun ina innana gardis, thatei ist prai-
17 toriaun, jah gahaihaitun alla hansa, Jah gawasidedun ina paurpurai, jah atlagidedun ana ina thaurneina wipja uswind-
18 andans, Jah dugunnun goljan ina : hails, thiudan Iudaie !
19 Jah slohun is haubith rausa, jah bispiwun ina, jah lagjand-
20 ans kniwa inwitun ina. Jah bithe bilailaikun ina andwasidedun ina thizai paurpurai, jah gawasidedun ina wastjom swesaim, jah ustauhun ina ei ushramidedeina ina.

21 Jah undgripun sumana manne, Seimona Kyreinaiu, kwimandan af akra, attan Alaiksandraus jah Rufaus, ei nemi
22 galgan is. Jah attauhun ina ana Gaulgautha stath thatei ist
23 gaskeirith hwairneins staths. Jah gebun imma drigkan wein
24 mith smyrna ; ith is ni nam. Jah ushramjandans ina dis-
dailjand wastjos is wairpandans hlauta ana thos, hwarjizuh
25 hwa nemi. Wasuh than hweila thridjo, jah ushramidedun
26 ina. Jah was ufarmeli fairinos is ufarmelith : sa thiudans
27 Iudaie. Jah mith imma ushramidedun twans waidedjans,
28 ainana af taihswon jah ainana af hleidumein is. Jah usfullnoda thata gamelido thata kwithano : jah mith unsibjaim
29 rahniths was. Jah thai faurgaggandans wajameridedun ina,
withondans haubida seina jah kwithandans : o sa gatairands
30 tho alh jah bi thrins dagans gatimrjands tho, Nasei thuk
31 silban jah atsteig af thamma galgin ! Samaleiko jah thai
auhumistans gudjans bilaikandans ina mith sis misso mith
thaim bokarjam kwethun ; antharans ganasida, ith sik silban
32 ni mag ganasjan. Sa Christus, sa thiudans Israelis, atsteigadau nu af thamma galgin, ei gasaihwaima jah galaubjaima.
Jah thai mith ushramidans imma idweitidedun imma.

---

24. MS. disdailjandans.   29. MS. fauragaggandans.

33   Jah bithe warth hweila saihsto, rikwis warth ana allai
34 airthai und hweila niundon.   Jah niundon hweilai wopida
Iesus stibnai mikilai kwithands : ailoe ailoe, lima sibakthanei,
thatei ist gaskeirith; guth meins, guth meins, duhwe mis
35 bilaist ? Jah sumai thize atstandandane gahausjandans kweth-
36 un :   sai,   Helian   wopeith.   Thragjands   than   ains   jah
gafulljands swam akeitis, galagjands ana raus, dragkida ina
kwithands : let, ei saihwam kwimaiu Helias athafjan ina.
37, 38 Ith Iesus aftra letands stibna mikila uzon.   Jah faurahah
39 al[h]s disskritnoda in twa iupathro und dalath.   Gasaihwands
than sa hundafaths sa atstandands in andwairthja is thatei
swa hropjands uzon, kwath : bi sunjai, sa manna sa sunus
40 was guths. Wesunuth-than kwinons fairrathro saihwandeins,
in thaimei was Marja so Magdalene jah Marja Iakobis this
41 minnizins jah Iosezis aithei jah Salome.   Jah than was in
Galeilaia, jah laistidedun ina jah andbahtidedun imma, jah
antharos managos thozei mith iddjedun imma in Iairusalem.
42   Jah juthan at andanahtja waurthanamma, unte was para-
43 skaiwe, saei ist fruma sabbato, Kwimands Iosef af Areima-
thaias, gaguds ragineis, saei was silba beidands thiudangardjos guths, anananthjands galaith inn du Peilatau jah
44 bath this leikis Iesuis.   Ith Peilatus sildaleikida ei is juthan
gaswalt ; jah athaitands than[a] hundafath frah ina juthan
45 gadauthnodedi.   Jah finthands at thamma hundafada fragaf
46 thata leik Iosefa.   Jah usbugjands lein jah usnimands ita
biwand thamma leina jah galagida ita in hlaiwa thatei was
gadraban us staina, jah atwalwida stain du daura this hlaiwis.
47 Ith Marja so Magdalene jah Marja Iosezis sehwun hwar
galagiths wesi.

---

38. MS. als.   44. MS. than.

CHAPTER XVI.

1 Jah inwisandin[s] sabbate dagis Marja so Magdalene jah
Marja so Iakobis jah Salome usbauhtedun aromata, ei at-
2 gaggandeins gasalbodedeina ina. Jah filu air this dagis
afarsabbate atidd[j]edun du thamma hlaiwa at urrinnandin
3 sunnin. Jah kwethun du sis misso: hwas afwalwjai unsis
4 thana stain af daurom this hlaiwis? Jah insaihwandeins
gaumidedun thammei afwalwiths ist sa stains; was auk
5 mikils abraba. Jah atgaggandeins in thata hlaiw gasehwun
juggalauth sitandan in taihswai biwaibidana wastjai hweitai;
6 jah usgeisnodedun. Tharuh kwath du im: ni faurhteith
izwis, Iesu sokeith Nazoraiu thana ushramidan; nist her,
7 urreis, sai thana stath tharei galagidedun ina. Akei gaggith
kwithiduh du siponjam is jah du Paitrau thatei faurbigaggith
izwis in Galeilaian; tharuh ina gasaihwith, swaswe kwath
8 izwis. Jah usgaggandeins af thamma hlaiwa gathlauhun;
dizuh-than-sat ijos reiro jah usfilmei, jah ni kwethun mannhun waiht; ohtedun sis auk.

9 Usstandands than in maurgin frumin sabbato ataugida
frumist Marjin thizai Magdalene, af thizaiei uswarp sibun
10 unhulthons. Soh gaggandei gataih thaim mith imma wis-
11 andam, kwainondam jah gretandam. Jah eis hausjandans
thatei libaith jah gasaihwans warth fram izai, ni galaubi-
dedun.
12 Afaruh than thata — —

NOTES.

The student should take an early opportunity of reading over and learning by heart the very common words, of constant occurrence, given in the list immediately preceding the Glossary, at p. 59.

The meaning of the longer words will be found in the Glossary, but it is by no means a bad plan to try to analyse each word, and hence to obtain the sense by comparison with the nearest cognate word in English. By this method many words can be thoroughly *understood*, and are then easily remembered.

In this analysis, it is requisite to divest each word of all suffixes and prefixes, leaving only the monosyllable which contains the root. Then, if the root be known, the word can again be put together in such a manner as to show the meaning. A few examples will make this clear.

Thus, in 1. 1, we have *anastodeins*, and in 1. 2, *insandja*. These are to be thus analysed.

Ana-stod-ein-s consists of the prefix *ana-*, on; the root-syllable *stod*, a derivative from *stoth*, pt. t. of *standan*, to stand, and therefore implying the idea 'stand'; the suffix *-ein-*, which has much the same force as the E. noun-suffix *-ing*; and, lastly, the final *-s*, the inflexion of the nom. case. The sense is, literally, an 'on-standing,' i. e. an entering upon, or, in a metaphorical sense, a beginning.

In-sand-ja consists of the prefix *in-*, i. e. in, to; *sand*, the root-syllable, is E. 'send'; and *-ja* is the 1st pers. sing. pres. from the infinitive form *-jan*, which is the ordinary form employed for weak verbs used in a transitive sense. The sense is, literally, 'I send in,' or 'I send to,' a slightly strengthened form of 'I send.'

A few more examples, explained more briefly, may be added.

Wop-jand-ins (1. 3) is the gen. of *wop-jand-s*, pres. part. of *wop-jan*, to cry aloud; allied to E. *weep*.

Af-lag-ein-ai (1. 4) is the dat. of *af-lag-ein-s*, an 'off-laying,' i. e. a putting off or aside, remission.

Ga-was-ith-s (1. 6) is the pass. pp. of *ga-was-jan*, where *ga-* is a *very* common prefix adding little or nothing to the sense of the word, whilst *-was-* contains the same root as the Lat. *ues-tire*, to clothe, and the E. *ves-ture*; the sense is, accordingly, 'clothed.'

If this method of analysis be frequently applied, the meanings of many words can be obtained, without reference to the glossary, by help of the well-known context. As the translation was made from the Greek, the best commentary on the Gothic version is a Greek Testament; for which the Authorized (or the Revised) English version is a very good substitute.

CHAPTER I.

1. **Aiwaggelj-ons**, gen. of *aiwaggelj-o*, wk. s. f., evangel, gospel. Note the use of *gg* for *ng*, precisely as the Gk. γγ is used for νγ. So also *aggilu* = *angilu*, angel, in verse 2.

Sun-aus, gen. of *sun-us*, str. s. m., son.

Guth-s is an exceptional form, standing for *guth-is*, gen. of *guth*, really a strong *neuter* form, though used in a masculine sense and considered as masculine.

2. **Ga-mel-ith**, neut. of *ga-mel-ith-s*, pp. of *ga-mel-jan*, to write. See the strong declension of adjectives.

'In Isaiah the prophet.' So in the Revised Version (1881), and in the best MSS. But the quotation is rather from Malachi iii. 1.

Literally, 'See, I in-send angel mine before thee.'

Sa-ei, he who, who. Particularly notice the use of the suffix *-ei*, with the force of an indeclinable relative. So again, in verse 7, *thiz-ei* = *this ei*, of the one who, i.e. whose. In all such cases, the suffix *ei* should be detached, and the declension of the rest of the word is then easily perceived.

Gamanweith, will prepare, lit. prepares; the present being used with a fut. sense, as in A.-S. In *ga-manw-eith*, we may neglect the prefix *ga-*, and we find *manw-eith* = *manw-jith*, 3 pers. sing. from *manw-jan*, where the suffix *-jan* shows that the verb is a secondary one, formed from the adj. *manw-us*, ready, with the sense 'to make ready.' The imper. pl. takes the very same suffix, so that in v. 3, we have *manweith* = prepare ye; *waurkeith*, work ye, make ye.

3. **Authidai**, dat. sing. of *authi-da*, str. sb. f., 'a waste place'; derived from *auths*, adj. waste, cognate with G. *öde*.

Fraujins, gen. of *frauja*, masc., a lord, A.-S. *fréa*; the fem. appears in the G. *frau*, lady.

Staigos, acc. pl. of *staiga*, str. sb. f., a path; cf. G. *steg*, and Cumberland *stee*, a ladder, *Sty head*, head of the pass; E. *sti-le*, a place to climb over.

Guths unsaris, of our God; but the usual Gk. text has simply αὐτοῦ, His. It is not my intention to compare the Greek text with the Gothic version, as the reader can do this without help.

4. **Daup-jands**, dipping, i. e. baptizing.

Fra-waurhte, mis-workings, misdeeds, sins. The prefix *fra-*, like G. *ver-*, A.-S. *for-*, has a sinister and intensive sense.

5. **And-hait-andans**, confessing; with a dative case. So also *and-bahtidedun* takes the dative in v. 13.

7. **Swinthoza mis**, stronger than me; the dative being used after the comparative. In the A.-S. *swíð*, strong, the *n* is dropped, the *i* being lengthened in consequence of the loss of *n*.

Sa afar mis, he after me, the one (who is) after me.

Thizei; see note to v. 2.

And-bindan, to un-bind; the E. *verbal* prefix *un-*, cognate with Goth. *and-* and Gk. ἀντί, is quite distinct from the E. *negative* prefix *un-*, cognate with Goth. *un-*, Lat. *in-*, Gk. ἀν-.

9. **Warth**, it became, it happened. Note the distinction between *wairthan* and *wisan*.

Jains, that; E. *yon*.

Fram Johanne, by John (not from, though *from* is the same word).

10. **Usluknans**, acc. pl. masc. of *uslukns*, adj., open, lit. ' unlocked.' Uppström suggests the reading *usluknandans*, acc. pl. masc. of pres. part. Massmann suggests *uslukanans*, acc. pl. masc. of past part. There seems no sufficient reason for emendation.

11. **Sunus meins sa liuba**, lit. son mine the dear one; my dear son.

12. 'And soon, behold, the Spirit,' &c. Massmann reads *suns sa ahma*, soon the Spirit. Here again, there seems no sufficient reason for emendation, which should seldom be resorted to.

13. **Dage**, gen. pl.; governed by *tiguns*; lit. forty of days.

Diuzam, dat. pl. of *dius*, a wild beast, E. *deer*, G. *thier*. Here we may note (1) the substitution of *r* for *s* in E. *deer*, and (2) the change of *s* to *z* between two vowels, precisely as in *thuzei*, v. 11, and in *thizei*.

15. **Usfullnoda**, has been fulfilled. The passive sense is due to the letter -*n*; verbs in -*nan* being so used. See note to 4. 37.

Atnehwida sik, has drawn itself near, has approached; the use of *sik* being reflexive.

16. **Is, this Seimonis**, lit. of him, of that Simon; i. e. of him, viz. Simon.

17. **Hirjats** is only used as an imperative dual, ' come here, ye two!' It only occurs in two other forms, viz. *hiri*, which is the corresponding singular, ' come thou here,' and *hirjith*, pl. ' come ye here.'

Gatauja, &c.; 'I will make you two to become catchers of men.'

18. **Laistidedun,** they followed; lit. 'they took the tracks'; from *laists,* sb. a track.

19. **Leitil,** a little, is the proposed reading in Gabelentz and Löbe, the MS. having *leita.* Uppström proposes *leitilata* as being the strict neuter form; but *leitil* will do as well, the suffix *-ata* being occasionally dropped.

20. **Hai-hait,** he called; here *hai-* is the reduplicating prefix, just as in Lat. *ce-cidi* and the Gk. *τέ-τυφα.* It is used to form the past tense of some (not all) of the strong verbs. It is obtained by adding *ai* to the first letter of the verb.

21. **Sabbato** is here indeclinable; or we may take *sabbato-daga* as a compound word in the dative case. See the expression again in 2. 23.

Laisida, he taught, pt. t. of *lais-jan,* secondary verb from a base *lais-,* appearing in the cognate A.-S. *lár* (=*lair* = *lais*), E. *lore.* Thus *laisida* = A.-S. *lǽrde* = G. *lehrte.*

27. **Swa-ei,** so that; cf. note on *saei,* v. 2.

Hwo, &c.; 'what is the teaching, the new?' = what is the new doctrine? This answers to the Gk. idiom, which admits of the expression *τίς ἡ διδαχὴ ἡ καινή*; and see 6. 2.

Jah after *waldufnja* has the force of 'even,' lit. 'also'; cf. v. 38.

28. **And allans bisitands Galeilaias,** throughout all the inhabitants of Galilee. The regular acc. pl. would be *bisitandans,* but certain pres. participles, when treated as substantives, make the acc. pl. in *-s* instead of *-ans.* See nouns in *-nds* in the Grammar.

29. **In garda,** in the house, where *garda* is the dative. We should rather have expected the accusative (as in Latin, after verbs of motion); and, indeed, *in gard* occurs in 2. 26 and 3. 20.

30. **Bi,** concerning; just as *by* was used in Middle English.

31. **Af-lai-lot,** left, lit. 'let'; here *af-* is the prefix, and *lai-* the reduplication; see note to v. 20. And see *fra-lai-lot* in v. 34.

32. The dative absolute in Gothic answers to the ablative absolute in Latin; hence **andanahtja than waurthanamma** = 'twilight being then come.' The following *than* = 'when.'

Ubil-habandans, evil-having, i. e. having an illness; precisely answering to the Gk. *κακῶς ἔχοντας* and the Latin *male habentes.* So also in 6. 55; but in 2. 17 we find *ubilaba habandans,* where *-aba* is the regular adverbial suffix.

36. **Galaistans waurthun,** were followers; a periphrasis for 'followed.' The same idiom recurs in Gal. 6. 16.

38. **Thaim bisunjane haimom,** the villages round about. Here *bisunjane* is an adverb; see 3. 34, 6. 6. The MS. reading *haimon* is

a mere slip on the part of the scribe, who put the sing. for the pl., although he had just written *thaim*.

40. **Thatei**, that, is constantly thus used to introduce a dependent clause, with a change of construction ; it here introduces the very words of the speech.

41. **Wiljau**, I am willing ; this verb, when used in the present tense, invariably takes the form of the subjunctive, not the indicative, mood.

42. **Aflaith af imma** ; the reduplication of *af* appears also in the Greek—ἀπῆλθεν ἀπ' αὐτοῦ.

44. **Gagg ataugjan**, go to show ; i.e. go and show. *At-aug-jan* is lit. ' to present to the eye '; from *augo*, the eye. This explains the A.S. *œtýwan*, to show, which is similarly derived from *éage*, the eye, by the usual vowel-change from *éa* to *ý*, and a change from *g* to *w*.

Fram, because of ; Gk. περί.

45. **Is**, he (the healed leper) ; but immediately after, *is* refers to Christ. This inartificial use of the pronouns is very common in A.S., so that it is not always easy to know the real subject of the sentence.

CHAPTER II.

1. **Ga-freh-un**, they learnt by inquiry. Such is frequently the sense of the corresponding A.S. verb *frignan* ; see Glossary to Sweet's A.S. Reader. **Ist**, is, i.e. was ; Gk. ἐστί.

2. **Ni gamostedun**, lit. were not able, could not ; but the meaning is extended, as in other passages, to the sense ' could not find room.' *Gamostedun* is from the strong-weak verb *gamotan*.

4. **Thar-ei**, where that, where. Cf. *sa-ei*.

Us-grab-and-ans, lit. graving or digging out, hence breaking through. The use of this peculiar word is due to the Gk. ἐξορύξαντες. Cf. 12. 1, where the Gk. has ὤρυξεν.

Insailidedun jah fralailotun, lowered by cords and let down ; but the usual Gk. text merely has χαλῶσι.

5. **Af-let-anda**, are let off, are remitted or forgiven. Notice the characteristic suffix *-da* of the passive voice. So also in v. 9.

6. **Thagk-jand-ans sis**, thinking to themselves. Here *gk* is for *nk* ; and *sis* is the dat. of the reflexive pronoun. Cf. Latin *sibi*.

7. **Niba ains guth**, except one, viz. God ; except God alone.

11. **Nimuh**, and take. The enclitic particle *uh* requires particular notice ; it is here used precisely like the Lat. *que*, being suffixed to the first word in the sentence which it joins to the preceding. It is also used like the Lat. *-que* in composition (as in *quis-que*), so that we have the

forms *sah*, short for *sa-uh*, *hwaz-uh* for *hwas-uh*, &c.   Cf. *kwathuh*,
i. e. and said, 14. 13.   And see notes to 3. 2, 8. 23.

12. **Aiw ni**, aye not, ever not, i. e. never; see 3. 29.

Gasehwun, *third* pers. pl.; not the *first* person, as in the Gk. and
A. V.

15. **Jah warth**, and it came to pass; lit. it became.

16. The words supplied are necessary to the sense; the scribe probably omitted them by accident.

17. **Ubilaba habandans**, they that are sick; see note to 1. 32.

19. **Ibai magun**, lit. if may, whether may, a way of introducing a
question; we drop the *if*.

Und thatei, unto (the time) that, i. e. as long as.

20. **Afnimada**, shall be taken away; here we may note (1) the
repetition of *af* after the verb; (2) the passive ending in *-da*; (3) the
use of the present for the future.

21. **Ibai afnimai**, &c.; lit. 'lest it may take away the fulness from
it, the new from the old.'   Here *sa ninja*, being feminine, agrees with
fullo understood; and *fairnjin*, being masculine, relates to *snaga*.   The
sentence is ill-constructed and, in fact, wrong, and is only intelligible when
compared with the Gk. text—εἰ δὲ μή, αἴρει τὸ πλήρωμα αὐτοῦ τὸ καινὸν
τοῦ παλαιοῦ, καὶ χεῖρον σχίσμα γίνεται.   The translator has taken τὸ
πλήρωμα to be an *accusative*, and has then translated every word just as
it stands.

22. **Giutand**, they pour, people pour.

23. Here we have a construction resembling the Latin accusative
with the infinitive.   'And it came to pass, that he is going through';
the present infinitive being used descriptively.

26. **Uf**, in the time of, lit. under; used to translate Gk. ἐπί.

Thanz-ei = *thans-ei*, which that.

Ainaim gudjam, for the priests alone; see v. 7.

Mith sis wisandam, being with himself, i. e. them that were
with him.

28. **Jah**, even; Gk. καί.

CHAPTER III.

2. **Hailidedi-u**, whether he would heal.   The sense of 'whether' is
given by the suffixed particle *-u*, which is omitted in the MS. in this
particular instance, but must be supplied as in other passages.   In the
very next verse, we have *skuld-u ist*, whether it is obligatory; and in
10. 38 we have *maguts-u*, whether are ye able.

6. **Us-kwem-eina**, pt. pl. subj. of *us-kwiman*.   So also *thraihcina*
from *thrcihan* in v. 9; *attaitokcina* in v. 10.

9. **Ei skip habaith wesi,** that a ship might be had, i. e. kept in readiness. Here *habaith* is the neuter of the pp. of *haban*.

11. **Thaih** = thai-uh, pl. of *sah* = sa-uh. *Thaih than* = whensoever they, as soon as they.

12. **Ga-swi-kunth-i-ded-eina**; here *ga-* is the prefix, *swi-* another prefix, *kunth-* a pp. with the sense 'known,' *-i-* the suffix helping to form a causal verb, *-ded-* the mark of the past tense of a weak verb, and *-eina* the suffix of the pl. of the pt. t. subjunctive. For *swikunth*, see 6. 14.

15. **Sauhtins,** diseases, lit. sicknesses. It is exactly represented by the obsolete E. *sought*. Thus Fitzherbert, in his Book of Husbandry, speaks of *longe-sought,* i. e. lung-disease, as incident to cattle.

17. **Gasatida im namna,** he set to them names, he gave them the names. *Namna* is the pl. of the neut. sb. *namo,* just as *watna* is pl. of *wato.*

20. **Ga-iddja sik,** lit. went themselves together, i. e. came together. Here *ai* is not the usual diphthong, but due to the juxta-position of two distinct vowels.

22. **Uswairpith** governs the dative; so also in 5. 40 and 9. 47.

27. **Kasa** is governed by *wilwan*.

Galeithands in gard is, entering into his house; εἰσελθὼν εἰς τὴν οἰκίαν αὐτοῦ.

Than, then, must be supplied; its omission is clearly due to the repetition of *than-* in the following *thana.*

28. **Af-let-ada,** shall be forgiven.

Allata, all, neut. sing.

Thata frawaurhte, the (kind) of sins; here *frawaurhte* is gen. pl. after the neut. sing. *thata,* and the two words form a phrase together.

31. **Standand-ona.** This use of the *neuter* pl. is very remarkable, as we should expect the masculine. Precisely the same construction occurs in the parallel passage in St. Luke viii. 20, where we have *gasaih-wan thuk gairnjandona*, desiring to see thee.

32. **Setun**; a pl. verb, to agree with *managei*, a noun of multitude. Cf. *thans sitandans,* those sitting, in v. 34; and see 4. 1.

35. **Saei allis,** for whosoever. Here *allis* translates the Gk. γάρ, as in other passages, and is the second word in the sentence. So also *sai allis* = for behold, Luke i. 44.

Sa, he.

Jah .. jah, both .. and.

CHAPTER IV.

1. **Ina,** acc. with infinitive; 'so that he, entering into a ship, is sitting in the sea.' The MS. *galeithan* is certainly a clerical error for

galeithandan ; cf. ὥστε αὐτὸν ἐμβάντα εἰς τὸ πλοῖον καθῆσθαι ἐν τῇ θαλάσσῃ.

2. **Manag,** many a thing, much; neut. acc. sing.

4. **Raihtis,** however; this is used with but little force, and answers to Gk. μέν, which it translates.

5. **Antharuth-than** = *anthar-uh than*, but then other; Gk. ἄλλο δέ. In **thiz-ei** = *in this ei*, on this account that, because; *in* with the genitive denotes ' on account of.' Cf. *in this waurdis*, 4. 17.

6. **At,** &c., at the sun then arising; here *at* with the dative is used with the force of the usual dative absolute. So also in v. 35, q. v.

8. The use of letters to denote numbers is borrowed from Gk. The Gothic *l*, like the Gk. λ', stands for 30; *r*, like Gk. ρ', means 100; whilst *j* occupies the same position in the alphabet as the Gk. ξ, and therefore means 60.

9. **Aus-ona haus-jand-ona,** hearing ears.

10. **Thai bi ina,** they (that were) beside him; οἱ περὶ αὐτόν. **Frehun** takes here a *double* accusative.

11. **At-gib-an,** not the infinitive, but neut. of the pp. **Jainaim thaim uta,** to them that are without; ἐκείνοις δὲ τοῖς ἔξω.

12. **Nibai hwan,** lest at any time. *Nibai* = *ni ibai*, if not.

15. **Unkarjans,** (being) careless. There is no such word in the Gk. text. According to Massmann, a few Latin texts have *negligenter*.

19. **Bi thata anthar lustjus,** lit. desires concerning the other thing, i. e. concerning other things; περὶ τὰ λοιπὰ ἐπιθυμίαι.

21. **Ibai . . duthe ei,** lit. if . . for the purpose that. Here *ibai* introduces a question. **Ni·u** = *ni-uh*, and not. In the next verse, *nih* also = *ni-uh*; but there is a difference in the syntax, *niu* being used in the *interrogative* clause (as in v. 38), but *nih* in the direct statement, the final *-h* having the force of γάρ.

22. **Nih allis ist hwa fulginis,** for there is not anything of that which is hidden. *Hwa* is a neuter nom., followed by a genitive.

24. **Mitath** occurs again as a *dative* form in 2 Cor. x. 13. **Izwis thaim galaubjandam,** to you that believe; lit. to you the believing.

25. **Jah thatei,** even that which.

33. **Hausjon** occurs, as a by-form of *hausjan*, in other passages also.

34. **Inuh,** prep. without. *Inuh* also occurs as a mere compound of *in*, in, with the enclitic particle *-uh*.

37. **Gafullnoda,** became full, was filled. The passive sense is given by the inserted *n*; we thus have *gafull-j-an*, to *make* full, *gafull-n-an*, to *become* full. This *n* evidently arose from the suffix of the pp. of a

strong verb; thus *and-bundn-an*, to become unbound = *and-bundan-an*, where *bundan-* is the stem of the pp.

38. **Niu kara thuk thizei,** is there not a care to thee of the fact that, does it not concern thee that? The word *ist* is omitted, though occurring in other passages; the phrase *kara ist* is used (as here) with the accusative of the person and the genitive of the thing. So also in 12. 14.

39. **Af-dumb-n,** become dumb. Verbs in *-nan* make the imperative singular in *-n*. Cf. note to verse 37.

41. **Ohtedun sis agis mikil,** they feared for themselves (with) a great fear. Here *agis* is the accusative; imitated from the Gk. ἐφοβή-θησαν φόβον μέγαν.

Sijai, lit. may be.

CHAPTER V.

4. **Eisarnam bi fotuns,** with irons by his feet; a periphrasis for 'fetters'; Gk. πέδαις. Just below the Gk. πέδας is rendered by **ana fotum eisarna**, irons on his feet.

7. **Hwa mis jah thus,** τί ἐμοὶ καὶ σοί;

Sunau may be either dat. or voc.; it is doubtless here a vocative; Gk. υἱέ.

10. **Usdrebi**; read *usdribi*, pt. s. subj. of *us-dreiban*. See 6. 13.

13. **And driuson,** down the slope. *Driuso* is 'that which falls away,' from *driusan*, to fall.

14. **Kwemun,** they (the villagers) came; the subject being changed, as in the Gk.

Hwa wesi thata waurthano, what that which was done might be.

15. The repetition of **thana** is due to that of τόν in the Gk.

18. The word **ina** (repeated) is governed by **bath,** the nom. to which is **sa,** understood from **saei.** 'And him, as (he was) entering the ship, he who had been mad prayed him.'

21. **Us-leith-and-in Iesua**; dative absolute. The Gk. has the gen. absolute.

23. **Aftumist habaith,** lit. hath (i. e. fares) at the last, lies in extremity, is at the point of death; a literal translation of ἐσχάτως ἔχει. After *habaith*, we must mentally supply *I pray thee*, as is actually done in the A. V.

Kwimands lagjais, coming thou mayst lay, i. e. thou mayst come and lay; ἐλθὼν ἐπιθῇς.

25. **Kwinona suma,** a certain one of women, i. e. a certain woman. So also *sumai thize bokarje*, certain of the scribes, Matt. 9. 3; and compare *ains* used with the gen. pl. in verse 22 above.

E

29. **Slaha**, stroke, i.e. plague; Gk. μάστιγος. The Lat. *plaga* has the same double sense.

30. **Tho us sis maht usgaggandein**, the might (virtue) going out of himself. So also *tho thata taujandein*, the woman that is doing this, in verse 32. The use of the pres. part. is very graphic.

34. **Sijais**, mayst thou be; the subj. used for the imperative.

36. **Rodith**, neut. of the pp. of *rodjan*; agreeing with *waurd*. So also *gaskeirith* is neut. in verse 41.

39. **Hwa**, why? Cf. the use of Gk. τί.

40. **Thans mith sis**, those with him, i.e. his chosen disciples.

41. **Kwath-uh**, and said. See note to 2. 11.

Taleitha kumei, Ταλιθά κοῦμι.

42. **Was jere twalibe**, was of twelve years; ἦν γὰρ ἐτῶν δώδεκα.

43. **Ei manna ni funthi thata**, that a man should not find it out, i.e. that no one should find out or know it.

CHAPTER VI.

2. **So handugeino so**; cf. 1. 27, and the note.

Wairthand, take place, i.e. are done or wrought.

7. **Hwanzuh** = *hwans-uh*, separately, severally; acc. pl. of *hwas-uh*, every one.

8. **Ei waiht ni nemeina**, lit. that a whit they should not take, i.e. that they should take naught (no whit).

9. **Wasjaith**, put ye on, wear; imp. pl. With dat. case.

11. **Janai**, as in the MS., is a mere clerical error for *jainai*.

14. **Allis**, for, Gk. γάρ; placed as the *second* word in the sentence, but to be taken *first*.

Sa daupjands, the baptizing one; Gk. ὁ βαπτίζων.

15. 'That he is a prophet as one of the prophets.' The A. V. has '*or* as.'

16. Lit. 'that to him I cut the head off, to John'; i.e. 'John, whose head I cut off.'

17. **Auk raihtis**, for also, for; which begins the sentence. So also in 7. 10; cf. 9. 41.

Gahabaida, seized; compare *haban* with Lat. *capere*.

In **Hairodiadins**, because of Herodias; *in* with the gen. has this sense; so also in verse 26.

19. **Naiw**, was angry with; Gk. ἐνεῖχεν. The word is very doubtful, but is assumed to be the pt. t. from a verb *neiwan*, to be angry. It has been supposed to be related to A. S. *niwol*, prostrate; but this is little better than conjecture, as the sense does not altogether suit.

20. **Ohta sis,** feared for himself, dreaded; followed by the acc. *Iohannen.*

21. 'And a fitting day taking place'; here we have a sort of *nominative* absolute, in place of the usual *dative.* But in verse 22, we have the datives *atgaggandein,* &c.

22. **Dauhtr**; such is the proper form of the dative; see 7. 26. The MS. has the nom. form *dauhtar.*

Thishwizuh = *this hwis-uh,* whatsoever; the gen. case, governed by *bidei.* Verbs of *asking* frequently take the gen. case, as in A.S. So also *hwis* in verse 24, and *haubidis* (which is in apposition with *hwis*), are both in the genitive.

27. **Spaikulatur**; Gk. σπεκουλάτωρα, which is merely a Gk. transcription of Lat. *speculatorem.*

55. **Thadei,** wherever; see 14. 14.

Ei is wesi, that he might be.

56. **Thau,** even, merely; Gk. κἄν.

Skauta, dat. case, governed by *attaitokeina.* So also *imma.*

CHAPTER VII.

1. **Gakwemun sik,** came together; here used reflexively, not as in 2. 2; Gk. συνάγονται. Cf. 10. 1.

3, 4. These verses are parenthetical, as in the A. V.

4. **Anthar ist manag,** lit. other (thing there) is many. Cf. verse 8.

5. **Bi thammei,** according to that which.

6. **Bi izwis than liutans,** with respect to you, the hypocrites; Gk. περὶ ὑμῶν τῶν ὑποκριτῶν.

11. **Thishwah thatei,** as to whatsoever.

Gabatnis, thou receivest benefit.

12. **Ni .. ni waiht**; a double negative; οὐκέτι .. οὐδέν.

18. **Frathjith** governs the dative, as in Luke 2. 50; hence, *ni frathjith thammei* = do ye not understand that thing, that, &c.

23. **Gagamainjand.** This curious reduplication of the prefix *ga-* occurs in some other verbs also.

31. **Mith tweihnaim markom,** lit. amid the two boundaries; Gk. ἀνά μέσον τῶν ὁρίων.

33. **In ausona imma,** upon the ears to him, i. e. upon his ears.

36. **Mann,** dat. case; always used instead of *mannin,* which would be the *regular* form.

Mais thamma, by that the more, so much the more.

CHAPTER VIII.

1. **At** with the dative signifies the time when; *at .. wisandein* = whilst the multitude was very great. Cf. 11. 11.

E 2

7. Jah thans, them also; καὶ αὐτά.

8. Spyreidans, merely a Gothic form of Gk. σπυρίδας.

11. Du imma, lit. to him; hence, at his hands, from him; παρ' αὐτοῦ.

12. Jabai, if; we must supply 'it will be strange' before it. The idiom is a Greek one, and due to the Gk. εἰ δοθήσεται.

Taikne, of tokens. gen. pl.; supply 'any.'

15. 'See that ye guard yourselves from,' &c.

23. Ga-u-hwa-sehwi = *hwa-uh-gasehwi*, if he could see anything. Here *u* = *uh* is used as the sign of interrogation, and is put after the prefix *ga-*, in order to introduce it as early as possible. *Hwa* is used indefinitely. Cf. 14. 44, 16. 8.

24. 'I see men, so that I see them as trees.' The word *see* only occurs *once* in the A. V., but the Gothic is nearer the Greek; βλέπω τοὺς ἀνθρώπους, ὅτι ὡς δένδρα ὁρῶ. See the Revised Version.

25. Aftra, again. For this sense, see also 9. 12.

26. Mannhun, to any one; dat. case. See note to 7. 36.

Wehsa should rather be *weihsa*; but the form occurs again in the following verse.

27. Mans, men, nom. pl.; we also find *mannans*.

31. Skulds ist uskiusan, is liable to be rejected. Here *uskiusan*, lit. 'to reject,' is used idiomatically with the passive sense. So also **uskwiman,** to be killed, lit. 'to kill.' But **usstandan,** being intransitive, is used in the usual manner. Cf. *frabugjan*, in 14. 5; and see 9. 45.

38. Meina, of me, gen. of *ik*. So also is, of him.

CHAPTER IX.

1. Thai ize, those of them who; agreeing with *sumai*.

3. Wullareis . . ni mag, a fuller cannot, i. e. no fuller can.

10. 'What is it, to arise from the dead?'

15. Managei, as a noun of multitude, takes the plural pres. part. and verb.

18. Thishwaruh thei, wheresoever that.

Usdreibeina should be *usdribeina*, pt. pl. subj. The vowel *i* is the same as in the pt. pl. indic. and the pp.

19. Und hwa, until what, until when.

At izwis, with you.

21. Hwan lagg mel ist, how long a time is it? πόσος χρόνος ἐστίν.

22. Unsara, gen. pl. of *ik*, governed by *hilp*; see verse 24.

Unsis, acc. pl. of *ik*.

23. Thata, this saying, viz. 'If thou canst,' &c. Gk. εἶπεν αὐτῷ τό, Εἰ δύνασαι, κ.τ.λ. Cf. 10. 40, 12. 33.

Allata mahteig, everything (is) possible; Gk. πάντα δυνατά (without any verb).

29. **In waihtai ni mag,** lit. in a whit can not, i. e. can by no means.

31. **Uskwimand,** they (i. e. men) will kill him.

41. **Saei auk allis,** for whosoever. *Auk* = Gk. γάρ; see 6. 17. *Allis,* wholly, is a mere expletive. Gk. ὃς γὰρ ἄν.

42. **Goth ist imma mais,** it is good for him rather; Gk. καλόν ἐστιν αὐτῷ μᾶλλον.

45. **Gawairpan** = to be cast; see note to 8. 31. So also *atwairpan* in verse 47.

49. **Hwazuh auk,** for every one.
Hwarjatoh hunsle, each one of sacrifices, i. e. every sacrifice. *Hwarjatoh* = *hwarjata-uh,* neut. of *hwarjizuh,* for which see 15. 24.

50. **Supuda,** put for *supoda,* shall be seasoned. The form *gasupoda* actually occurs in Luke, 14. 34; but we have one other instance of the use of *u* for *o* in the form *gakrotuda,* shall be broken, Luke 20. 18.

CHAPTER X.

2. **Skuld-u sijai,** whether it may be right. Here -*u* asks the question, as usual.

7. **Inuh this,** on account of this.

13. Understand *imma* after the second *du.*

17. **Arbja wairthau,** I may become an inheritor.

21. **Ainis thus wan ist,** it is lacking to thee of one thing.

23. **Faiho** = *faihu;* see verse 22.

24. **Hugjandam afar faihau,** thinking after (i. e. upon) wealth. *Hugjandam,* though an uncertain reading, is probably the right one.

25. **Azitizo;** better *azetizo;* see 2. 9.

29. **In meina,** for the sake of me, for my sake.

32. **Aftra,** again; Gk. πάλιν.
Thoei habaidedun ina gadaban, the things which had to befall him. Gk. τὰ μέλλοντα αὐτῷ συμβαίνειν. This use of E. *had* precisely represents the Gothic idiom. Cf. *thatei habaida taujan,* that which he had to do, was about to do; John 6. 6.

33. **Thatei sai,** namely, lo! Here *thatei* represents the Gk. ὅτι. The verse is unfinished in the Gothic; the Gk. has καὶ παραδώσουσιν αὐτὸν τοῖς ἔθνεσι, which Massmann translates into Gothic by *jah atgiband ina thaim thiudom.*

35. **Wileima** is the 1st pers. pl.; we should expect *wileiwa,* the 1st pers. *dual,* but a mixture of the dual and plural is not surprising. But

bidjos is really a dual form; and so is *uggkis*. In the next verse we have the dual forms *wileits* and *igkwis*; but in verse 37 we have the plurals *eis* and *kwethun*, followed by the duals *ugkis* and *sitaiwa*. So also in verses 38, &c.

38. **Maguts-u**, could ye two? Here -*u*, as usual, introduces a question. *Maguts* is the 2 p. pt. dual; and *magu*, in verse 39, is the 1 p. pt. dual.

39. The MS. omits **daupjanda**, but it must be supplied; Gk. βαπτισθήσεσθε.

40. **Ith thata, du sitan**, but this thing, viz. to sit. Cf. 9. 23.

42. **Thaiei** must be supplied; it was probably omitted owing to its likeness to *thatei*. Gk. ὅτι οἱ δοκοῦντες.

45. **At andbahtjam**, lit. for services, i.e. to receive services; Gk. διακονηθῆναι.

46. Read *Bartcimaius*, as being a nom. form; cf. *Nazoraius*.

49. **Haihait atwopjan ina**, commanded (them) to call him.

CHAPTER XI.

1. **Bethsfagein;** so also in Luke, 19. 29. Massmann mentions the reading Βηθσφαγή.

2. **Gaggats**, go ye two; see note to 10. 35. Observe the numerous dual forms. Cf. 14. 13.

3. **This gairneith**, desires this (foal); *gairnjan* governs the genitive.

7. **Ana**, upon, is here (at first) used adverbially; cf. *du* at the end of 10. 13. But *ana ina* = upon him.

11. **At** with the dat. expresses the time when; see note to 8. 1.

21. **Frakwast**, thou cursedst. Here *kwast* is a phonetic substitution for the regular (but scarcely pronounceable) form *kwatht*.

22. **Galaubein guths**, faith in God, lit. faith of God; Gk. πίστιν Θεοῦ.

23. **Wairp thus**, cast thyself. *Wairpan* sometimes governs the dative case, as here. See 12. 4.

Thata, ei thatei, this (thing), that that which.

Thishwah thei, this, whatever it be, that.

29. Here **fraihna** takes the acc. *izwis*, and the gen. *waurdis*; 'I also ask you one word.'

30. **Uzuh**, whether from. *Uz-uh* = *us-uh*, where the enclitic -*uh* introduces a question, as usual. See notes to 8. 23, 10. 38.

32. **Uhtedun** is for *ohtedun*; see 12. 12. Cf. *supuda* for *supoda*; see note to 9. 50.

CHAPTER XII.

1. **Dal uf mesa**, a hollow place for a wine-vat. *Mes* also means a table, dish; hence a wide vat.

2. **Nemi akranis**, he might receive (some) of the fruit; *akranis* being in the gen. case. Gk. λάβῃ ἀπὸ τοῦ καρποῦ.

4. 'Him they maltreated, throwing stones.' Here *wairpan* governs the dative; see 11. 23.

Haubith wundan brahtedun, lit. brought (i. e. made) him wounded in the head. *Wundan* is the acc. masculine, and governs *haubith*, which is also an accusative, indicating the place in which the wound was felt.

5. **Sumanzuh** = *sumans-uh*, and some.

6. **Liubana sis**, dear to himself.

10. **Warth du haubida**, has become for the head; a lit. translation of ἐγενήθη εἰς κεφαλήν.

14. 'And there (is) no care to thee of any one'; see note to 4. 38.

19. **Kwenai** is the dat. after *bileithai*; so also *fraiwa* is dat. sing. in verse 20. But *barne* is the gen. pl., so that *ni barne* must be taken as equivalent to 'none of children,' i. e. no child.

30. Understand **ist**, is. The verb is omitted in the Gk. also, which has αὕτη πρώτη ἐντολή. So also in the next verse.

32. **Kwast**, thou hast said; see note to 11. 21.

33. **Thata, du frijon**, this thing, viz. to love. Cf. 9. 23, 10. 40.

38. The chapter ends with the syllable *bo-*, the rest being lost.

CHAPTER XIII.

16. The verse is lost all but the two last words; it must have ended with **niman wastja seina**, to take his garment.

19. The Gothic literally follows the Gk., making **thai dagos jainai** (those days) the *nominative* case. 'For those days shall be such affliction'; ἔσονται γὰρ αἱ ἡμέραι ἐκεῖναι θλίψις; see the Revised Version.

Und hita, up to this time.

20. **Ainhun leike**, anybody; lit. 'any of bodies'; *leike* being gen. plural.

25. **Wairthand driusandeins**, shall be falling; ἔσονται ἐκπίπτοντες.

28. **Uskeinand laubos**, leaves shoot forth. Here *laubos* is the nominative, not the accusative as in the A. V. The Gk. ἐκφύῃ τὰ φύλλα may have been misunderstood by the translator.

29. The verse may easily be completed by adding the word *haurdim*, the doors. The Gk. has θύραις; and in Matt. 6. 6, *haurdai* corresponds to θύραν.

CHAPTER XIV.

4. The first legible syllable is -teins. The whole sentence should be
—*Du hwe so frakwisteins this balsanis warth,* wherefore was this waste
of the balsam?   .

5. Maht wesi auk, for the balsam might be able to be sold (lit. to
sell), &c.   See note to S. 31.

8. 'What she had, she did.'

13. Gaggats, go ye two.   Note the use of the dual.

16. The verse ends with sipon; add -*jos* to complete the word, and
also *is,* lit. of him.   *Thai siponjos is* = his disciples.   We next pass on
to v. 41, 'See, the Son of man is betrayed into the hands of sinners.'

44. At-uh-than-gaf, put for *than-uh at-gaf,* but then gave (or, had
given).   From the verb *at-giban.* See a similar construction in 16. 8.

51. Leina, with linen; dat. case.
Gripun is, seized him; *is* being the gen. case.

61. Waiht ni = ni waiht, no whit, nothing.

64. Skulan wisan, to be deserving; εἶναι ἔνοχον.

65. Gabaurjaba, gladly; there is no such word in the Greek texts.

66. Paitrau being in the dative absolute, the word jah before atiddja
is superfluous.

68. Ni wait, ni kann, I know not, nor do I understand.

69. Thatei sa thizei ist, that he is (one) of them.   It is clear that
thizei is here used as equivalent for *thize,* gen. pl. of *sa.*   So in verse 70,
thizei is = *thize is,* thou art (one) of them.   Gk. ἐξ αὐτῶν, in both places.

CHAPTER XV.

7. Thaiei gatawidedun.   Cf. the *Revised* Version, 'men who had
committed murder.'   The A. V. is indistinct as to the *number* of the
pronoun and verb.

9. Wileid-u = wileith-u, do ye wish?   Here -*u* is the enclitic
particle indicating a question; and *wileith* is the subjunctive form, used
in place of the indicative.   In verse 12, the form *wileith* occurs; for
the change of final *th* to *d* before *u,* see note to 16. 7.

14. Hwa allis ubilis, for what evil?   *Hwa ubilis* is, literally, 'what
of evil.'

16. Praitoriaun; Gk. Πραιτώριον.

17. Uswindandans, plaiting it; i.e. having plaited it; Gk. πλέξαντες.

19. Lagjandans kniwa; Gk. τιθέντες τὰ γόνατα.

20. Andwasidedun, they unclothed him.   The E. verbal prefix *un-*
is cognate with Goth. *and-*; see note to 1. 7.

21. Sumana manne, some one of men, a certain man.

32. **Atsteigadau,** let him descend. Here the passive voice is used with the force of a *middle* voice. There are a few other similar instances.

34. **Ailoe** ; Gk. 'Ελωί, 'Ελωί, λαμμᾶ σαβαχθανί.
Bilaist, hast thou forsaken ; put for *bilaiht,* which was hard to pronounce.

36. **Dragkida ina,** gave him to drink. Observe the difference between the strong verb *drigkan,* to drink, and the weak causal verb *dragkjan,* to make to drink.

Ei saihwam, that we see ; the indicative, where we might expect the subjunctive.

Kwimai-u Helias, if Helias may come ; where *-u* is the enclitic particle, signifying ' if ' or ' whether.'

39. In **andwairthja is,** in his presence, before him, near him ; ἐξ ἐναντίας αὐτοῦ.

41. ' And when he was in Galilee, they also followed him,' &c.

42. **Paraskaiwe** ; Gk. Παρασκευή ; preparation.

43. **Anananthjands galaith,** taking courage, he went ; τολμήσας εἰσῆλθε.

44. **Thana** ; MS. *than.* Possibly for *than',* the *a* being elided before the following *h* in quick speech.

CHAPTER XVI.

4. **Gaumidedun thammei,** they perceived the fact that. *Gaumjan* takes the dative.

6. **Ni faurhteith izwis,** do not fear for yourselves.

7. **Kwithuduh** = kwithuth uh, and say ye. Cf. note to 15. 9.

8. **Diz-uh-than-sat** = than-uh dis-sat, for then . . . seized upon them. The nominative is *reiro,* trembling. The verb *dis-sat* must be again supplied after *usfilmei.* Cf. note to 14. 44.

Ohtedun sis auk, for they feared for themselves.

9. As ' the two oldest Gk. MSS., and some other authorities, omit from verse 9 to the end,' the occurrence of these verses in the Gothic is noteworthy.

10. **Wisandam,** lit. being, Gk. γενομένοις. But the sense is really ' that had been,' as in the A.V.

12. ' And then, after this.' Here the MS. ceases, the rest of the gospel being lost.

LIST OF WORDS
OF COMMON OCCURRENCE.

af, of, off, from, by, &c.
afar, after, according to.
aftra, again, back.
ains, one.
ak, but.
alls, all.
ana, on, upon, in, &c.
and, towards, to, throughout.
at, at, by, &c.
aththan, but.
atta, father.
auk, for, also.
bi, by, about, near, &c.
bithe, whilst, when.
dags, day.
dis-, apart; also as intensive prefix.
du, to, towards.
duhwe, wherefore.
duthe, therefore.
ei, that.
eis, they; *eizei*, they that.
faur, for, before, &c.
faura, before, because of.
filu, much.
fram, from, by, on account of.
fruma, first.
ga-, a common prefix; scarcely affecting the sense.
gaggan, to go.
-h, enclitic; see *uh*.
haban, to have.
hails, whole.
haubith, head.
her, here.

himins, heaven.
hwa, what.
hwan, when.
hwar, where.
hwas, who.
iba, *ibai*, perhaps, lest.
iddja, went.
ik, I.
im, am; to them.
imma, him; dat.
in, in, into, to, by, &c.
ina, him; acc.
ins, them.
is, art; he.
ist, is.
ita, it.
ith, but.
izai, to her.
ize, of them.
izos, of her.
izwar, your.
jabai, if.
jah, and.
jai, yea.
jains, that (yon).
ju, now.
jus, ye.
kunnan, to know.
kwam, came.
kwath, quoth, said.
mais, more; adv.
manags, much, many.
manna, a man.
meina, of me.

meins, mine.

mik, me; acc.

mis, me; dat.

mith, with, by, near.

ni, nih, not, nor.

niba, nibai, except, unless.

nu, now.

sa, he; who (rel.); the.

saei, who (lit. he who).

sama, same.

seins, his, their.

sis, to himself, themselves.

so, she; the.

sums, some.

sunna, sun.

suns, soon, at once.

sunus, son.

swa, so, also.

swaei, so that, that.

swaswe, just as, so that.

swe, as.

thai, the; nom. m. pl.

thaim, the, those; dat. pl.

thairh, through, by.

thamma, to the; dat. m. n. s.

than, then, when.

thana, the; acc. m. s.

thans, the; acc. m. pl.

thata, thatei, that.

thau, though, than.

thei, that.

theins, thy.

this, of the; gen. m. n. s.

thizai, to the; dat. f. s.

thize, of the; gen. m. n. pl.

tho, her, it, the, that; acc. f. s. and n. and acc. pl.

thos, the; nom. and acc. f. pl.

thu, thou; dat. *thus*; acc. *thuk*.

ufar, over.

uh, u, 'h; enclitic particle.

und, until.

undar, under.

uns, unsis, us.

unsar, our.

unte, for, because, till.

us, out, from.

ut, uta, out, without; adv.

waila, well.

warth, became, happened, was.

was, was.

weis, we.

wesi, might be.

wesun, were.

withra, over against, in return for, near, towards.

GLOSSARIAL INDEX.

The words are arranged in alphabetical order. Thus *hw* follows *h* ; *kw* follows *k* ; and *th* follows *te*, and precedes *ti*.

In compound words, the composition is indicated by a hyphen. Thus, in *af-letan*, the *af-* is a mere prefix, and the word is to be compared with the simpler form *letan*.

The references are given to the *chapters* and *verses* of St. Mark's Gospel. Numerous words are added, without references, which do not occur in that gospel. Thus the Index includes all the more important words in the language.

Forms marked *, as **Agan***, are unauthorised, but may be inferred.

The contractions are such as will be readily understood. Thus *wk. s. m.* = weak substantive, masculine; *str. v.* = strong verb; *adj.* = adjective; *gen.* = genitive; &c.

Aba, *wk. s. m.* a man; or, rather, a husband, 10. 12 ; *gen. pl.* abne ; *dat. pl.* abnam.

Abraba, *adv.* strongly, excessively, very, 16. 4.

Abrs, *adj.* strong, mighty. · Cf. A. S. *abal*, strength.

Af, *prep. with dat.* of, from, out of, off, by, &c.; 1. 42 ; 2. 20 ; 3. 22 ; 5. 4, &c.; af taihswon, on my right hand, 10. 37. E. *of*.

Af-aikan, *str. v. (pt. t.* aiaik), to deny vehemently, imprecate curses on oneself, to deny, 14. 71 ; *pt. t.* af-aiaik, 14. 68.

Af-airzjan, *wk. v.* to lead astray, to deceive, 13. 22.

Afar, *prep. with dat. and acc.* after (both of place and time), 1. 7 ; according to, 5. 24. Afar thata, thereafter ; afar thatei, after that ; afar leitil, after a little while ; afaruh than, but after, 16. 12. Comparative of *af*.

Afar-gaggan, *str. v.* to go after, follow, 5. 37.

Afar-laistjan, *wk. v.* to follow after ; *with dat. case*, 10. 32.

Afar-sabbatus, *s.* the week following, 16. 2.

Afar-uh than, but after, 16. 12. See **Afar** and **Uh.**

Af-dauthjan, *wk. v.* to kill, put to death, 14. 55 ; *pass.* to die, 7. 10.

Af-dumbnan, *wk. v.* to hold one's peace, to be still, 4. 39.

Af-hwapjan, *wk. v.* to quench; to choke, 4. 7.

Af-hwapnan, *wk. v.* to be quenched, 9. 44, 46; to be choked, 5. 13.

Af-lageins, *str. s. f.* a laying aside, remission, 1. 4.

Af-lailot, left, 1. 31.

Af-lailotum, we have left, 10. 28. See **Af-letan.**

Af-leithan, *str. v.* (laith, lithans), to go away, depart, leave, 1. 42 ; 3. 7 ; *pt. s.* aflaith, went, 12. 1.

Af-letan, *str. v.* (lailot, letans), to leave, forsake, 1. 18; to put away (a wife), 10. 4; to send away, 4. 36; to let off, forgive, 3. 28; *pt. s.* aflailot, left, 1. 31; *pt. pl.* 1 *p.* aflailotum, 10. 28.,

Af-maitan, *str. v.* (maimait, maitans), to cut off, 9. 43; af-maitan haubith, to behead, 6. 16, 27; *pt. s.* afmainnait, 6. 16.

Af-marzeins, *str. s. f.* deceitfulness, 4. 19.

Af-niman, *str. v.* to take away, remove, take away from, 2. 20, 21; 4. 25.

Af-sateins, *str. s. f.* divorcement, 10. 4.

Af-satjan, *wk. v.* to divorce, 10. 2.

Af-slahan, *str. v.* (sloh, slahans), to slay, 12. 5; *pt. s.* afsloh, struck off, 14. 47; *pt. pl.* afslohun, killed, 12. 5.

Af-slauthnan, *wk. v.* to be beside oneself, to be amazed, 1. 26; 10. 24.

Afta, *adv.* behind. A. S. *æft.*

Aftana, *adv.* behind, from behind, 5. 27. A. S. *æftan.*

Af-tiuhan, *str. v.* (tauh, tauhum, tauhans), to draw away, push off; to take, draw aside, 8. 32.

Aftra, *adv.* back, backwards; again, once more, 2. 1; 3. 1; *hence* aftra gabotjan, to restore, 9. 12; aftra gasatjan, to heal, 8. 25.

Aftuma, *adj.* the hindmost, the last, 10. 31. See **Afta.**

Aftumists, *adj.* the last, 9. 35; aftumist haban, to be at the point of death, 5. 23.

Af-wairpan, *str. v.* to cast away, put away, 10. 50. See **Wairpan.**

Af-walwjan, *wk. v.* to roll away, 16. 3, 4.

Agan*, *root verb,* to fear; *hence* un-agands, fearless.

Aggilus, *str. s. m.* an angel, 8. 38; messenger, 1. 2; *pl.* aggileis, 1. 13; aggiljus, 12. 25. Gk. ἄγγελος.

Aggwus, *adj.* narrow, strait; aggwitha, *s.* anguish. A. S. *ange,* strait.

Agis, *str. s. n.* fright, fear, terror, awe, 4. 41. E. *awe.*

Agjan, *wk. v.* to terrify; *only in compounds.*

Aglaitei, *wk. s. f.* lasciviousness, 7. 22. *From* aglus.

Aglo, *wk. s. f.* anguish, tribulation, affliction, 4. 17; 13. 24.

Agluba, *adv.* hardly, with difficulty, 10. 23. See below.

Aglus (*also* agls), *adj.* difficult, hard; aglu ist, it is hard, 10. 24. Cf. E. *ail.*

Aha, *wk. s. m.* understanding.

Ahaks, *str. s.* (*f. or m.?*), a dove, 1. 10.

Ahjan, *wk. v.* to think.

Ahma, *wk. s. m.* the spirit, the Holy Ghost, 1. 8, 10, 12, &c.

Ahs (*gen.* ahsis), *str. s. n.* an ear of corn, 2. 23; 4. 28. E. *ear.*

Ahtau, *num.* eight.

Ahwa, *str. s. f.* a river, 1. 5. A. S. *ía. ℓ. a c̣ r̤ ı ·*

Aibr, *str. s. n.* an offering.

Aigan, Aihan, *v. anom.* (*of which are found the principal forms* aih *or* aig; aihum *or* aigum; aihta; *pres. pt.* aigands), to have, own, possess, 12. 6; *pt. pl.* aihtedun, 12. 23. Cf. E. *own.*

Aigin, *str. s. n.* property.

Aihtedun, they owned, had, 12. 23. (*ai*) See **Aigan.**

Aihtron, *wk. v.* to desire, beg for, pray; to beg, 10. 46. *Desiderative from* aigan.

Aihwa-tundi (βάτος), *str. s. f.* a bramble-bush; a bush, 12. 26.

Aikklesjo, *wk. s. f.* (Gk. ἐκκλησία), a church.

Ainlif, *num.* eleven.

Ainnohun, Ainohun, *adj.* any one, 5. 37; 9. 8. See **Ainshun.**

Ains, *adj.* (*fem.* aina, *neut.* ain *or*

ainata?), one, single, only, 2. 7, 26; ains—jah ains, the one—and the other, 10. 37.

Ains-hun, *adj.* (hun *being a suffix*); *only used with* ni *preceding*; ni ainshun, not any one, none, 5. 37.

Air, *adv.* early, 1. 35; filu air, very early, 16. 2. A. S. *ǽr.*

Airkns, *adj.* good, holy, sincere.

Airtha, *str. s. f.* earth, region, land, 2. 10; 4. 5. E. *earth.*

Airthakunds, *or* **Airtheins**, *adj.* earthly.

Airus, *str. s. m.* a messenger. A. S. *ár*, a messenger.

Airzeis, *adj.* astray, going astray; airzeis wisan, *or* wairthan, to go astray, be deceived; to err, 12. 24. Cf. Lat. *errare.*

Airzjan, *wk. v.* to deceive.

Aithei, *wk. s. f.* a mother, 3. 32; 5. 40.

Aiths, *str. s. m.* an oath, 6. 26. E. *oath.*

Aiththau, *conj.* or, 3. 4. A. S. *oððe.*

Aiw, *adv.* ever, aye, 2. 12; ni aiw, never, 3. 29. A. S. *á.*

Aiwaggeljo, *wk. s. f.* evangel, gospel, 1. 1, 14. Gk. *εὐαγγέλιον.*

Aiweins, *adj.* eternal, 3. 29. See **Aiws.**

Aiwiski, *str. s. n.* shame.

Aiws, *str. s. m.* time, a long time, an age, eternity, the world, 10. 30. A. S. *á.*

Aiz, *str. s. n.* brass, coin, money, 6. 8. E. *ore.*

Ajukduths, *str. s. f.* an age, eternity.

Ak, *conj.* but; *gen. used after a negative*, 1. 44. A. S. *ac.*

Akei (ἀλλά), *conj.* but, 9. 13.

Akeit, Aket, *str. s. n.* vinegar, 15. 36. Lat. *acetum.*

Akran, *str. s. n.* fruit, 4. 7; — matjan, to eat fruit, 11. 14; — giban, to bear fruit, 4. 7; — bai-

ran, to bear fruit, 4. 28. E. *acorn.*

Akrana-laus, *adj.* unfruitful, 4. 19.

Akrs, *str. s. m.* a field, 15. 21. E. *acre.*

Akwisi, *str. s. f.* an axe. E. *axe.*

Ala-brunsts, *str. s. f.* a holocaust, whole burnt-offering, 12. 33.

Alakjo, *adv.* together, collectively; allai alakjo (πάντες), all together, 11. 32.

Alan, *str. v.* to nourish. Lat. *alere.*

Alds, Alths, *str. s. f.* age, generation, life.

Aleina, *str. s. f.* a cubit. Cf. E. *ell.*

Alew, *str. s. n.* olive oil, 6. 13. Gk. *ἔλαιον.*

Alewis, *adj.* belonging to the olive-tree; fairguni alewi (ὄρος ἐλαιῶν), the Mount of Olives, 11. 1.

Alhs, *str. s. f.* (*dat.* alhai *and* alh), temple, 11. 11; 12. 35. A. S. *alh.*

Alids, *pp.* fatted; *from* alan.

Alja (εἰ μή, ἐὰν μή), *conj.* than, except, unless, save, 9. 8; *prep. with dat.* (πλήν), except, 10. 18; 12. 32. *From* aljis.

Aljan, *str. s. n.* zeal. A. S. *ellen.*

Aljath, *adv.* other-whither, in another direction; *hence* afleithan aljath, to go away, 12. 1. *From* aljis.

Aljis, *adj.* other. Cf. E. *else.*

Allathro, *adv.* from all sides, from every quarter, 1. 45. *From* alls.

Allis, *adv.* wholly, altogether, 6. 14; however, for, *as in* allis than, for when, 12. 25; hwa allis, but what, 15. 14; for, 3. 35. *From* alls.

Alls, *adj.* all, 1. 5, 27; 7. 14; much, 12. 37. E. *all.*

Althan, *str. v.* to grow old.

Altheis, *adj.* old. E. *old.*

Amen, amen, verily, 3. 28; 6. 11. Gk. *ἀμήν.*

Amsa, *wk. s. m.* shoulder.

Ana, *prep. with dat. and acc.* on, in, upon, over, to, towards, 1. 10, &c.; at, 1. 22. E. *on.*

Ana, *adv.* upon, on, 2. 4; atlagjan aua, to lay on, 8. 23; galagjan ana, to lay on, 11. 7. *E. on.*

Ana-biudan, *str. v.* to command, 1. 27; *pt. s.* anabauth, 1. 44; 5. 43.

Ana-busns, *str. s. f.* a command, commandment, 7. 7. See above.

Ana-filh, *str. s. n.* a tradition, 7. 3. 5.

Ana-filhan, *str. v.* to hand down as tradition, observe as tradition; *pt. pl.* anafulhun, 7. 5; *pt. pl.* 2 *p.* anafulhuth, 7. 13; *pt. s.* anafalh, entrusted, let out, 12. 1.

Ana-fulhano, *wk. s. n.* a tradition, 7. 9.

Anafulhun, *pt. t. pl.* 7. 5. See **Anafilhan.**

Ana-hneiwan, *str. v.* to stoop down, 1. 7.

Anaks, *adv.* suddenly, 9. 8.

Ana-kumbjan, *wk. v.* to lie down, recline, sit at meat, 2. 15; to sit down, recline, 8. 6.

Ana-laugns, *adj.* secret, 4. 22.

Ana-mahtjan, *wk. v.* to use one's might against any one; to defraud, 10. 19.

Ana-nanthjan, *wk. v.* to have courage, to dare, to be bold, 15. 43.

Ana-silan, *wk. v.* to be silent, grow still, 4. 39.

Ana-stodeins, *str. s. f.* beginning, 1. 1; 10. 6.

Ana-stodjan, *wk. v.* to begin; *title.*

Ana-wairths, *adj.* about to come, future, 10. 30.

And, *prep. with acc.* to, towards, through, 1. 28; throughout, 1. 39; 14. 9. (Takes also the form *anda* in composition.) A. S. *and,* prep.

Anda-nahti, *str. s. n.* twilight, gloaming, evening, 1. 32; 11. 11, 19.

And-augjo, *adv.* openly, 1. 45. *From* augo.

And-bahti, *str. s. n.* service, ministry. Cf. G. *amt*; E. *embassy.*

And-bahtjan, *wk. v.* to serve, minister, 1. 13, 31. See above.

And-bahts, *str. s. m.* a servant, minister, 9. 35; 14. 54. A. S. *ambeht.*

And-beitan, *str. v.* (bait, bitum, bitans),to reprove, rebuke, threaten, 1. 25; 3. 12; 8. 32; *pt. s.* andbait, 8. 33.

And-bindan, *str.v.*(band, bundum, bundans). to unbind, unloose, 1. 7; to explain, 4. 34.

And-bundnan, *wk. v.* to be unbound, to be loosened. 7. 35.

Andeis, *str. s. m.* an end, 3. 26; 13. 27. E. *end.*

And-hafjan, *str. v.* (*pt. t.* and-hof), to reply, 3. 33, 7. 28.

And-haitan, *str. v.* to call to one, 7. 14; to profess, confess, 1. 5.

And-hausjan, *wk. v.* to listen, to hear (a prayer); to hear, 6. 20.

And-hof, answered, replied, 3. 33; 7. 28. See **And-hafjan.**

And-huljan, *wk. v.* to uncover, 2. 4.

And-niman, *str.v.* to receive, take, 4. 20; 6. 11; *pt. pl.* andnemun, 7. 4.

And-rinnan, *str. v.* (rann, runnum, runnans), to compete in running; *hence* to strive, dispute, 9. 34.

And-staurran, *wk. v.* to murmur against, 14. 5.

And-wairthi, *str. s. n.* presence; faura *or* in andwairthja, in presence of, before, 2. 12; 9. 2.

And-wasjan, *wk. v.* to unclothe, take off clothes, 15. 20.

Ans, *str. s. m.* a beam.

Ansts, *str. s. f.* favour, grace. A. S. *ést.*

Anthar, *adj.* another, other, the rest, 3. 21; 12. 21. E. *other.*

Antharuh, *adj.* the other, 4. 5.

Apaustaulus, Apaustulus, *str.*

s. m. an apostle, messenger, 6. 30.
Gk. ἀπόστολος.

Ara, *wk. s. m.* an eagle. A. S.
earn.

Arbaiths, *str. s. f.* labour. A. S.
earſoð.

Arbi, *str. s. n.* a heritage, inherit-
ance, 1. 7. A. S. *yrſe.*

Arbi-numja, *wk. s. m.* an inheritor,
heir, 12. 7.

Arbja, *wk. s. m.* an heir; arbja
wairthan, to inherit, 10. 17.

Arhwazna, *str. s. f.* an arrow.

Arjan, *wk. v.* to plough. A. S.
erian.

Arman, *wk. v. with acc.* to pity,
have mercy on, 10. 47.

Arms, *adj.* poor, wretched. A. S.
earm.

Arms, *str. s. m.* the arm; ana
armins niman, to take up in the
arms, 9. 36. E. *arm.*

Arniba, *adv.* surely, safely, 14. 44.

Aromata (ἀρώματα), sweet spices,
16. 1.

Asans, *str. s. f.* harvest, harvest
time, 4. 29; summer, 13. 28.

Asilu-kwairnus, *str. s. f.* a mill-
stone, 9. 42. From *asilus,* an ass,
and *kwairnus,* a mill-stone (cf. E.
quern).

Asneis, *str. s. m.* a servant, hired
servant, 1. 20. A. S. *esne.*

Asts, *str. s. m.* a bough, a twig, a
branch, 4. 32; 11. 8; 13. 28.

At, *prep. with dat.* at, by, 4. 1;
from, 12. 2; *with acc.* at, 12. 2.
E. *at.*

At-augjan, *wk. v.* to bring before
the eyes, shew, 1. 44; to appear,
16. 9; *pass.* to appear, 9. 4.
From augo. A.S. *ætýwan.*

At-bairan, *str. v.* (bar, berum,
baurans), to bring, offer, 1. 44;
6. 28; *pt. s.* at-bar, 6. 28.

At-gaggan (at-iddja), *anom. v.* to
go to, come; *hence,* to descend,
come down, 1. 10; to enter, 4.
19; 5. 39.

At-giban, *str. v.* (gaf, gebum, gibans), to give over, deliver up,
put in prison, 1. 14; to give, 4.
11; *pt. s.* atgaf, gave, delivered,
6. 28; 8. 6; 15. 15; *pt. pl.* atgebun, 15. 10.

At-haban, *wk. v.* to have at; *hence,*
refl. to come towards, 10. 35.

At-hafjan, *str. v.* to take down,
15. 36.

At-haitan, *str. v.* to call to one,
3. 13; *pt. s.* athaihait, 6. 7.

Athn, *str. s. n.* a year.

Aththan, *conj.* but, 1. 7; 2. 10.

At-iddjedun, came, 2. 18. See
At-gaggan.

Atisk, *str. s. n.* a corn-field, 2. 23.

At-ist, is at hand, 4. 29. See **At-
wisan.**

At-lagjan, *wk. v.* to lay, lay on;
to put on clothes, 15. 17; at-
lagjan faur, to lay before, set before,
8. 6.

At-nehwjan, *wk. v. refl.* to draw
near, be at hand, 1. 15; 14. 42.

At-saihwan, *str. v.* (sahw, sehwum,
saihwans), *with gen. and acc.* to
take heed, give heed, 8. 15.

At-standan, *str. v.* to stand near,
14. 47, 70.

At-steigan, *str. v.* (staig, stigum,
stigans), to descend, come down,
15. 30, 32.

Atta, *wk. s. m.* father, 1. 20; 5. 40.

At-tauhun, they led, brought, 15.
22. See **At-tiuhan.**

At-tekan, *str. v.* (taitok, tekans),
to touch, 1. 41; *pt. s.* attaitok,
1. 41; 5. 27; 7. 33; *pt. s. subj.*
attaitoki, 8. 22; *pt. pl. subj.* attaitokeina, 3. 10; 6. 56.

At-tiuhan, *str. v.* (tauh, tauhum,
tauhans), to pull towards, to bring,
11. 2; *pt. pl.* attauhun, 15. 22.

At-wairpan, *str. v.* (warp, waurpum, waurpans), to cast, cast
down, 9. 22; *app. with pass. sense,*
to be cast, 9. 47.

At-walwjan, *wk. v.* to roll to, 15. 46.

At-wisan, *str. v.* to be present, be at hand; *pr.* s. atist, 4. 29.

At-wopjan, *wk. v.* to call, 9. 35.

Audags, *adj.* happy, blessed. A. S. *éadig*.

Aufto, *adv.* perhaps, probably; ibai aufto, if so, 2. 22; ei aufto, if haply, 11. 13.

Auga-dauro, *wk. s. f.* window (eye-door).

Augjan, *wk. v.* to shew, lit. bring before the eyes.

Augo, *wk. s. n.* the eye, 7. 22. E. *eye*.

Auhjodus, *str. s. m.* tumult, 5. 38; insurrection, 15. 7.

Auhjon, *wk. v.* to cry aloud, make a noise, 5. 39.

Auhns, *str. s. m.* an oven. E. *oven*.

Auhsa, *wk. s. m.* an ox. E. *ox*.

Auhuma, *adj.* high, orig. highest; *hence superl. adj.* auhumists, the highest, chief, 8. 31.

Auk, *conj.* (*commonly after the first, or first closely-connected, words of the sentence; and very rarely at the beginning*), for, also, 1. 16; auk raihtis, for, 6. 17. E. *eke*.

Aukan, *str. v.* to grow, increase. E. *eke*, v.

Aurahi, *str. s. f.* a grave, tomb, 5. 2.

Aurali, *str. s. n.* a napkin.

Aurkeis, *str. s. m.* a cup, 7. 4, 8.

Aurti-gards, *str. s. m.* an orchard, garden.

Aurtja, *wk. s. m.* a gardener.

Auso, *wk. s. n.* the ear, 4. 9; 14. 47. E. *ear*.

Authida, *str. s. f.* a desert, 1. 3, 4, 12; 8. 4.

Auth(i)s, *adj.* desert, waste, 1. 35. Icel. *auðr*, G. *öde*.

Awethi, *str. s. n.* a flock of sheep. Cf. E. *ewe*.

Awiliud, *str. s. n.* giving of thanks.

Awiliudon, *wk. v.* to thank, to give thanks, 8. 6.

Awistr, *str. s. n.* a sheepfold.

Awo, *wk. s. f.* a grandmother. Cf. Lat. *auus*.

Azets, *adj.* light, easy; *only in compar.* azetizo, easier, 2. 9; *spelt* azitizo, 10. 25.

Azgo, *wk. s. f.* ash, cinder. E. *ash*.

Azgo, *str. s. m.* unleavened bread; azyme = τῶν ἀζύμων, 14. 12.

B.

Badi, *str. s. n.* a bed, 2. 4; 2. 9; ana badjam bairan, to carry about on beds, 6. 55. E. *bed*.

Bagms, *str. s. m.* a tree, 8. 24. E. *beam*.

Bai, *adj.* both.

Baidjan, *wk. v.* to compel.

Bairan, *str. v.* (bar, berum, baurans), *with acc.* to bear, carry, bring, 1. 32; akran bairan, to bear fruit, 4. 28; *pt. pl.* berun, q. v. E. *bear*.

Bairgahei, *wk. s. f.* hill country. Cf. G. *berg*.

Bairgan, *str. v.* (barg, baurgum, baurgans), to keep. A.S. *beorgan*.

Bairhtaba, *adv.* brightly, clearly, 8. 25.

Bairhts, *adj.* bright. E. *bright*.

Baitrs, *adj.* bitter. E. *bitter*.

Balgs, *str. s. m.* (*pl.* balgeis), a wine-skin, 2. 22. E. *bag*.

Balsan (μύρον), balsam, balm, ointment, 14. 5.

Balthei, *wk. s. f.* boldness (as if from adj. *balths**).

Balwjan, *wk. v.* to torment, plague, 5. 7. Cf. E. *bale*.

Bandi, *str. s. f.* a band, 7. 35. E. *band*.

Bandja, *wk. s. m.* a prisoner, 15. 6. *From* bindan.

Bandwo, *str. s. f.* a sign, token; a signal, 14. 44. *From* bindan.

Banja, *str. s. f.* wound. E. *bane*.

Bansts, *str. s. m.* a barn.

Barizeins, *adj.* of barley (as if from a sb. *baris**).

Barms, *str. s. m.* bosom, lap. A. S. *bearm.*

Barn, *str. s. n.* a child, 5. 39; 7. 27. E. *bairn.*

Barnilo, *wk. s. n.* a little child, son, 2. 5; 10. 24.

Barniski, *str. s. n.* childhood, 9. 21.

Basi, *str. s. n.* a berry. E. *berry.*

Bath, prayed, asked, besought, 1. 35; 5. 10. See **Bidjan.**

Batists, best. E. *best.*

Batiza, better. E. *better.*

Bauains, *str. s. f.* a dwelling, dwellingplace, 5. 3.

Bauan, *v.* (*both wk. and str.*) to build, inhabit, dwell in. A. S. *búan.*

Baudana, *acc. of* Bauths, *adj.* deaf, 7. 32.

Baur, *str. s. m.* a child. *From* bairan.

Baurd, *str. s. n.* a board. E. *board.*

Baurgs, *str. s. f.* a burgh, borough, town, city, 1. 33. E. *borough.*

Baurthei, *wk. s. f.* a burden. *From* bairan.

Bauths, *adj.* deaf, 7. 32.

Bedun, prayed, 5. 12; 7. 32; asked for, 15. 6. See **Bidjan.**

Beidan, *str. v.* (baid, bidnm, bidans), *with gen.* to abide, await, look for, expect, 15. 43. E. *bide.*

Beist, *str. s. n.* leaven, 8. 15. Prov. E. *beistings.*

Berun, they bore, 1. 32; brought, 7. 32. See **Bairan.**

Berusjos, *str. s. m. pl.* parents.

Bi, *prep. with acc.* by, about, 1. 6; concerning, 1. 30; 3. 6; near, 3. 32; *with dat.* by, at, after, according to, 5. 7; *with instrumental,* as in bithe, q. v. E. *by.*

Bi-aukan, *str. v.* (*pt. t.* biaiauk), to increase, add to, 4. 24.

Bida, *str. s. f.* a request, exhortation, prayer, 9. 29.

Bidagwa, *wk. s. m.* a beggar. Cf. E. *beg.*

Bidjan, *str. v.* (bath, bedum, bidans), to pray, ask, 1. 35; 6. 22, 24; *pt. s.* bath, 1. 35; 5. 10; *pt. pl.* bedun, q. v. A. S. *biddan.*

Bi-gitan, *str. v.* to find, 1. 37; *pt. s.* bigat, 7. 30.

Bi-hlahjan, *str. v.* (hloh, hlohum, hlahans), to laugh at, laugh to scorn; *pt. pl.* bihlohun, 5. 40.

Bi-laikan, *str. v.* (lailaik, laikans), to mock, 10. 34; *pt. pl.* bilailaikun, 15. 20.

Bi-leithan, *str. v.* (*pt. t.* bi-laith: *pp.* bi-lithans), to leave, forsake, 10. 7; 12. 19; *pt. s. 2 p.* bilaist, 15. 34.

Bindan, *str. v.* (band, bundum, bundans), to bind. E. *bind.*

Bi-rinnan, *str. v.* to run about, 6. 55.

Bi-saihwan, *str. v.* to look round on, 3. 34; 10. 23.

Bi-satjan, *wk. v.* to beset, set round anything, 12. 1.

Bi-sitan, *v. only used in pres. part.* bi-sitands, a neighbour, one who dwells near, 1. 28.

Bi-speiwan, *str. v.* to spit upon; *pt. pl.* bispiwun, 15. 19. See **Speiwan.**

Bi-sunjane, *adv.* near, round about, 1. 38; 3. 34; 6. 6.

Bi-swaran, *str. v.* to conjure, adjure, 5. 7.

Bitauh, went about, 6. 6. See **Bi-tiuhan.**

Bithe, *adv.* whilst, 1. 42. *From* bi *and* the.

Bi-tiuhan, *str. v.* to go about, visit; *pt. s.* bitauh, 6. 6.

Biudan, *str. v.* (bauth, budum, budaus), to bid. E. *bid.*

Biuds, *str. s. m.* a holy table, altar; *hence* any table, 7. 28. A.S. *b'od.*

Biugan, *str. v.* (baug, bugum, bugans), to bow, bend. E. *bow,* v.

Biuhts, *adj.* accustomed, wont; biuhts wisan, to be wont, 10. 1 (*where* was *is omitted*).

Bi-waibjan, *wk. v.* to weave round, wind about, 14. 51 ; to clothe, 16. 5.

Bi-windan, *str. v.* (wand, wundum, wundans), to wind round, enwrap, swathe ; *pt. s.* biwand, 15. 46.

Blandan, *v.* to blend. E. *blend.*

Blauthjan, *wk. v.* to abrogate, make void, 7. 13.

Bleiths, *adj.* merciful. E. *blithe.*

Bliggwan, *str. v.* (*pt. t.* blaggw, *pl.* bluggwum, *pp.* bluggwans), to beat, cut, 5. 5 ; 10. 34.

Blinds, *adj.* blind, 8. 23. E. *blind.*

Bloma, *wk. s. m.* a flower. E. *bloom.*

Blotan, *v.* (*pt. t.* bai-blot ?), to reverence, worship, 7. 7.

Bloth, *str. s. n.* blood, 5. 25. E. *blood.*

Boka, *str. s. f.* a letter ; *pl.* bokos, the writings, the scriptures, 14. 49 ; bokos af-sateinais, a bill of divorcement, 10. 4. E. *book.*

Bokareis, *str. s. m.* a bookman, a scribe, 1. 22.

Bota, *str. s. f.* advantage. E. *boot,* sb.

Botjan, *wk. v.* to boot, advantage, profit, 5. 26 ; 8. 36. E. *boot,* v.

Brahta, I brought, 9. 16. See Briggan.

Brahw, *str. s. n.* twinkling (of an eye). Cf. E. *brow.*

Braids, *adj.* broad. E. *broad.*

Briggan, *wk. v.* (*pt. t.* brahta), *with acc.* to bring, 6. 27. E. *bring.*

Brikan, *str. v.* (brak, brekum, brukans), to break. E. *break.*

Brinnan, *str. v.* (brann, brunnum, brunnans), to burn. E. *burn.*

Brinno, *wk. s. f.* a fever, 1. 30. Lit. 'a burning.'

Brothar, *s. m.* a brother, 1. 16 ; 3. 35 ; *pl.* brothjus, 3. 31. E. *brother.*

Brothrahans, *pl.* brethren, 12. 20.

Brukjan, *wk. v.* to make use of. E. *brook,* v.

Bruks, *adj.* useful.

Brunjo, *wk. s. f.* a breast-plate. A. S. *byrne.*

Brunna, *wk. s. m.* a spring, well ; *hence* the issue, 5. 29. E. *bourn.*

Brusts, *str. s. f.* breast. E. *breast.*

Bruth-faths, Bruth-fads, *str. s. m.* (1) bridegroom, 2. 19, 20 ; (2) *in phrase* sunjus bruth-fadis, sons of the bride-chamber.

Bruths, *str. s. f.* bride. E. *bride.*

Bugjan, *wk. v.* (*pt. t.* bauhta), to buy, sell, 11. 15. E. *buy.*

D.

Daddjan, *wk. v.* to give suck, suckle, 13. 17.

Dags, *str. s. m.* a day, time, 1. 9, 13 ; naht jah dag, nahtam jah dagam, 4. 27 ; 5. 5 ; daga hwammeh, daily, 14. 49. E. *day.*

Daigs, *str. s. m.* dough. *From* deigan. E. *dough.*

Dailjan, *wk. v.* to deal out. E. *deal,* v.

Dails, *str. s. f.* a deal, portion. E. *deal,* sb.

Dal, *str. s. n.* a dale, a valley ; a ditch, 12. 1. E. *dale.*

Dalath, *adv.* down, 9. 9 ; und dalath, to the bottom, 15. 38.

Dalatha, *adv.* below, 14. 66.

Daubitha, *str. s. f.* deafness ; *hence* dulness, hardness of heart, 3. 5.

Daubs, *adj.* deaf ; *hence* hardened, dull, 8. 17. E. *deaf.*

Dauhtar, (*pl. acc.* dauhtruns), *str. s. f.* a daughter, 5. 23. E. *daughter.*

Dauhts, *str. s. f.* a feast.

Dauns, *str. s. f.* scent, odour.

Daupeins, *str. s. f.* a dipping, washing, baptism, 1. 4 ; 7. 4 ; 10. 38 ; 11. 30.

Daupidai, 1. 5, *pl. of* daupiths, *pp.* of Daupjan.

Daupjan, *wk. v.* to dip, to baptize, 1. 4, 9 ; 10. 38 ; to wash oneself, 7. 4. E. *dip.*

Daupjands, the Baptist, 6. 14, 24; 8. 28.

Daur, *str. s. n.* a door, 1. 33. E. *door.*

Dauro, *wk. s. f.* a door, 16. 3.

Daursan, *v.* to dare; see **Gadaursan.** E. *dare.*

Dauths, *adj.* dead, 9. 26. E. *dead.*

Dauthus, *str. s. m.* death, 6. 14; 9. 1. E. *death.*

Deds, *str. s. f.* deed. E. *deed.*

Deigan, Digan, *str. v.* (daig, digum, digans), to knead, mould.

Dis-, *prefix,* apart; also used intensively.

Dis-dailjan, *wk. v.* to divide, 15. 24.

Dis-sitan, *str. v.* to settle upon, to seize upon, 16. 8 (*where the verb is separated*).

Dis-skreitan, *str. v.* (skrait, skritum, skritans), to tear (to shreds), rend, 14. 63.

Dis-skritnan, *wk. v.* to become torn to shreds, to be rent apart, 15. 38.

Dis-tairan, *str. v.* to tear asunder, burst, 2. 22.

Dis-wilwan, *str. v.* to plunder completely, 3. 27.

Diups, *adj.* deep, 4. 5. E. *deep.*

Dius, *str. s. n.* a wild beast, 1. 13. E. *deer.*

Diz-uh-than-sat, *put for* thanuh dissat, 16. 8. See **Thanuh** *and* **Dis-sitan.**

Diwan, *str. v.* (dau, diwum, diwans), to die. E. *die.*

Domjan, *wk. v.* to deem, judge. E. *deem.* From **Doms.**

Doms, *str. s. m.* judgment. E. *doom.*

Draban, *str. v.* See **Ga-draban.**

Dragan, *str. v.* (drog, drogum, dragans), to draw. E. *draw.*

Draggk, Dragk, *str. s. n.* drink.

Dragkjan, Draggkjan, *wk. v.* to give to drink, 15. 36. E. *drench.*

Draibjan, *wk. v.* to trouble, vex, 5. 35. *From* dreiban.

Drauhsna, Drausna, *str. s. f.* that which falls, a crumb, fragment, 7. 28. Cf. E. *dross, drizzle.*

Draus, fell, 7. 25. See **Driusan.**

Dreiban, *str. v.* (draib, dribum, dribans), to drive. E. *drive.*

Driggkan, Drigkan, *str. v.* (draggk, druggkum, druggkans), *with acc.* to drink, 2. 16; 10. 38. E. *drink.*

Driugan, *str. v.* (drauh, drugum, drugans), to serve as a soldier, fight. Scotch *dree.*

Driusan, *str. v.* (draus, drusum, drusans), to fall down, fall upon, press against, crowd upon, 3. 10; 5. 33; 7. 25; 9. 20. Cf. E. *drizzle.*

Driuso, *wk. s. f.* place where the ground falls, steep slope, 5. 13.

Drobjan, *wk. v.* to cause trouble, excite to uproar, 15. 7.

Drunjus, *str. s. m.* a droning noise, voice. E. *drone.*

Drus, *str. s. m.* fall. *From* driusan.

Du, *prep. with dat.* to, towards, for, 1. 4; 2. 8; bairan du, to bring to, 10. 13. Cf. E. *to.*

Du-at-gaggan, *wk. v.* (du-atiddja), to go to, 1. 31; 10. 2.

Du-at-rinnan, *str. v.* to run to, 10. 17.

Du-at-sniwan, *str. v.* (snaw, snewum, sniwans), to hasten towards, run on (shore), 6. 53.

Dubo, *wk. s. f.* a dove. E. *dove.*

Dugan, *anom. v.* to avail. E. *do,* in phr. ' that will *do.*'

Du-ginnan, *str. v.* (gann, gunnum, gunnans), to begin, undertake, 1. 45; 2. 23; *pt. s.* dugann, 1. 45; 4. 1; *pt. pl.* dugunnun, 8. 11.

Duhwe, wherefore, 2. 8; 15. 34. See **Duthe.** *From du* and *hwe.*

Dulths, *str. s. f.* (*dat.* dulthai *and* dulth), a feast, 15. 6.

Dumbs, *adj.* dumb. E. *dumb.*

Du-rinnan, *str. v.* (rann, runnum, runnans), to run to. 9. 15.

Duthe, duththe, duhthe, *prep.* (*lit.* thereto), therefore, 1. 38; 12.

24; duthei ei, in order that, 4. 21. *From* du *and* the.

Dwals, *adj.* foolish. E. *dull.*

E.

Ei, *conj.* (1) that, *with* '*indic. and subj.* 1. 27; (2) *forming relatives; as* saei, he that, he who, who (*in fem.* soei, sei; *in neut.* thatei). *It is also used to begin dependent clauses, in the sense of* if, whether, *as in* 11. 13; 15. 44.

Eis, they, 8. 5. See **Is.**

Eisarn, *str. s. n.* iron; ei. bi fotuns *or* ei. ana fotum (πέδη), a fetter, 5. 4. E. *iron.*

Eisarneins, *adj.* iron, 5. 3.

F.

Fadar, *s. m.* father. E. *father.*

Faginon, *wk. v.* (*with dative, or followed by* fram, ana, in), to re-joice, 14. 11. Cf. E. *fain.*

Fagrs, *adj.* suitable. E. *fair.*

Fahan, *str. v.* (faifah, fahans), to catch, seize. A. S. *fón.*

Faheds, Faheths, *str. s. f.* joy, 4. 16.

Faihu, Faiho, *str. s. n.* cattle, pro-perty; *hence* possessions, 10. 22, 23, 24; a fee, money, 14. 11. E. *fee.*

Faihu-frikei, *wk. s. f.* covetous-ness, 7. 22. See **Faihu** and **Friks.**

Fair-greipan, *str. v.* (graip, grip-um, gripans), to grip, catch hold of, 8. 23; *pt. s.* fairgraip, 5. 41.

Fairguni, *str. s. n.* a mountain, 3. 13. A. S. *firgen.*

Fairhwus, *str. s. m.* the world, 8. 36. A. S. *feorh,* life.

Fairina, *str. s. f.* charge, accusa-tion, 15. 26. Cf. A. S. *firen,* crime.

Fairneis, *adj.* old, 2. 21. A. S. *fyrn.*

Fairra, *adv.* far, 7. 6. E. *far.*

Fairrathro, *adv.* from far, 5. 6; 8. 3; 11. 13.

-falths, -fold; *as in* R-falths, etc.; 10. 30. E. *-fold.*

Fana, *wk. s. m.* a bit of cloth; a patch, 2. 21. E. *vane.*

Fani, *str. s. n.* clay, mud. E. *fen.*

Faran, *str. v.* (for, forum, farans), to fare, go. E. *fare.*

Fareisaius, *str. s. m.* a Pharisee, 7. 1.

Fastan, *wk. v.* (*with acc.*) to hold fast, observe, keep, 7. 9; to fast, 2. 18. E. *fast.*

Fastubni, *str. s. n.* observance, fasting, 9. 29.

Fatha, *str. s. f.* a hedge, 12. 1. Cf. E. *fathom.*

Faths, *str. s. m.* a leader, chief.

Fauho, *wk. s. f.* a fox.

Faur, *prep. with acc.* for, before, to, along, by, 1. 16. A.S. *for.*

Faura, *prep. with dat.* before, 1. 2; because of, 2. 4. A. S. *fore.*

Faura-gaggan, *v. anom.* to go be-fore, 11. 9.'

Faura-gateihan, *str. v.* (taih, taih-ans), to inform beforehand, fore-tell; *pt. s.* 1 *p.* fauragataih, 13. 23.

Faura-hah, *str. s. n.* that which hangs before, a curtain, a veil, 15. 38.

Faura-standan, *str. v.* to stand before; *hence,* to rule, govern; also, to stand near, 14. 69. See **Standan.**

Faura-tani, *str. s. n.* a sign, wonder, 13. 22.

Faur-bauth, he forbade; see **Faur-biudan.**

Faur-bi-gaggan, *v. anom.* to go before, precede, 10. 32; 16. 7. See **Gaggan.**

Faur-biudan, *str. v.* to command; to forbid, command not to do; *pt. s.* faurbauth, 6. 8; 8. 30.

Faur-gaggan, *v. anom.* to go by, pass by, 11. 20; 15. 29.

Faurhtei, *wk. s. f.* fright, fear, 5. 42. E. *fright.*

Faurhtjan, *wk. v.* to be frightened, to fear, 5. 36.

Faurhts, *adj.* fearful, 4. 40; faurhts waiithan, to be afraid, 10. 32. A. S. *fyrht.*

Faur-lageins, *str. s. f.* a setting or laying forth; *hence* hlaibos faurlageinais, shew-bread, 2. 26.

Faur-sniwan, *str. v.* (snau, snewum, sniwans), to hasten before, anticipate; *pt. s.* faursnau, 14. 8.

Faur-this, *adv.* first of all, beforehand, before, 3. 27; 9. 11; faurthizei, before that, 14. 72.

Faws, Faus, *adj.* few (*gen. with pl. nouns*), 6. 5; 8. 7; *comp.* fawiza. E. *few.*

Fera, *str. s. f.* a country, region, coast, 8. 10.

Fetjan, *wk. v.* to adorn, deck. E. *fit,* v.

Fidwor, *num.* four, 1. 13; 2. 3; 8. 9; 13. 27. E. *four.*

Fif, *num.* five. See **Fimf.**

Figgrs, *str. s. m.* a finger, 7. 33. E. *finger.*

Fijan, Fian, *v.* to hate.

Fijands, Fiands, *s. m.* (*pres. pt. of* fijan, to hate), an enemy, 12. 36. F. *fiend.*

Fijathwa, Fiathwa, *str. s. f.* hatred. E. *feud.*

Filhan, *str. v.* (falh, fulhum, fulhans), *with acc.* to hide, conceal; to bury. Icel. *fela,* prov. E. *feal,* to hide.

Filigri, Filegri, *str. s. n.* a hidden place, a cave, den, 11. 17.

Filleins, *adj.* made of skin, leathern, 1. 6. Cf. E. *fell.*

Filu(s), *adj.* much; *also* filu, *adv.* much. *It is generally used in neuter* filu, *and often followed by gen. case of sb.*; 1. 45; 3. 7; 5. 21. A. S. *fela.*

Fimf, *num.* five, 8. 19. E. *five.*

Finthan, *str. v. with acc.* (faith, funthum, funthans), to find out,

know, 15. 45; *pt. s. subj.* funthi, should know, 5. 43. E. *find.*

Fiskja, *wk. s. m.* a fisher, 1. 16.

Fisks, *str. s. m.* a fish, 8. 7. E. *fish.*

Fitan, *str. v.* (fat, fetum, fitans), to travail.

Flahta, Flahto, *wk. s. f.* a plait, plaiting.

Flauhtjan, *wk. v.* to vaunt oneself.

Flekan, *str. v.* (faiflok, flekans), to lament.

Flodus, *str. s. f.* flood, river. E. *flood.*

Fodjan, *wk. v.* to feed. E. *feed.*

Fodr, *str. s. n.* a sheath. Cf. E. *fur.*

Fon, *str. s. n.* (*gen.* funins, *dat.* funin), fire, 9. 22, 47, 49.

Fotu-baurd, *str. s. n.* a foot-board, footstool, 12. 36.

Fotus, *str. s. m.* the foot, 5. 4, 22; *gen. pl.* fotiwe, 12. 36. E. *foot.*

Fra-, a prefix of verbs, giving an intensive or destructive force. Cf. G. *ver-;* A. S. *for-.*

Fra-bugjan, *wk. v.* to sell, 10. 21; 14. 5.

Fra-giban, *str. v.* to give, grant, 10. 37.

Fraihnan, *str. v.* (frah, frehum, fraihans), *with an acc.* to ask; *pt. s.* frah, 5. 9; 8. 23; 12. 28; *pt. pl.* frehun, 4. 10. A. S. *frignan.*

Fraisan, *str. v. with acc.* (faifrais, faifraisum, fraisans), to tempt, 1. 13; 10. 2; 12. 15. A. S. *frásian.*

Fra-itan, *str. v.* (fret, fretum), to eat up, devour; *pt. pl.* fretun, 4. 4. E. *fret.*

Fraiw, *str. s. n.* seed, 4. 3, 26, 27. E. *fry,* spawn.

Fra-kunnan, *v. anom.* to despise, 9. 12.

Fra-kwiman, *str. v.* to expend, spend, 5. 26.

Fra-kwisteins, *str. s. f.* waste, 14. 4.

Fra-kwistjan, *wk. v.* to destroy, 1. 24 ; 8. 35.

Fra-kwistnan, *wk. v.* to be destroyed, to perish, 2. 22.

Fra-letan, *str. v.* to let go, release, let alone, 1. 24 ; *pt. s.* fralailot, permitted, 1. 34 ; 5. 37 ; dismissed, 8. 9 ; *pt. pl.* fralailotun, let down, 2. 4.

Fra-lets, *str. s. m.* remission, forgiveness, 3. 29.

Fram, *prep. with dat.* from, 1. 9 ; by, 1. 5 ; on account of, 1. 44. E. *from.*

Framatheis, *adj.* foreign, strange. A. S. *fremde.*

Framis, *adv.* further, onward, 1. 19. *Comp. of* fram.

Frathi, *str. s. n.* understanding, mind, 12. 33.

Frathjan, *str. v.* (froth, frothum, frathans), to perceive, think, know, understand, 4. 12 ; 5. 15 ; 7. 18 ; 12. 12 ; *pt. pl.* frothun, 9. 32. Cf. A. S. *fród,* wise.

Frauja, *wk. s. m.* a lord, master, 1. 3 ; 2. 38. A. S. *fréa.*

Fra-wairpan, *str. v.* (warp, waurpum, waurpans), to cast away, 9. 42.

Fra-waurhts, *adj.* (*as sb.*) a sinner, sinful man, 2. 15, 17 ; 14. 41.

Fra-waurhts, *str. s. f.* evil working, evil doing, sin, 1. 4 ; 3. 28 ; 4. 12.

Fra-waurpans, *pp.* cast, 9. 42. See **Fra-wairpan.**

Frehun, asked. See **Fraihnan.**

Freidjan, *wk. v.* to spare.

Freis, *adj.* free. E. *free.*

Fretun, ate. See **Fra-itan.**

Frijon, *wk. v.* to love, 10. 21 ; 12. 30.

Frijonds, *str. s. m.* a friend ; *orig.* pres. pt. of the above. E. *friend.*

Friks, *adj.* greedy ; *only in* faihu-friks, 7. 22. A. S. *frec.*

Frithon, *wk. v.* to make peace.

Frius, *str. s. n.* frost.

Frodaba, *adv.* wisely, 12. 34.

Frods, Froths, *adj.* wise. A. S. *fród.* See **Frathjan.**

Frothun, they understood. See **Frathjan.**

Fruma, *adj.* the first, first (*fem.* frumei), 10. 31 ; fruma sabbato, first day of the week, 15. 42 ; 16. 9. A. S. *forma.*

Frumist, *adv.* first, 4. 28 ; 16. 9.

Frumists, *superl. adj.* first, principal, chief (men), 6. 21. E. *foremost.*

Frums, *str. s. m.* beginning.

Fugls, *str. s. m.* a bird, fowl, 4. 4, 32. E. *fowl.*

Fula, *wk. s. m.* a foal, 11. 2. E. *foal.*

Fulgins, *adj.* hidden, 4. 22. See **Filhan.**

Fulla-fahjan, *wk. v.* to satisfy, 15. 15.

Fulleiths, *s.* fulness, 4. 28.

Fulljan, *wk. v.* to fill. E. *fill.*

Fullnan, *wk. v.* to become full.

Fullo, *wk. s. f.* fulness, 2. 21.

Fulls, *adj.* full ; *often followed by gen.* 8. 19. E. *full.*

Fuls, *adj.* foul. E. *foul.*

Funins, Funin. See **Fon.**

Funthi. See **Finthan.**

Fynikiska (φοινίκισσα), *adj.* Phoenician, 7. 26.

G.

Ga-, a very common prefix to verbs, sbs., and adjs. ; sometimes found repeated ; it makes no appreciable difference to the sense. A. S. *ge-,* G. *ge-,* M. E. *y-* or *i-.*

Ga-aistan, *wk. v.* to reverence, respect, 12. 6.

Ga-aiwiskon, *wk. v.* to make ashamed, to shame ; to maltreat, 12. 4.

Ga-arman, *wk. v. with acc.* to have pity on, pity, 5. 19.

Ga-bairan, *str. v.* to bear (children) ; to compare, 4. 30.

Ga-bairhtjan, *wk. v.* to make

bright *or* clear, to manifest, 4. 22.

Ga-band, he had bound. See **Ga-bindan.**

Ga-batnan, *wk. v.* to profit, boot, benefit, 7. 11. See **Batiza.**

Ga-bauan, *v.* to make *or* build nests, to dwell, 4. 32.

Ga-baurjaba, *adv.* with pleasure, willingly, gladly, 6. 20 ; 12. 37 ; heartily, gladly (*not expressed in the Greek*), 14. 65.

Ga-baurths, *str. s. f.* birth, 7. 26 ; mel ga-baurthais, birthday, 6. 21 ; native country, 6. 4 ; generation, 8. 38.

Gabei, *wk. s. f.* riches, 4. 19.

Gabigs, Gabeigs, *adj.* rich, 10. 25. *From* giban.

Ga-bindan, *str. v.* to bind, 3. 27 ; 5. 3 ; 11. 4 ; 15. 7 ; *pt. s.* gaband, he had bound, 6. 17.

Ga-biugan, *str. v.* to bow, bend ; eisarnam gabuganaim, with bent irons, 5. 4.

Ga-bleithjan, *wk. v.* to pity, 9. 22.

Ga-botjan, *wk. v.* to make useful ; aftra gabotjan, to restore, 9. 12.

Ga-brikan, *str. v.* to break ; *pt. s.* gabrak, 5. 4 ; 8. 6.

Ga-bruka, *str. s. f.* a broken bit, a fragment, 8. 8. See above.

Ga-daban, *str. v.* (gadob) to happen, befall, 10. 32.

Ga-daila, *wk. s. m.* a partaker.

Ga-dailjan, *wk. v.* to divide, 3. 24, 26.

Ga-daursan, *anom. v.* to dare ; *pt. s.* gadaúrsta, 12. 34.

Ga-dauthnan, *wk. v.* to die, 5. 39 ; 9. 48 ; 12. 19.

Ga-dobs, *adj.* fitting, fit.

Ga-domjan, *wk. v.* to doom, judge, condemn, 14. 64.

Ga-draban, *str. v.* (drof, drobum, drabans), to hew out, 15. 46.

Ga-dragkjan, Ga-draggkjan, *wk. v.* to give to drink, 9. 41.

Ga-drauhts, *str. s. m.* a soldier, 15. 16. *From* driugan.

Ga-driusan, *str. v.* to fall ; *pt. s.* gadraus, 4. 4, 7, 8 ; 5. 22.

Gaf, gave. See **Gibau.**

Ga-fahan, *str. v.* (faifah, faifahum, fahans) *with acc.* to catch, take, apprehend as a criminal, 9. 18.

Ga-fastan, *wk. v.* to hold fast, keep, 10. 20.

Ga-faurds, *str. s. f.* chief council, Sanhedrim, 14. 55 ; 15. 1.

Ga-fraihnan, *str. v.* to ask, seek, 2. 1 ; *pt. pl.* gafrehun, q. v.

Ga-fraujinon, *wk. v.* to exercise lordship, 10. 42.

Ga-frehun, they found out by inquiry, they heard (A. V. it was noised), 2. 1. See **Ga-fraihnan.**

Ga-fulljan, *wk. v.* to fill, 15. 36.

Ga-fullnan, *wk. v.* to become full, be filled, 4. 37.

Ga-gaggan, *v. anom.* (*pt. t.* ga-iddja), to come together, resort, 6. 30 ; *refl.* 3. 20 ; to come to pass, 11. 23.

Ga-ga-mainjan, *wk. v.* to make common, defile, 7. 23.

Ga-geigan, *wk. v.* to win, gain, 8. 36.

Gaggan, *anom. v.* (iddja, iddjedum, gaggans), to gang, go, go one's way, 1. 38 ; 3. 6 ; 7. 29 ; 10. 21 ; 16. 7 ; gaggan afar, to go after, to follow, 2. 14 ; 5. 24 ; 14. 13. E. *gang,* go.

Gaggs, *str. s. m.* a way, a street, 6. 56 ; 11. 4.

Ga-guds, *adj.* godly, pious, 15. 43.

Ga-haban, *wk. v.* to have, hold, possess, 10. 23 ; to lay hold on, 3. 21 ; 6. 17.

Ga-haihaitun, 14. 11 ; 15. 16. See **Ga-haitan.**

Ga-hailjan, *wk. v.* to heal, 1. 34 ; 3. 10 ; 6. 13.

Ga-hailnan, *wk. v.* to become whole, to be healed, 5. 29.

Ga-haitan, *str. v.* (haihait, haihaitum, haitans), to call together ;

pt. pl. gahaihaitun, promised, 14. 11; called together, 15. 16.

Ga-hausjan, *wk. v.* to hear, 2. 17; 3. 8; 5. 27; 7. 25.

Ga-hraineins, *str. s. f.* cleansing, 1. 44.

Ga-hrainjan, *wk. v.* to cleanse, make clean, 1. 40; 7. 19.

Ga-hugds, *str. s. f.* a thought; the thought, *i. e.* the mind, 12. 30.

Ga-hweitjan, *wk. v.* to whiten, 9. 3.

Ga-hwotjan, *wk. v.* to rebuke, 9. 25; strictly charge, 1. 43.

Gaianna, *wk. s.* Gehenna, 9. 43, 45, 47. Gk. γέεννα.

Ga-iddja, gathered themselves together, 3. 30. See **Ga-gaggan.**

Gairda, *str. s. f.* a girdle, 1. 6; 6. 8. Cf. E. *gird.*

Gairnjan, *wk. v. with gen.* to yearn for, long for, desire, wish for, 11. 3. E. *yearn.*

Gaitein, *str. s. n.* a kid.

Gaits, *str. s. f.* a goat. E. *goat.*

Ga-juko, *wk. s. f.* that which is yoked or paired; *hence* a comparison, parable, 3. 23; 4. 2; 12. 1.

Ga-kunnan, *wk. v.* to know, to consider; to read, 12. 26.

Ga-kwiman, *str. v.* to come together, come; *pt. pl.* gakwemun, 2. 2; 5. 21; 7. 1.

Ga-lagjan, *wk. v.* to lay, lay down, set, place, make (*with double acc.*), 6. 5; 11. 7; 12. 36.

Ga-laistjan, *wk. v. with acc.* to follow, 1. 36.

Ga-laith, went. See **Galeithan.**

Ga-laubeins, *str. s. f.* belief, faith, 2. 5; 5. 34; 10. 52.

Ga-laubjan, *wk. v.* to believe, 1. 15; 4. 24; 11. 31.

Ga-laugnjan, *wk. v.* to be hid, lie hid, 7. 24.

Ga-lausjan, *wk. v.* to loose, loosen, 5. 4.

Ga-leikan, *wk. v.* to please, 6. 22; to take pleasure in, 1. 11.

Ga-leikon, *wk. v.* to liken, 4. 30.

Ga-leiks, *adj.* like, 7. 8; 14. 70.

Ga-leithan, *str. v.* (laith, lithans), to go, come, 1. 20; 5. 38; 11. 11; 12. 12; 14. 10; *pt. s.* galaith, 1. 35; 2. 13; 3. 1; 7. 17.

Galesun; see **Ga-lisan.**

Ga-lewjan, *wk. v.* to betray, 3. 19; 14. 10.

Galga, *wk. s. m.* a cross (lit. gallows), S. 34; 15. 21. E. *gallows.*

Ga-lisan, *str. v.* (las, lesum, lisans), to collect, gather together, 13. 27; *pt. pl.* galesun, 4. 1.

Ga-liug, *str. s. n.* a lie; galiug weitwodjan, to bear false witness, 14. 56.

Ga-liuga-christus, *str. s. m.* a false Christ, 13. 22.

Ga-liugan, *wk. v.* to marry, 6. 17.

Ga-liuga-praufetus, *str. s. m.* a false prophet, 13. 22.

Galiuga-weitwods, *str. s. m.* a false witness, 10. 19.

Ga-mainjan, *wk. v.* to make common, defile, 7. 15, 18, 20.

Ga-mains, *adj.* common, unclean, 7. 2. A. S. *gemǽne.*

Ga-manwjan, *wk. v.* to prepare, make ready, 1. 2.

Ga-marzjan, *wk. v.* to offend; *pass.* to be offended, 4. 17.

Ga-matjan, *wk. v.* to eat, 8. 8.

Ga-maurgjan, *wk. v.* to curtail, cut short, 13. 20.

Ga-meljan, *wk. v.* to write, 1. 2.

Ga-motan, *anom. v.* (*pres. sing.* ga-mot, *pl.* ga-motum; *pt. t.* ga-mosta, *pp.* ga-mosts), to have room, find room, have place, 2. 2.

Ga-motjan, *wk. v.* to meet, 5. 2; 14. 13.

Ga-munan, *v. anom.* (gamunaida), to mind, to remember, 8. 18.

Ga-munds, *str. s. f.* remembrance, 14. 9.

Ga-nam, took, 9. 2. See **Ga-niman.**

Ga-nasjan, *wk. v.* to save, 5. 34; 8. 35; 10. 52.

Ga-nesi, Ga-nesun; see Ga-nisan.

Ga-niman, *str. v.* to take, take with one, 5. 40; *pt. s.* ganam, 9. 2.

Ga-nipnan, *wk. v.* to mourn, to be sorrowful, 10. 22.

Ga-nisan, *str. v.* (nas, nesum, nisans), to be saved, 10. 26; to become whole, 5. 23, 28; *pt. pl.* ganesun, they became whole, 6. 56; *pt. s. subj.* ganesi, should be saved, 13. 20.

Ga-nithjis, *str. s. m.* a kinsman, 6. 4.

Ga-niutan, *str. v.* (naut, nutum, nutans), to net, catch with nets, catch; *pt. pl. subj.* ganuteina, 12. 13.

Ga-nohs, *adj.* sufficient, numerous, 10. 46. E. *enough.*

Ga-nuteina; see Ga-niutan.

Ga-raihts, *adj.* right, just, righteous, 6. 20.

Gards, *str. s. m.* a house, 1. 29; 3. 20. E. *yard.*

Ga-rinnan, *str. v.* (rann, runnum, runnans), to run together, come together, 1. 33; *pt. pl.* garunnun, 14. 33.

Ga-runi, *str. s. n.* counsel, 3. 6; 15. 1.

Ga-saggkw; see Ga-siggkwan.

Ga-saihwan, *str. v.* to see, behold, 1. 10; 3. 11; 5. 15; *pt. s.* gasahw, 1. 16; 2. 14; *p:. pl.* gasehwun, 9. 8.

Ga-sakan, *str. v.* to reprove, rebuke; *pt. s.* gasok, 4. 39.

Ga-salbon, *wk. v.* to salve, anoint, 6. 13; 16. 1.

Ga-sat; see Ga-sitan.

Ga-satjan, *wk. v.* to set, place, lay, found; restore, 8. 25; gasatida namo, he surnamed, 3. 16.

Ga-sehwun; see Ga-saihwan.

Ga-siggkwan, *str. v.* to sink; *pt. s.* gasaggkw, 1. 32.

Ga-sitan, *str. v.* to sit down, to sit, 4. 1; *pt. s.* gasat, 11. 7.

Ga-skafts, *str. s. f.* shaping, formation, creation, things created, 10. 6.

Ga-skapjan, *str. v.* to shape, create, make; *pt. s.* gaskop, 13. 19; *pass.* to be made, 2. 27.

Ga-skeirjan, *wk. v.* to make sheer or clear, to interpret, 5. 41; 15. 22.

Ga-skohs, *adj.* shod, 6. 9.

Ga-skop, created, 13. 19. See Ga-skapjan.

Ga-slawan, *wk. v.* to be silent, 4. 39.

Ga-sleithjan, *wk. v.* to slight, injure; *with* sik, to be injured in, suffer the loss of, 8. 36.

Ga-sok; see Ga-sakan.

Ga-sothjan, *wk. v.* to fill, satisfy, 8. 4.

Ga-standan, *str. v.* to stand still, 10. 49. See Ga-stoth.

Ga-staurknan, *wk. v.* to dry up, pine away, 9. 18.

Ga-stoth, stood firm, *i. e.* became whole, was restored, 3. 5. See Ga-standan.

Ga-straujan, *wk. v.* to strew, straw, furnish, 14. 15.

Gasts, *str. s. m.* a stranger. E. *guest.*

Ga-swalt; see Ga-swiltan.

Ga-swikunthjan, *wk. v.* to manifest, make known, 3. 12.

Ga-swiltan, *str. v.* to die, 12. 20; *pt. s.* gaswalt, is dead, 5. 35; 9. 26.

Ga-swogjan, *wk. v.* to sigh, 7. 34.

Ga-taihun; see Ga-teihan.

Ga-tairan, *str. v.* (tar, terum, taurans), *lit.* to tear; to break, destroy, 14. 58; 15. 29.

Ga-tamjan, *wk. v.* to tame, 5. 4.

Ga-tauhun; see Ga-tiuhan.

Ga-taujan, *wk. v.* (*pt. t.* ga-tawida), to do, make, 1. 17; *pt. s.* ga-tawida, 2. 25; 5. 19; 6. 20; *pt. pl.* gatawidedun, 6. 30; 9. 13.

Ga-taura, *wk. s. m.* a tear, rent, 2. 21.

Ga-tawida; see Ga-taujan.

Ga-teihan, *str. v.* (taih, taihum, taihans), to teach, tell, announce to, make known to; *pt: s.* gataih, 16. 10; *pt. pl.* gataihun, 5. 14; 6. 30.

Ga-tilaba, *adv.* conveniently, 14. 11.

Ga-tils, *adj.* convenient, 6. 21.

Ga-timrjan, *wk. v.* to build, 12. 1; 14. 58; 15. 29.

Ga-tiuhan, *str. v.* to draw, lead, bring, take; *pt. pl.* gatauhun, 14. 53; 15. 16.

Ga-thahan, *wk. v.* to be silent, 10. 48.

Ga-thairsan, *str. v.* (thars, thaursum, thaursans), to wither, 3. 1, 3.

Ga-thaursnan, *wk. v.* to become dry, to wither away, 4. 6; 5. 29; 11. 21.

Ga-thiuthjan, *wk. v.* to bless, 8. 7.

Ga-thlaihan, *str. v.* to take in the arms, caress, 10. 16.

Ga-thliuhan, *str. v.* to flee; *pt. pl.* gathlauhun, 5. 14; 14. 50; 16. 8.

Ga-thulan, *wk. v.* to suffer, endure, 5. 26.

Gatwo, *wk. s. f.* a street. North E. *gate,* a street.

Ga-u-hwa-sehwi, whether he saw ought, 8. 23; *compounded of* ga, uh, hwa, *and* saihwan.

Gaumjan, *wk. v. with dat.* to see, perceive, behold, observe, 4. 12. A. S. *gýman.*

Gaunon, *wk. v.* to lament.

Gaurs, *adj.* sorrowful, sad, grieved, 3. 5; 6. 26; 10. 22.

Ga-wagjan, *wk. v.* to make to wag, stir, shake, 13. 25.

Ga-wairpan, *str. v.* to cast, cast down, throw down, 9. 18, 45. See Wairpan.

Ga-wairtheigs, *adj.* at peace, peaceably disposed, 9. 50.

Ga-wairthi, *str. s. n.* peace, 5. 34.

Ga-waldan, *str. v.* (waiwald, waiwaldum, waldans), to rule, bear rule, 10. 42.

Ga-waliths, *pp.* chosen, elect, 13. 20. See below.

Ga-waljan, *wk. v.* to choose, 13. 20.

Ga-wandjan, *wk. v.* to turn; *refl.* to turn oneself, to be converted, 4. 12.

Ga-wargjan, *wk. v.* to condemn, 10. 33.

Ga-wasjan, *wk. v.* to clothe, 1. 6; 5. 15.

Ga-wath; see Ga-widan.

Ga-waurkjan, *wk. v.* to work, make, 9. 5; to appoint, 3. 14.

Gawi, *str. s. n.* a province, country, region, 6. 55. Cf. G. *gau.*

Ga-widan, *str. v.* (wath, wedum, widans), to join together; *pt. s.* gawath, 10. 9.

Gazds, *str. s. m.* goad, sting. E. *goad.*

Giba, *str. s. f.* a gift. A.S. *gifu.*

Giban, *str. v.* (gaf, gebum, gibans), to give; *pt. s.* gaf, 2. 26; 4. 7; *pp. fem.* gibano, 6. 2. E. *give.*

Gibla, *wk. s. m.* gable, pinnacle. E. *gable.*

Gild, *str. s. n.* tribute.

Gildan, *str. v.* (gald, guldum, guldans), to yield, pay. E. *yield.*

Gilstr, *str. s. n.* tribute.

Giltha, *str. s. f.* a sickle, 4. 29. Cf. E. *geld.*

Ginnan, *str. v.* (gann, gunnum, gunnans), to begin. A.S. *ginnan.*

Giutan, *str. v.* (gaut, gutum, gutans), *with acc.* to pour, 2. 22. A. S. *géotan.*

Glitmunjan, *wk. v.* to shine, glitter, glister, 9. 3. Cf. E. *glitter.*

Gods, *adj.* good. 4. 20. E. *good.*

Goljan, *wk. v. with acc.* to salute, greet, 15. 18.

Graban, *str. v.* (grof, grobum, grabans), to grave, dig. E. *grave.*

Gramjan, *wk. v.* to make angry.

Gras, *str. s. n.* grass, a blade of grass, a herb, 4. 28, 32. E. *grass.*

Gredags, *adj.* greedy, hungry; gr. wisan, to hunger, 2. 25; 11. 12. E. *greedy.*

Gredus, *str. s. m.* hunger. E. *greed.*

Greipan, *str. v.* (graip, graipum, gripans), to gripe, grip, seize, lay hold of, take (prisoner), 14. 44, 48, 49, 51. E. *gripe.*

Gretan, Greitan, *str. v.* (gaigrot, gretans), to weep, lament, 5. 38; 14. 72. Scotch *greet.*

Grundus, *s.* ground. E. *ground.*

Gudja, *wk. s. m.* a priest, 1. 44. *From* guth.

Gulth, *str. s. n.* gold. E. *gold.*

Guma, *wk. s. m.* a man. A. S. *guma,* M. E. *gome.*

Gumeins, *adj.* manlike, male, 10. 6.

Gunds or Gund, *str. s. n.* a cancer.

Guth, *str. s. m.* God, 1. 1; 5. 7. E. *God.*

H.

Habaith, *neut. of* habaiths, *pp. of* haban; h. wesi, might be had in readiness, 3. 9. See below.

Haban, *wk. v.* (habaida), to have, 1. 22; 7. 3; to hold, esteem, 11. 32; to be able to do, 14. 8; to be about to, 10. 32; ubil habands (=Lat. *male habentes*), ill, 1. 34; *pt. s.* habaida, 7. 25. E. *have.*

Hafjan, *str. v.* (hof, hofum, hafans), to heave, heave up, carry, bear, 2. 3. E. *heave.*

Haftjan, *wk. v.* to cleave to.

Hafts, *adj.* joined. Cf. E. *haft.*

Hahan, *str. v.* (haihah, haihans), to hang, leave in suspense. A. S. *hón.*

Haidus, *str. s. m.* manner, way. A. S. *hád*; E. *-hood,* suffix.

Haifsts, *str. s. f.* strife.

Haihait; see **Haitan.**

Haihs, *adj.* half-blind, with one eye, 9. 47. Cf. Lat. *cæcus.*

Hailjan, *wk. v.* to heal, 3. 2, 15. E. *heal.*

Hails, *adj.* hale, whole, 5. 34; be hale, i. e. hail! 15. 18. E. *whole, hale.*

Haimothli, *str. s. n.* a homestead, landed possession, 10. 29, 30.

Haims, *str. s. f.* (*pl.* haimos), a village, country place, 1. 38; 6. 56. E. *home.*

Hairda, *str. s. f.* a herd, flock, 5. 11. E. *herd* = flock.

Hairdeis, *str. s. m.* a herd, or shepherd. E. *herd* = shepherd.

Hairto, *wk. s. n.* the heart, 2. 6. E. *heart.*

Hairus, *str. s. m.* a sword, 14. 43. A. S. *heoru.*

Haitan, *str. v.* (haihait, haihaitum, haitans), to name, call; *pt. s.* haibait, called, 1. 20; commanded, 5. 43; haitada, *pr. s.* (as *fut. s.*) *pass.* shall be called, 11. 17. A. S. *hátan.*

Haithi, *str. s. f.* heath. E. *heath.*

Haithiwisks, *adj.* of or belonging to a heath; wild, 1. 6.

Haithno, *wk. s. f.* a heathen woman, a Gentile woman, 7. 26. E. *heathen.*

Haiti, *str. s. f.* a command, hest. *From* haitan.

Hakuls, *str. s. m.* a cloak. A. S. *hacele.*

Halba, *str. s. f.* the half.

Halbs, *adj.* half, 6. 23. E. *half.*

Haldan, *str. v.* (*perf.* haihald, *pl.* haihaldum, *pp.* haldans), to hold, keep; *hence* to feed, keep sheep or swine, 5. 11. E. *hold.*

Haldis, *adv. comp.* rather. Icel. *heldr.*

Halja, *str. s. f.* hell. E. *hell.*

Halks, *adj.* needy, poor.

Hallus, *str. s. m.* a rock, stone.

Hals, *str. s. m.* neck. A. S. *heals.*

Hals-agga(?), *wk. s. m.* the neck, *a proposed reading in* 9. 42. [*The*

MS. *has* bals-agga; but cf. A. S. *heals*, neck.]

Halts, *adj.* halt, lame, 9. 45. E. *halt*.

Hamfs, *or* Hanfs, *adj.* one-handed, maimed, 9. 43. [Whether *m* or *n* is the right letter, seems uncertain.]

Hamon, *wk. v.* to clothe.

Hana, *wk. s. m.* a cock, 14. 68. A. S. *hana*.

Handugei, *wk. s. f.* handiness, cleverness, wisdom, 6. 2.

Handugs, *adj.* clever. E. *handy*.

Handus, *str. s. f.* the hand, 1. 31. E. *hand*.

Handu-waurhts, *adj.* wrought by hand, 14. 58.

Hansa, *str. s. f.* a company, a band of men, 15. 16. Cf. *Hanse-towns*.

Hardu-hairtei, *wk. s. f.* hard-heartedness, hardness of heart, 10. 5.

Hardus, *adj.* hard. E. *hard*.

Harjis, *str. s. m.* an army. A. S. *here*.

Hatan, Hatjan, *wk. v.* to hate. E. *hate*.

Hatis, *str. s. n.* hate.

Haubith (*gen.* haubidis), *str. s. n.* the head, 6. 16, 24; h. afmaitan, to behead, 6. 16, 27; b. waihstins, corner-stone, 12. 10. E. *head*.

Hauhei, *wk. s. f.* height.

Hauheins, *str. s. f.* glory.

Hauh-hairtei, *s.* pride, 7. 22. See Hauhs *and* Hairto.

Hauhista, highest, 5. 7. See Hauhs.

Hauhisti, *str. s. n.* the highest point, highest height, 11. 10.

Hauhitha, *str. s. f.* height. E. *height*.

Hauhjan, *wk. v.* to exalt, lift on high, glorify, magnify, 2. 12.

Hauhs, *adj.* (*comp.* hauhiza, *sup.* hauhista), high, 9. 2; *superl.* 5. 7. E. *high*.

Haunjan, *wk. v.* to humiliate.

Hauns, *adj.* base, contemptible. A. S. *héan*.

Haurds, *str. s. f.* a door. Cf. E. *hurdle*.

Hauri, *str. s. n.* a glowing coal. Cf. E. *hearth*.

Haurn, *str. s. n.* a horn. E. *horn*.

Hausjan, Hausjon, *wk. v. with acc.* to hear, 4. 16; *with dat.* to listen to, 6. 11; 7. 14; 9. 7; *with prep.* fram, 3. 21. E. *hear*.

Hawi, *str. s. n.* grass. E. *hay*.

Hazjan, *wk. v.* to praise. A. S. *herian*.

Heito, *wk. s. f.* heat, fever. E. *heat*.

Heiwa-frauja, *wk. s. m.* a master of a house, 14. 14.

Her, *adv.* here, hither, 6. 3. E. *here*.

Hethjo, *wk. s. f.* a chamber.

Hidre, *adv.* hither, 11. 3. E. *hither*.

Hilms, *str. s. m.* a helmet. E. *helm*.

Hilpan, *str. v. with gen.* (halp, hulpum, hulpans), to help, 9. 22. E. *help*.

Himins, *str. s. m.* heaven, 1. 10, 11. Cf. G. *himmel*.

Hindana, *prep. with gen.* behind, on that side of, beyond, 3. 8. Cf. E. *be-hind*.

Hindar, *prep. with dat. and acc.* on that side of, beyond, 5. 1; behind, 8. 33.

Hindumists, *adj. superl.* hindmost. E. *hindmost*.

Hiri, *interj.* come here, 10. 21. See below.

Hirjats, *interj.* come here, you two! 1. 17; *dual form of* hiri.

Hirjith, *interj.* come ye here! 12. 7; *plural form of* hiri.

His, *pron. of* which the fem. is hija, *neut.* hita, this; —und hita, till this time, till now, 13. 19.

Hita, *neut. of* his, this, 13. 19. See His. E. *it*, A. S. *hit*.

Hiufan, *str. v.* (hauf, hufum, hufans),

to sigh, mourn, lament. A. S. *heofan.*

Hiuhma, *wk. s. m.* a crowd.

Hiwi, *str. s. n.* hue, appearance. E. *hue.*

Hlahjan, *str. v.* (hloh, hlohum, hlahans), to laugh. E. *laugh.*

Hlaifs, Hlaibs, *str. s. m.* a loaf, bread, 2. 26; 7. 5. E. *loaf.*

Hlains, *str. s. m.* a hill.

Hlaiw, *str. s. n.* a grave, tomb, 6. 20; 15. 46; 16. 2. A. S. *hlǽw.*

Hlamma, *str. s. f.* a snare.

Hlas, *adj.* joyful, merry.

Hlathan, *str. v.* (hloth, hlothum, hlathans), to load. E. *lade.*

Hlaupan, *str. v.* (hlaihlaup), to run, leap. E. *leap.*

Hlauts, *str. s. m.* a lot, 15. 24. E. *lot.*

Hleibjan, *wk. v.* to assist.

Hleiduma, *adj.* left, on the left hand, 10. 37.

Hleithra, *str. s. f.* hut, tent. Cf. E. *lid?*

Hlifan, *str. v.* (hlaf, hlefum, hlufans), to steal, 10. 19.

Hliftus, *str. s. m.* a thief. Cf. E. *shop-lifter.*

Hlija, *wk. s. m.* tent, tabernacle, 9. 5.

Hliuma, *wk. s. m.* hearing, 7. 35. Cf. E. *li-sten.*

Hlutrs, *adj.* pure. A. S. *hlutor.*

Hnaiws, *adj.* lowly. *From* hneiwan.

Hnaskwus, *adj.* soft, tender. E. *nesh.*

Hneiwan, *str. v.* (hnaiw, hniwum, hniwans), to bend down, sink. A. S. *hnigan.*

Hniupan, *str. v.* (hnaup, hnupum, hnupans), to break.

Hnuto, *wk. s. f.* a thorn, sting.

Hoha, *wk. s. m.* a plough.

Holon, *wk. v.* to treat with violence.

Horinassus, *str. s. m.* whoredom, adultery, 7. 21.

Horinon, *wk. v.* to commit adultery, 10. 11. See below.

Horinondei, adulterous (*pt. pres.*

fem. from horinon, *v.* to commit adultery), 8. 38.

Hors, *str. s. m.* a whoremonger. Cf. E. *whore.*

Hrains, *adj.* pure, clean, 1. 41. Cf. E. *rinse.*

Hramjan, *wk. v.* to crucify.

Hrisjan, *wk. v.* to shake. A. S. *hrysian.*

Hropjan, *wk. v.* to call out, cry out, 1. 26; 3. 11. A. S. *hrópan.*

Hrot, *str. s. n.* a roof, 2. 4.

Hrotheigs, *adj.* triumphant. Cf. A. S. *hróðor,* joy.

Hrugga, *str. s. f.* a staff, 6. 8. E. *rung.*

Hrukjan, *wk. v.* to crow (as a cock), 14. 72. Cf. E. *rook.*

Huggrjan, *wk. v.* to hunger. E. *hunger.*

Hugjan, *wk. v.* to think, imagine, trust, 10. 24. A. S. *hogian.*

Hugs, *str. s. m.* thought. A. S. *hyge.*

Huhrus, *str. s. m.* hunger.

Hulistr, *str. s. n.* a veil. E. *holster.*

Huljan, *wk. v. with acc.* to hide, cover, 14. 65. Cf. prov. E. *hull,* husk.

Hulths, *adj.* gracious. A. S. *hold.*

Hun, *indef. suffix, as in* ains-hun, any one, hwas-hun, any one.

Hund, *s. n.* (*pl.* hunda), a hundred, *only used in pl. preceded by* twa, etc.; — twa h., 200; — thrija h., 300; — fimf hunda, 500; — niun hunda, 900; 14. 5. E. *hund-red.*

Hunda-faths, *str. s. m.* a centurion, 15. 39.

Hunds, *str. s. m.* a dog, hound, 7. 27. A. S. *hund,* E. *hound.*

Hunsl, *str. s. n.* a sacrifice, 9. 49. E. *housel.*

Hunsljan, *wk. v.* to offer.

Hunths, *str. s. f.* captivity. *From* hinthan.

Hups, *str. s. m.* the hip, loins, 1. 6. E. *hip.*

Hus, *str. s. n.* house. E. *house.*

Huzd, *str. s. n.* a treasure, 10. 21. E. *hoard.*

HW.

Hwa, what. See Hwas.

Hwadre, *adv.* whither.

Hwairban, *str. v.* (hwarb, hwaurbum, hwaurbans), to walk. A.S. *hwéorfan.*

Hwairnei, *wk. s. f.* skull, 15. 22. [Unless we consider *hwarneins* as an adj., 'belonging to a skull.']

Hwaiteis, *str. s. m.* wheat. E. *wheat.*

Hwaiwa, *adv.* how, 2. 26; 3. 23. See Hwe.

Hwan, *adv.* when; hwan lang mel, for how long a time, 9. 21; nibai hwan, lest at any time, 4. 12; hwan filu, how much, 3. 8. E. *when.*

Hwanzuh, *acc. of* Hwazuh, *q. v.*

Hwapjan, *wk. v.* to quench.

Hwar, *adv.* where, 14. 12.

Hwarbon, *wk. v.* to go about, walk, 1. 16; 11. 27. *Allied to* hwairban.

Hwarjis, *pron.* who? which? (*out of many*), 9. 34; 12. 23.

Hwarjizuh, *adj.* every, each one, 15. 24. *From* hwarjis *and* uh.

Hwas, *pron. inter. and rel.* (hwo, hwa), who, what, which, what sort of, 1. 24; any one, anything, 2. 9; 7. 16. E. *who.*

Hwas-hun, *pron.* any one; ni hw., no one, 10. 18, 29.

Hwassei, *wk. s. f.* sharpness.

Hwathar, *adj.* whether (of two), which (of two), 2. 9. E. *whether.*

Hwathjan, *wk. v.* to foam, 9. 18, 20.

Hwatho, *wk. s. f.* foam.

Hwathro, *adv.* from whence, whence, 6. 2; 8. 4. E. *whither.*

Hwazuh, *pron. indef.* (*fem.* hwo'h, *neut.* hwa'h), each, every: *from* hwas *and* uh, 9. 49; twans hwanzuh, two and two, 6. 7.

Hwe, *adv.* how, *instr. case of* hwas, 4. 30. Cf. E. *how.*

Hweila, *str. s. f.* a while, a time, a season, 2. 19; time, hour, 15. 25. E. *while.*

Hweila-hwairbs, *adj.* enduring only for a while, 4. 17.

Hweits, *adj.* white, 9. 3. E. *white.*

Hwileiks, Hweleiks, what sort of. E. *which.*

Hwis, *gen. m. n. of* hwas, 6. 24.

Hwo, *fem. of* hwas, who, what, 1. 27; 3. 33.

Hwota, *str. s. f.* a threat.

Hwotjan, *wk. v.* to threaten, rebuke, charge, 10. 48.

I.

Iairusaulymim, Jerusalem, 7. 1.

Ibai, *conj.* perhaps; *answers in questions to* Greek μή, 2. 19; lest, 2. 21. E. *if.*

Ibns, *adj.* even. E. *even.*

Ibuks, *adj.* backwards.

Iddjedun, they went, 5. 24. See Gaggan. A.S. *eode,* pl. *eodon.*

Idreiga, *str. s. f.* repentance, 1. 4.

Idreigon, *wk. v.* (*with and without* sik), to repent, 1. 15; 6. 12.

Id-weitjan, *wk. v.* to reproach, revile, 15. 32. A.S. *ed-witan.*

Iftuma, *adj.* the one after, the following; iftumin daga, on the morrow, 11. 12.

Igkwis, *dat. and acc. dual,* you two, 1. 17; 10. 36. A.S. *inc.*

Ija, her, *acc. f. of* is, 1. 30; 5. 33.

Ijos, them, *acc. fem. pl. of* is, 16. 8.

Ik, *pron.* I, 1. 2; 6. 16. E. *I.*

Im, to them; *from* is, 1. 31.

Im, am. See Wisan.

Imma, him, *pron. dat. of* is, 1. 5.

In, *prep.* (*with dat. and acc.*) in, 1. 2; towards, into, to, 5. 1; *with gen.* on account of, about, through, by; — in this, (*or* in-uh-this), on this account; — in thizei, because, for the reason that. *It is a common prefix.* E. *in.*

Ina, him; *acc. of* is, 1. 10, 26, 43.

In-feinan, *wk. v.* to pity, have compassion on, 1. 41 ; 8. 2.

In-maideins, *str. s. f.* a change, exchange. 8. 37.

In-maidjan, *wk. v.* to change, exchange, transfigure, 9. 2.

Inn, *adv.* in, 1. 19.

Innana, *adv.* within ; *prep. with gen.* within, inside. 15. 16.

Innathro, *adv.* within, 7. 21, 23.

Inn at-gaggan, *str. v.* to enter, enter into, go into, 4. 19 ; 5. 39. See **Gaggan.**

Inn gaggan, *wk. v.* to go in, enter ; i. framis, to go on, 1. 19.

Innuma, *adj. comp.* inner.

Ins, them ; *pl. acc. m. of* is, 1. 20 ; 2. 13 ; 6. 7.

In-saian, *str. v.* to sow in, 4. 15.

In-saihwan, *str. v.* (sahw, sehwum, saihwans), to look upon, regard, behold, 10. 21 ; to look round, 9. 8.

In-sailjan, *wk. v.* to let down, lower with cords, 2. 4.

In-sandjan, *wk. v.* to send, 1. 2 ; 3. 14 : 5. 12.

Inuh, Inu, *prep.* without, 4. 34 ; *from* in, *followed by the enclitic* u *or* uh inuh ; this, therefore, 10. 7.

In-wagjan, *wk. v.* to stir up, 15. 11.

In-weitan, *str. v.* to worship, reverence, salute ; *pt. s.* inwait, 5. 6 ; *pt. pl.* inwitun, 9. 15.

In-widan, *str. v.* to reject, frustrate, 7. 9 ; to deny, refuse, 8. 34 ; 14. 72.

In-wisan, *v. anom.* to be present ; *hence* to be present and gone again, to be just past, 16. 1.

Is, *pron.* he, 1. 8 ; *fem.* si ; *neut.* ita, 4. 37 ; *gen. m.* is, 1. 7, 16 ; *gen. f.* izos, of her, 1. 31 ; *dat. m.* imma, 1. 5 ; *dat. f.* izai, 5. 34 ; *acc. m.* ina, 1. 10 ; *acc. f.* ija, 1. 30 ; *gen. pl.* ize, 1. 23 ; *dat. pl.* im, 1. 31 ; *acc. pl. m.* ins, 1. 20.

Is, thou art, 1. 11, 24. See **Wisan.**

Ist, is, 7. 2. See **Wisan.** E. *is.*

Ita, it ; *nom. n.* of is, 4. 37.

Itan, *str. v.* (at, etum, itans), to eat. E. *eat.*

Ith, *conj.* but, 1. 8, 41 ; except, 4. 34.

Iudaieis, Jews, 7. 3.

Iup, *adv.* upwards. F. *up.*

Iupa, *adv.* above.

Iupathro, *adv.* from above, 15. 38.

Izai, to her, *dat. f.* of is, 5. 34.

Ize, of them, *gen. pl. m. of* is, 1. 23 ; 5. 37.

Izos, of her ; *gen. fem. sing. of* is, 1. 31.

Izwar, *pos. pron.* your, 2. 8 ; 6. 11 ; 7. 9.

Izwis, to you, you ; *dat. and acc. pl. of* thu, 1. 8 ; 4. 11.

J.

J, the fifteenth letter of the alphabet. *As a numeral it means* 60 ; 4. 8.

Ja, *adv.* yes. E. *yea.*

Jabai, *conj.* if, even if, although, 1. 40 ; 4. 26.

Jah, *conj.* and, 1. 4 ; even, also, 2. 28.

Jai, *adv.* yes, verily, 7. 28.

Jainar, *adv.* there, 1. 35 ; 5. 11. See **Jains.**

Jaind, Jaindre, *adv.* there. Cf. E. *yonder.*

Jains, *pron. dem.* that, (*fem.* jaina, *neut.* jainata), 1. 9 : 4. 35. E. *yon.*

Jainthro, *adv.* thence, 1. 19 ; 6. 1 ; 10. 1.

Jer, *str. s. n.* a year, 5. 25. E. *year.*

Jiuka, *str. s. f.* strife.

Jiukan, *wk. v.* to contend, fight.

Ju, *adv.* now, already, 8. 2. A.S. *iu.*

Jugga-lauths, *str. s. m.* a young lad, a young man. 14. 51 ; 16. 5. *From* juggs *and* liudan.

Juggs, *adj.* young, new, 2. 22. E. *young.*

Juk, *str. s. n.* a yoke. E. *yoke.*

Junda, *str. s. f.* youth, 10. 20.

Jus, *pron.* ye, 7. 11; *pl. of* thu, thou; *gen.* izwara; *dat. and acc.* izwis, 1. 8: 4. 11. E. *ye.*

Juthan, *adv.* already, 1. 45; 4. 37; 11. 11; 13. 28;'15. 42.

K.

Kaisar, *str. s. m.* Cæsar, 12. 14.

Kaisara-gild, *str. s. n.* tribute-money, 12. 14.

Kalbo, *wk. s. f.* a calf. E. *calf.*

Kalds, *adj.* cold. E. *cold.*

Kalkinassus, *str. s. m.* fornication, adultery, 7. 21.

Kalkjo, *wk. s. f.* a harlot.

Kann, I know, I can; *from* kunnan, 1. 24. E. *can.*

Kannjan, *wk. v.* to make known. E. *ken.*

Kant, *for* Kannt, thou knowest, 10. 19. See Kunnan.

Kara, *str. s. f.* care; *hence* kar' ist, *with acc. of pers. and gen. of thing,* it concerns; *used without* ist, 4. 38; ni kara thuk, there is no care to thee, thou carest not, 12. 14. E. *care.*

Karkara, *str. s. f.* a prison, 6. 17, 27. Lat. *carcer.*

Karon, *wk. v.* to be concerned about.

Kas, *str. s. n.* a vessel, pot (for holding liquids, etc.), 3. 27, (A. V. goods); 11. 16. Icel. *ker.*

Kasja, *wk. s. m.* a potter.

Katils, *str. s. m.* a kettle, vessel for water, 7. 4. E. *kettle.*

Kaupatjan, *wk. v.* to strike with the palm of the hand, to cuff, 14. 65.

Kaupon, *wk. v.* to traffic, trade. E. *cheapen.*

Kaurban, Corban, 7. 11.

Kauritha, *str. s. f.* a burden.

Kaurjan, *wk. v.* to lade, burden.

Kaurn, *str. s. n.* corn. E. *corn.*

Kaurno, *str. s. f.* corn, a grain of corn, 4. 28, 31.

Kaurus, *adj.* burdensome.

Kausjan, *wk. v.* to prove, test; to taste, 9. 1. *Causal of* kiusan.

Keinan, *wk. v.* to spring up, grow (of plants), 4. 27.

Kelikn, *str. s. n.* a tower, 12. 1; upper room, 14. 15.

Kilthei, *wk. s. f.* womb. Cf. E. *child.*

Kindins, *str. s. m.* a governor.

Kinnus, *str. s. f.* the cheek. Cf. E. *chin.*

Kintus, *str. s. m.* a farthing.

Kiusan, *str. v.* (kaus, kusum, kusans), to choose. A. S. *céosan.*

Klismjan, *wk. v.* to tinkle.

Klismo, *wk. s. f.* a cymbal.

Kniu, *str. s. n.* (*gen.* kniwis), the knee, 1. 40; 15. 19. E. *knee.*

Knoda, *or* Knods, *s. f.* a race, stock.

Knussjan, *wk. v.* to kneel, 10. 17; k. kniwam, to kneel, 1. 40.

Kriustan, *str. v.* (kraust, krustum, krustans), to gnash with the teeth, grind the teeth, 9. 18. E. *crush.*

Krusts, *str. s. f.* gnashing of teeth.

Kukjan, *wk. v. with dat.* to kiss, 14. 44, 45.

Kuni, *str. s. n.* kin, race, generation, tribe, 8. 12; 9. 19. E. *kin.*

Kunnan, *anom. v.* (*first perf. as pres.* kann, *pl.* kunnum; *pt. t.* kuntha; *pp.* kunths), to know, 4. 11; *pt. pl.* kunthedun, 1. 34. A. S. *cunnan.*

Kunthi, *str. s. n.* knowledge.

Kunths, *pp. as adj.* known. A. S. *cúð.*

Kustus, *str. s. m.* a proof, test. Cf. A. S. *costian,* to tempt.

KW.

Kwainon, *wk. v.* to mourn, weep, lament, 16. 10. E. *whine.*

Kwairnus, *str. s.* a mill-stone. E. *quern.* See Asilu-kwairnus.

Kwairrus, *adj.* gentle.

Kwam, came ; *from* kwiman ; 1. 9 ; 7. 31.

Kwast, thou sayest, 12. 32. See **Kwithan.**

Kwath, said, 4. 30 ; 7. 6. See **Kwithan.** E. *quoth.*

Kwemun, came, 1. 29 ; 4. 4. See **Kwiman.**

Kwethun, spoke, told, 1. 30 ; 4. 38. See **Kwithan.**

Kwens, Kweins, *str. s. f.* a woman, a wife, 6. 17 ; 10. 2. E. *queen, quean.*

Kwiman, *str. v.* (kwam, kwemum, kwumans), to come, arrive, 1. 7 ; *pt. pl.* kwemun, 1. 29 ; 4. 4. E. *come.*

Kwineins, *adj.* female, 10. 6.

Kwino, *wk. s. f.* a woman, 5. 25.

Kwistjan, *wk. v.* to destroy. A.S. *cwysan.*

Kwithan, *str. v.* (kwath, kwethun, kwithans), to say, speak, call, name ; *pt. s.* kwath, 4. 30 ; *pt. pl.* kwethun, 1. 30 ; 4. 38 ; ubil kwithan, to speak evil of one, 7. 10.

Kwithiduh, *for* kwithith uh, and say ye, 16. 7.

Kwithu-hafta, *wk. s. f.* a woman with child, 13. 17.

Kwithus, *str. s. m.* womb. A.S. *cwið.*

Kwius, *adj.* quick, living, alive, 12. 27. Cf. E. *quick.*

Kwrammitha, *str. s. f.* moisture.

Kwums, *str. s. m.* coming. *From* kwiman.

L.

L, the twelfth letter of the Gothic alphabet. *As a numeral, it signifies* 30 ; 4. 8.

Lag, lay ; *from* ligan, 1. 30 ; 2. 4.

Laggs, *adj.* long (*only used with ref. to time*) ; swa lagga hweila swe, so long as, 2. 19 ; hwan lagg mel, how long, 9. 21. E. *long.*

Lagjan, *wk. v.* to lay, set, place, 5. 23 ; 6. 56 ; 10. 16 ; 15. 19 ;

lagjan ana, to lay upon, 5. 23. E. *lay.*

Laian, *str. v.* to revile. A.S. *léan.*

Laiba, *str. s. f.* a thing left, a leaving, remnant, 8. 8. Cf. E. *leave.*

Laigaion, *s.* a legion (*from* Gk. λεγεών), 5. 9, 15.

Laikan, *str. v.* (lailaik, laikans), to leap for joy.

Laiks, *str. s. m.* sport, dance. A.S. *láic.*

Lailot, he permitted, suffered, 5. 19. See **Letan.**

Laisareis, *str. s. m.* a teacher, master, 4. 38.

Laiseins, *str. s. f.* a teaching, doctrine, 1. 22 ; 4. 2.

Laisjan, *wk. v.* to teach, 1. 21. A. S. *léran.*

Laistjan, *wk. v.* to follow (*with acc. ; also with prep.* afar), 1. 18 ; 8. 34 ; 9. 38.

Laists, *str. s. m.* a track, footstep. E. *last, sb.*

Lamb, *str. s. n.* a lamb. E. *lamb.*

Land, *str. s. n.* land, field. E. *land.*

Lasiws, *adj.* weak.

Lathon, *wk. v.* to call, invite, 2. 17. A. S. *laðian.*

Latjan, *wk. v.* to tarry.

Lats, *adj.* slothful. E. *late.*

Laubjan, *wk. v.* to believe. Cf. E. *be-lieve.*

Laufs, Laubs, *str. s. m.* a leaf, 11. 13 ; *pl.* laubos, 13. 28. E. *leaf.*

Laugnjan, *wk. v.* to lie, deny, 14. 70. *From* liugan.

Lauhatjan, *wk. v.* to shine as lightning.

Lauhmuni, Lauhmoni, *str. s. f.* lightning.

Laun, *str. s. n.* pay, reward. A. S. *léan.*

Laus, *adj.* empty. E. *loose.*

Laus-handja, *adj.* empty-handed, 12. 3.

Lausjan, *wk. v.* to make of none effect.

Laus-kwithrs, *adj.* with empty stomach, fasting, 8. 3.

Leihts, *adj.* light (not heavy).

Leihwan, *str. v.* (laihw), to lend. Cf. E. *lend, loan.*

Leik, *str. s. n.* the body, 5. 29; a dead body, carcase, 15. 43; flesh, 10. 8; 13. 20. A. S. *lic.*

Leikan, *wk. v.* to please. E. *like.*

Leikeis, *str. s. m.* a physician. See **Lekeis.**

Lein, *str. s. n.* linen, 14. 51, 52; 15. 46. Lat. *linum.*

Leisan, *str. v.* (lais, lisum, lisans), to learn. Cf. E. *learn.*

Leithan, *str. v.* (laith, lithum, lithans), to go. A. S. *li'an.*

Leithus, *str. s. m.* strong drink.

Leitils, *adj.* (*comp.* minniza, *superl.* minnists), little, I. 19; 9. 42; 14. 70. E. *little.*

Lekeis, Leikeis, *str. s. m.* a leech, physician, 2. 17; 5. 26. E. *leech.*

Letan, *str. v.* (*also spelt* leitan, 15. 9, etc.; *pt. t.* lailot, *pp.* letans), to let, permit, suffer, allow, 5. 19. E. *let.*

Lew, *str. s. n.* occasion, opportunity.

Lewjan, *wk. v.* to betray, 14. 42, 44.

Libains, *str. s. f.* life, 4. 19; 9. 43; 10. 17. See below.

Liban, *wk. v.* to live, 5. 23. E. *live.*

Ligan, *str. v.* (lag, legum, ligans), to lie, I. 30; 2. 4. E. *lie.*

Ligrs, *str. s. m.* a couch, bed, 4. 21; 7. 4, 30. E. *lair.*

Lisan, *str. v.* (las, lesum, lisans), to gather. Prov. E. *lease,* to glean.

Lists, *str. s. f.* craftiness. A. S. *list.*

Lita, *str. s. f.* a prayer.

Lithus, *str. s. m.* limb, member. A S. *lið.*

Liubs, *adj.* dear, beloved, 1. 11; 9. 7; 12. 6. E. *lief.*

Liudan, *str. v.* (lauth, ludum, ludans), to grow, spring up. 4. 27.

Liugan, *str. v.* (laug, lugum, lug-

ans), to lie, tell falsehoods. E. *lie.*

Liugan, *wk. v.* (*pt. t.* liugaida), to marry, to take a wife, 10. 11; 12. 25; to be married, take a husband, 10. 12.

Liugn, *str. s. n.* a lie.

Liuhath, *str. s. n.* (*gen.* liuhadis), light, 13. 24; 14. 54. E. *light.*

Liuta, *wk. s. m.* a dissembler, hypocrite, 7. 6.

Liutei, *wk. s. f.* deceit, pretence, hypocrisy, 7. 22; 12. 15.

Liuts, *adj.* deceitful. A. S. *lytig.*

Liuthon, *wk. v.* to sing.

Lofa, *wk. s. m.* the flat or palm of the hand;—lofam slahan, to strike with the palms of the hands, 14. 65. Prov. E. *loof,* palm of the hand.

Lubains, *str. s. f.* hope.

Ludja, *str. s. f.* the face.

Luftus, *str. s. m.* the air. Cf. E. *a-loft.*

Lukarn, *str. s. n.* a light, candle (Lat. *lucerna*), 4. 21.

Lukarna-statha, *wk. s. m.* a candle-stick, 4. 21. *From* lukarn *and* staths.

Lun, *str. s. n.* a ransom, 10. 45.

Lustus, *str. s. m.* lust, desire, 4. 19. E. *lust.*

Luton, *wk. v.* to betray; see **Liuts.**

M.

Magan, *v. anom.* (*old pt. t. as pres.* mag, *pt. t.* mahta, *pp.* mahts), to be able, 1. 40; maguts-u, are ye able, 10. 38. And see **Mahta.** E. *may.*

Magaths, *str. s. f.* a maid. E. *maid.*

Magus, *str. s. m.* a boy. A. S. *maga.*

Mahta, *pt. s.* might, could, 1. 45; mahtedun, *pt. pl.* were able, 3. 20; see **Magan.** E. *might.*

Mahteigs, *adj.* mighty, great, possible, 9. 23; 10. 27. E. *mighty.*

Mahts, *adj.* possible.

Mahts, *str. s. f.* might, power, strength, virtue, 5. 30; miracle, 6. 2. E. *might.*

Maidjan, *wk. v.* to change, falsify.

Maihstus, *str. s. m.* a dunghill.

Mail, *str. s. n.* a spot. E. *mole.*

Maimaitun; see Maitan.

Mais, (μᾶλλον), *adv.* more, rather, 5. 26;—mais thamma, so much the more, 7. 36;—filaus mais, *or* filu mais, much more; thanamais, more still, longer, 5. 35; rather, 15. 11. Cf. E. *more.*

Maists, *superl. adj.* the greatest, 4. 32; 9. 34; *as a sb.* a chief man, man of rank, 6. 21. E. *most.*

Maitan, *str. v.* (maimait, maitans), to cut; *pt. pl.* maimaitun, 11. 8.

Maithms, *str. s. m.* a gift, Corban, 7. 11. A. S. *maiðm.*

Maiza, *comp. adj.* (*f.* maizei, *n.* maizo), greater, 12. 31. E. *more.*

Malan, *v.* to grind. Cf. E. *meal.*

Malma, *wk. s. m.* sand.

Malo, *wk. s. f.* a moth.

Mammo, *wk. s. f.* flesh.

Managei, *wk. s. f.* a crowd, multitude, the people, 2. 4; 3. 7.

Managiza, *compar. adj.* more, 12. 33. See **Manags.**

Manags, *adj.* much, many, 1. 34; 12. 26. E. *many.*

Mana-seths, Mana-seds, *str. s. f.* a multitude; the world, 14. 9. Lit. *man-seed,* i. e. generation of men.

Man-leika, *wk. s. m.* the image or likeness (of a man), 12. 16.

Manna, *wk. s. m.* a man, 1. 17; *gen. s.* mans, 2. 10; 7. 15; *dat. s.* mann, 7. 15; *acc. s.* mannan, 7. 15; *gen. pl.* manne, 7. 7. E. *man.*

Manna-hun, *adj.* any one; ni m., no one, 1. 44; 8. 26; 9. 9. *From* manna, *with suffix* hun.

Manwjan, *wk. v.* to prepare, 1. 3, 19; 10. 40; 14. 12.

Manwus, *adj.* ready, 14. 15.

Marei, *wk. s. f.* the sea, 1. 16; 3. 7; hindar marein, across the sea, 5. 1. E. *mere.*

Marka, *str. s. f.* border-country, coast, 5. 17; 7. 31. E. *march-es.*

Marzjan, *wk. v.* to offend, hinder, cause to stumble, 9. 43. Cf. E. *mar.*

Matha, *wk. s. m.* a worm, 9. 44, 46, 48. Cf. E. *moth.*

Mathl, *str. s. n.* a market, marketplace, 7. 4.

Mathljan, *wk. v.* to speak. A. S. *maðelian.*

Mati-balgs, *str. s. m.* a meat-bag, wallet, scrip, 6. 8. *From* mats *and* balgs.

Matjan, *wk. v.* to eat, 1. 6; 2. 26; 14. 14. *From* mats.

Mats, *str. s. m.* (*pl.* mateis), meat, food, 7. 19. E. *meat.*

Maudjan, *wk. v.* to remind.

Maujai, *dat. of* Mawi, q. v.

Maurgins, *str. s. m.* morn, morning, 11. 20; 15. 1. E. *morn.*

Maurnan, *wk. v.* to mourn, be grieved about. E. *mourn.*

Maurthr, *str. s. n.* a murder, 7. 21; 15. 7. E. *murder.*

Maurthrjan, *wk. v.* to murder, kill, 10. 19.

Mawi, *str. s. f.* (*gen.* maujos, *dat.* maujai), a maid, maiden, damsel, 5. 42; 6. 22. *Allied to* magus.

Mawilo, *wk. s. f.* a young maiden, damsel, 5. 41.

Megs, *str. s. m.* a son-in-law.

Meina, *gen. of* ik, 8. 35. A. S. *min.*

Meins, *poss. pron.* my, 1. 2, 11. E. *mine, my.*

Meki, *str. s. n.* a sword.

Mel, *str. s. n.* time, 1. 15; 9. 21; season, 11. 13; mela gabaurthais, birthday, 6. 21. E. *meal,* a time for food.

Mela, *wk. s. m.* a measure, a bushel, 4. 21.

Meljan, *wk. v.* to write, 10. 4.

Mena, *wk. s. m.* the moon, 13. 24. E. *moon.*

Menoths, *str. s. m.* a month. E. *month.*

Meritha, *str. s. f.* fame, report, 1. 28. A.S. *mærð, mærðu.*

Merjan, *wk. v.* to proclaim, announce, preach, 6. 12; noise abroad, 1. 4.

Mes, *str. s. n.* a table, 11. 15; a dish, charger, 6. 25: dal uf mesa, a ditch or receptacle for a wine-vat, 12. 1. A.S. *mýse.*

Midjis, *adj.* middle, midst, 9. 36. E. *mid.*

Midjun-gards, *str. s. m.* the earth. A.S. *middangeard.*

Miduma, *str. s. f.* the midst, 3. 3.

Mik, me; *acc. of* ik, 1. 40. E. *me.*

Mikiljan, *wk. v.* to magnify, extol, glorify, praise, 2. 12.

Mikils, *adj.* mickle, great, much, 1. 26. E. *mickle.*

Milds, *adj.* mild. E. *mild.*

Milhma, *wk. s. m.* a cloud, 9. 7; 13. 26; 14. 62.

Milith, *str. s. n.* honey, 1. 6. Lat. *mel.*

Miluks, *str. s. f.* milk. E. *milk.*

Mimz, *str. s. n.* flesh, meat.

Minnists, *superl. adj.* most minute, smallest, least, 4. 31.

Minniza, *compar. adj.* smaller, less, 15. 40. *From* mins.

Mins, *adv.* less.

Mis, to me, me, *dat. of* ik, 1. 17; 5. 7.

Missa-deds, *str. s. f.* a misdeed, sin, 11. 25. E. *misdeed.*

Missa-leiks, *adj.* various, divers, 1. 34. A.S. *mislic.*

Misso, *adv.* reciprocally, *gen. after a pers. pron.* one another, 1. 27; 4. 41.

Mitan, *str. v. (pt. t.* mat, *pl.* metum, meitum, *pp.* mitans), to mete, measure, 4. 24. E. *mete.*

Mitaths, Mitads, *str. s. f.* a measure, a bushel, 4. 24.

Mith, *prep. with dat.* with, amongst, together with, through, by, near, in reply to, 1. 13; mith tweihnaim markom, amid the two boundaries, in the midst of the region, 7. 31. A.S. *mid.*

Mith anakumbjan, *wk. v.* to lie down together with, to recline at meat with, 2. 15.

Mith iddjedun, they went with, 15. 41. See **Gaggan.**

Mith-sokjan, *wk. v.* to dispute, 8. 11.

Mith-thanei, *conj.* when, whilst, 4. 4.

Mith ushramjan, *wk. v.* to crucify with, 15. 32.

Miton, *wk. v.* to measure; *hence,* to weigh a matter, consider, reason upon, ponder, 2. 8.

Mitons, *str. s. f.* a measuring; *hence,* a reasoning, consideration, thought, 7. 21.

Mizdo, *wk. s. f.* meed, reward, 9. 41. E. *meed.*

Mods, *str. s. m.* moodiness, anger, wrath, 3. 5. E. *mood.*

Mota, *str. s. f.* toll, custom, 2. 14.

Motan, *anom. v. (pt. t.* mosta), to be obliged to. A.S. *mótan.*

Motareis, *str. s. m.* a receiver of custom, toll-taker, publican, 2. 15. *From* mota.

Motjan, *wk. v.* to meet. E. *meet.*

Mulda, *str. s. f.* dust, 6. 11. E. *mould.*

Munan, *wk. v.* to consider, intend.

Muns, *str. s. m.* mind, meaning. Cf. E. *mind.*

Munths, *str. s. m.* mouth. E. *mouth.*

N.

Nadrs, *str. s. m.* adder, viper. E. *adder* (for *nadder*).

Nagljan, *wk. v.* to nail. Cf. E. *nail.*

Nahan*, *str. v. (pres.* nah, *pt. t.*

nahta, *pp.* nauhts), to suffice. *Hence* ganohs, *adj.*

Nahta-mats, *str. s. m.* (*lit.* night-meat), an evening meal, supper, 6. 21.

Nahts, *str. s. f.* night, 4. 27. E. *night.*

Naiteins, *str. s. f.* blasphemy, 2. 7; 3. 28. Cf. A. S. *nátan*, to vex.

Naiw, was angry, *pt. s. from an infin.* neiwan, 6. 19. [The reading is very doubtful, and little more than conjectural.]

Nakwaths, *adj.* (*gen.* nakwadis), naked, 14. 51. E. *naked..*

Namnjan, *wk. v.* to name.

Namo, *wk. s. n.* (*pl.* namna, *gen.* namne, *dat.* namnam), name, 5. 9. E. *name.*

Nanthjan, *wk. v.* to dare. A. S. *nédan.*

Nasjan, *wk. v.* to save, 3. 4. A. S. *nerian. From* nisan.

Nati, *str. s. n.* a net, 1. 16, 18. E. *net.*

Natjan, *wk. v.* to wet. Cf. Du. *nat*, G. *nass*, wet.

Naudi-bandi, *str. s. f.* a fetter, 5. 3, 4. *From* nauths *and* bindan.

Nauh, *adv.* still, yet; ni nauh, or nauh ni, not yet, not as yet, 4. 40. Cf. G. *noch.*

Nauh-thanuh, **Nauh-than**, *adv.* still, yet, 5. 35.

Naus, *str. s. m.* a corpse. Icel. *nár.*

Nauths, *str. s. f.* need. E. *need.*

Ne, *adv.* no. E. *no.*

Nehwa, *adv.* near, 2. 4; 11. 1; 13. 28. E. *nigh.*

Nehwundja, *wk. s. m.* a neighbour, 12. 31.

Nei, *adv.* not.

Neith, *str. s. n.* envy, 15. 10. A. S. *nið.*

Nemeina, that they might take, 6. 8. See **Niman.**

Nethla, *str. s. f.* a needle, 10. 25. E. *needle.*

Ni, *conj.* nor, not, 1. 7, 22; 4. 27. A. S. *ne.*

Niba, **Nibai**, *conj.* if not, except, 2. 7, 26: 3. 27; 7. 3; 8. 14. *From* ni *and* ibai.

Nidwa, *str. s. f.* rust.

Nih, *conj.* nor, not even, 2. 2. *From* ni *and* uh; cf. Lat. *ne-c.* See also **Niu.**

Niman, *str. v.* (nam, nemum, ninans), to take, take away, receive, 2. 9; 7. 27; 8. 6; *pt. pl. subj.* nemeina, 6. 8. A. S. *niman.*

Nimuh, and take, 2. 10. See **Niman** and **Uh.**

Nisan, *str. v.* (nas, nesum, nisans), to heal. A. S. *nesan, ge-nesan.*

Nist, is not, 6. 3; 9. 40. *From* ni *and* ist.

Nithan, *str. v.* (*pt. t.* nath), to help.

Nithjis, *str. s. m.* a kinsman; *fem.* nithjo.

Niu, *adv.* and not, 4. 21; niu aiw, never, 2. 25. *From* ni *and* uh; *put for* ni-uh. See **Nih.**

Niuhseins, *str. s. f.* a visitation.

Niujis, *adj.* new, 1. 27. E. *new.*

Niun, *num.* nine. E. *nine.*

Niunda, *ord. adj.* the ninth, 15. 33.

Niutan, *str. v.* (naut, nutum, nutans), to enjoy. A. S. *néotan.*

Nota, *wk. s. m.* stern, hinder part of a ship, 4. 38.

Nu, *adv.* now, 10. 30; 15. 32. A. S. *nu.*

Nuh, *adv.* then (in asking questions), 12. 9. *From* nu *and* uh.

Nuta, *wk. s. m.* a fisher, catcher of fishes, 1. 17. *From* niutan.

O.

O, *interj.* oh! 9. 19; 15. 29.

Ogan, *str. v.* (*pres.* og, *pt. t.* ohta, *pl.* ohtedum), to fear, 5. 15; 9. 32; *refl.* to fear, to be afraid of, 4. 41. *From* agan.

Ogjan, *wk. v.* to terrify.

Osanna, Hosannah, 11. 9.

P.

Paida (χιτών), *str. s. f.* a coat, outer body-garment, 6. 9. Cf. E. *pea*-jacket.

Paraskaiwe (παρασκευή), *s.* the day of the preparation, 15. 42.

Paska (πάσχα), the Passover, 14. 12.

Paurpura, *s.* purple, 15. 17, 20. Gk. πορφύρα.

Plats, *str. s. m.* a patch, new piece put in, 2. 21. E. *patch* (for *platch*).

Plinsjan, *wk. v.* to dance, 6. 22.

Praitoriaun, *s.* Pretorium, 15. 16.

Praggan, *v.* to press.

Praufetes, *s.* prophet, 6. 15; 11. 32.

Praufetjan, *wk. v.* to prophesy, 7. 6; 14. 65.

Praufetus, *s. m.* a prophet, 1. 2; 6. 4; 8. 28.

Puggs, *str. s. n.* a purse. A. S. *pung.*

Pund, *str. s. n.* a pound. E. *pound*; from Lat. *pondus.*

R.

R, the 18th letter of the Gothic alphabet. *As a numeral, it means* 100; 4. 8; 10. 30.

Ragin, *str. s. n.* counsel. E. *reyn-* in *reyn-ard.*

Ragineis, *str. s. m.* a counsellor, 15. 43. *From* ragin.

Rahnjan, *wk. v.* to reckon, count up; to number, 15. 28.

Raidjan, *wk. v.* to appoint.

Raihtaba, *adv.* rightly; straightway, 7. 35.

Baihtis, *conj.* (*always used in the position of an enclitic*), however, indeed, 4 4.

Raihts, *adj.* right, direct, straight, 1. 3. E. *right.*

Raips, *str. s. m.* a rope. A. S. *ráp.*

Raisjan, *wk. v.* to raise. E. *raise.*

Rakjan, *wk. v.* to reach. Cf. E. *rack,* to torture.

Rann, he ran, 5. 6. See **Rinnan.**

Rasta, *str. s. f.* rest; a stage, mile. E. *rest.*

Raths, *adj.* ready, easy.

Raubon, *wk. v.* to rob. Cf. E. *rob.*

Rauds, *adj.* red. E. *red.*

Raupjan, *wk. v.* to pluck, 2. 23. E. *reap.*

Raus, *str. s. n.* a reed, 15. 19. G. *rohr.*

Razda, *str. s. f.* a speech, a tongue, language, 14. 70. A. S. *reord.*

Razn, *str. s. n.* a house, 11. 17. E. *ran-* in *ran-sack.*

Redan, *str. v.* to counsel. E. *read.*

Reiki, *str. s. n.* power, authority. A. S. *rice.*

Reikinon, *wk. v.* to rule, govern, 10. 42. *From* reiks.

Reikista, *superl. adj.* most powerful; *hence as s.* a prince, 3. 22.

Reiks, *adj.* powerful. A. S. *rice.*

Reiran, *wk. v.* to tremble, 5. 33.

Reiro, *wk. s. f.* a trembling, 16. 8.

Reisan*, *str. v.* to rise; *see* urreisan.

Rign, *str. s. n.* rain. E. *rain.*

Rignjan, *v.* to rain.

Rikan, *str. v.* (rak, rekum, rikans), to collect.

Rikwis, Rikwiz, *str. s. n.* darkness, 15. 33. Perhaps allied to E. *reek.*

Rikwizjan, *wk v.* to become dark, to be darkened, 13. 24.

Rimis, *str. s. n.* rest, quietness.

Rinnan, *str. v.* (*pt. t.* rann, *pl.* runnum, *pp.* runnans), to run, 5. 6;—samath rinnan, to run together, 9. 25. E. *run.*

Riurs, *adj.* mortal, temporal.

Rodjan, *wk. v.* to speak, 1. 34. See **Redan.**

Rohsns, *str. s. f.* a hall, 14. 66.

Rums, *str. s. m.* room, place. E. *room.*

Rums, *adj.* roomy, broad.

Runa, *str. s. f.* a rune, a mystery, 4. 11. E. *rune.*

Runs, *str. s. m.* a running, an issue, 5. 25. *From* rinnan.

S.

Sa, *pron.* he, the one, 1. 7; *def. art.* the, 1. 11; 2. 4; *fem.* so, 1. 27. A. S. *se.*

Sabbato, *s. m. indecl.* the Sabbath, 2. 27, 28; sabbato-dags, the Sabbath-day, 1. 21.

Sabbatus, *str. s. m. (gen. pl.* sabbate, -o; *dat.* -um, -um), the Sabbath, 2. 24; 3. 4; 16. 1.

Sada, *pl. n. of* **Saths,** q v.

Saei, *pron.* (*put for* sa ei), who, *lit.* he who, 1. 2.

Saggkwjan, *wk. v.* to make to sink.

Sah (*for* sa-uh; *fem.* soh, *neut.* thatuh), and this, this, that. See **Sa.**

Sa-hwazuh, *pron.* each one, every one; sa-hwazuh saei, whosoever, 9. 37. *From* sa. hwas, *and* uh.

Sai, *adv.* see! lo! behold! 1. 2, 12; 2. 24.

Saian, Saijan, *str. v.* (*pt. t.* saiso, *pp.* saians), to sow, 4. 3, 4, 14. E. *sow.*

Saihs, *num.* six, 9. 2. E. *six.*

Saihsta, *ad* . (*fem.* saihsto), the sixth, 15. 33.

Saihwan, *str. v.* (sahw, schwum, saihwans), to see, 1. 44; 5. 6; s. faura, to beware of, 12. 38. E. *see.*

Sail*, a cord, rope. A. S. *sail.*

Sainjan, *wk. v.* to tarry. Cf. A. S. *scene,* slow.

Sair, *str. s. n.* sorrow, travail. A. S. *sair,* E. *sore.*

Saiwala, *s'r. s. f.* the soul, the life, 3. 4. E. *soul.*

Saiws, *str. s. m.* sea, lake. E. *sea.*

Sakan, *str. v.* (sok, sakans), to rebuke, 10. 13 A. S. *sacan.*

Sakjo, *wk. s. f.* strife. A. S. *sacu,* E. *sake.*

Sakuls, *adj.* quarrelsome.

Salbon, *wk. v.* to anoint, 14. S. Cf. E. *salve.*

Saldra, *str. s. f.* jesting.

Salithwa, *str. s. f.* (*only in pl.* salithwos), a mansion; guest-chamber, 14. 14. *From* saljan.

Saljan, *wk. v.* to dwell, abide, remain, 6. 10.

Saljan, *wk. v.* to bring an offering, to sacrifice, 14. 12. E. *sell.*

Salt, *str. s. n.* salt, 9. 49, 50. E. *salt.*

Saltan, *v.* to salt, 9. 49.

Sama, Sa sama, *adj.* the same, 10. 10; *in comp.* together. E. *same.*

Sama-leiko, *adv.* equally, likewise, 4. 16; 12. 21; 15. 31.

Sama-leiks, *adj.* alike, agreeing together, 14. 56, 59. *From* sama *and* leiks.

Samana, *adv.* together, in the same place, 12. 28. Cf. A. S. *æt-samne,* together.

Samath, *adv.* to the same place, together; — s. rinnan, to run together, 9. 25. A. S. *samod.*

Samjan, *wk. v.* to please. Cf. E. *seem.*

Sandjan, *wk. v.* to send, 9. 37. E. *send.*

Sarwa, *n. pl.* arms, armour. A. S. *searu.*

Sat, sat, 11. 2. See **Sitan.**

Saths, *adj.* (*gen.* sadis), full; s. wairthan, to be filled, to be full, 7. 27; 8 8. E. *sad.*

Satjan, *wk. v.* to set, place, put, 4. 21. E. *set.*

Sauhts, *str. s. f.* sickness, disease, 1. 34. A. S. *suht.*

Sauil, *str. s. n.* the sun, 1. 32; 13. 24. Cf. Lat. *sol.*

Sauls, *str. s. f.* a pillar. A. S. *syll.*

Saurga, *str. s. f.* sorrow, grief, care, 4. 19. E. *sorrow.*

Sauths, *str. s. m.* a sacrifice, burnt-offering, 12. 33. Cf. E. *seethe.*

Seins, *poss. pron.* his, theirs, their, 1. 5; 6. 21. A.S. *sin.*

Seithu, *adv.* late. A.S. *sið,* adv.

Sels, *adj.* good. A.S. *sél.*

Setun, sat, 3. 32. See Sitan.

Si, *pers. pron. f.* she, 6. 24; 7. 28. *From* is.

Sibja, *str. s. f.* relationship.

Sibun, *num.* seven, 8. 5; 12. 20; 16. 9. E. *seven.*

Sidus, *str. s. m.* a custom, manner. A.S. *sidu.*

Sifan, *wk. v.* to rejoice.

Siggkwan, *str.v.* (saggkw, suggkwans), to sink. E. *sink.*

Siggwan, *str. v.* (saggw, suggwum, suggwans), to sing. E. *sing.*

Sigis, *str. s. n.* victory. A.S. *sige.*

Sigljo, *wk. s. n.* seal. Lat. *sigillum.*

Sijai, may be, 1. 27; sijau, I may be, 9. 19; sijuth, ye are, 4. 40; 7. 18. See Wisan. A.S. *sý.*

Sik, *acc. of reflex. pron.* self, himself, herself, itself, 1. 15; 3. 20.

Silba, *pron.* self, 1. 44; *fem.* silbo, 4. 28. E. *self.*

Silda-leikjan, *wk. v.* to wonder, 1. 27; 5 20.

Silda-leiks, *adj.* wonderful, 12. 11. Cf. E. *seld-om.*

Silubr, *str. s. n.* silver, money. E. *silver.*

Simle, *adv.* once, at one time. A.S. *simle.*

Sinap, *str. s. n.* mustard, 4. 31. Gk. σίναπι.

Sind, they are, 4. 15. See Wisan. A.S. *sind.*

Sineigs, *adj.* old. Cf. E. *seneschal;* Lat. *sen-ex.*

Sinista, *sup. adj.* the eldest, an elder, 7. 3; 8. 31. *As if from* sins*.

Sinteino, *adv.* ever, always, continually, 5. 5; 14. 7.

Sinteins, *adj.* daily.

Sinths, *str. s. m.* a journey; *hence*

a time; *in the phrases* ainamma sintha, once; twaim sintham, twice, etc.; *also* antharamma sintha, a second time, 14. 72. A.S. *sið.*

Siponeis, *str. s. m.* a pupil, disciple, 2. 15.

Sis, *dat. of reflex. pron.* to himself, to themselves, 2. 6; 3. 14; mith sis, among themselves, 1. 27.

Sitan, *str. v.* (sat, setum, sitans), to sit, 2. 6; *pt. s.* sat, 11. 2; *pt. pl.* setun, 3. 32. E. *sit.*

Sitls, *str. s. m.* a settle, seat, 11. 15. E. *settle.*

Siujan, *wk. v.* to sew, 2. 21. E. *sew.*

Siukan, *str. v.* (sauk, sukum, sukans), to be sick, to be ill.

Siuks, *adj.* sick, ill, diseased, 6. 5; — siuks wisan, to be sick, fall sick. E. *sick.*

Siuns, *str. s. f.* sight.

Skaban, *str.v.* (skof, skobum, skabans), to shave. E. *shave.*

Skadus, *str. s. m.* a shade, shadow, 4. 32. E. *shade.*

Skaftjan, *wk. v.* to shape.

Skaidan, *str. v.* (*pt. t.* skaiskaid), to divide, sever, separate, put asunder, 10. 9. E. *shed.*

Skal, shall, must, 8. 31. See Skulan. E. *shall.*

Skalja, *str. s. f.* a scale, tile. E. *scale.*

Skalks, *str. s. m.* a servant, 10. 44. E. *-schal* in *sene-schal.*

Skaman, *wk. v. refl. with gen.* to be ashamed of, be ashamed, 8. 38. E. *shame.*

Skanda, *str. s. f.* shame.

Skapjan, *str. v.* (skop, skopum, skapans), to shape. E. *shape.*

Skathis, *str. s. n.* scathe, wrong. E. *scathe.*

Skathjan, *str. v.* (skoth, skothum, skathans), to do scathe to.

Skathuls, *adj.* hurtful, harmful.

Skattja, *wk. s. m.* a money-changer, 11. 15.

Skatts, *str. s. m.* money, 12. 15. A. S. *sceat.*

Skauda-raips, *str. s. m.* a shoe-latchet (lit. a shoe-rope), 1. 7.

Skauns, *adj.* beautiful. Cf. E. *sheen.*

Skauts, *str. s. m.* the hem of a garment, 6. 56. A. S. *scéat.*

Skawjan, *wk. v.* to look at, see. E. *show.*

Skeinan, *str. s.* (skain, skinum, skinans), to shine. E. *shine.*

Skeirs, *adj.* sheer, clear, evident. E. *sheer.*

Skewjan, *wk. v.* to go along, 2. 23.

Skildus, *str. s. m.* a shield. E. *shield.*

Skilja, *wk. s. m.* a butcher.

Skilliggs, *str. s. m.* a shilling. E. *shilling.*

Skip, *str. s. n.* a ship, boat, 1. 19. E. *ship.*

Skiuban, *str. v.* (skauf, skubum, skubans), to shove. E. *shove.*

Skohs, *str. s. m.* a shoe, sandal, 1. 7. E. *shoe.*

Skreitan, *str. v.* (skrait, skritum, skritans), to tear.

Skuft, *str. s. n.* the hair of the head.

Skuggwa, *wk. s. m.* a mirror.

Skula, *wk. s. m.* a debtor; liable to, in danger of, 3. 29; skula wisan, to be a debtor, to deserve, 14. 64. *From* skulan.

Skulan, *v. anom.* (*pres.* skal, *pt. t.* skulda, *pp.* skulds), to owe; *pt. s.* skal, must, 8. 31. A. S. *sculan*; whence E. *shall, should.*

Skulds, *adj.* owing; skulds wisan, to be lawful, 3. 5; ni skuld ist, is not lawful to do, 2. 24.

Skura, *str. s. f.* a shower; skura windis, a storm of wind, 4. 37. E. *shower.*

Slahan, *str. v.* (sloh, slahans), to strike, beat, hit, 15. 19;—lofam slahan, to strike with the palms of the hands, to buffet, 14. 65; *pt. s.* sloh, 14. 47. E. *slay.*

Slahs, *str. s. m.* (*pl.* slaheis), a stroke, stripe; a plague. 5. 29.

Slaihts, *adj.* smooth. E. *slight.*

Slauhts, *str. s. f.* slaughter. E. *slaught-er.*

Slawan, *wk. v.* to be silent, be still, 9. 34.

Sleithis, *adj.* perilous.

Slepan, *str. v.* (*pt. t.* saislep *or* saizlep, *pl.* saislepum, *pp.* slepans), to sleep, fall asleep, 4. 27. E. *sleep.*

Sleps, *str. s. m.* sleep.

Slindan, *str. s.* (sland, slundum, slundans), to gulp down.

Sliupan, *str. v.* (slaup, slupum, slupans), to slip into, creep. E. *slip.*

Sloh, he struck, 14. 47. See **Slahan.**

Smairthr, *str. s. n.* fatness.

Smakka, *wk. s. m.* a fig, 11. 13.

Smakka-bagms, *str. s. m.* a fig-tree, 11. 13, 20.

Smals, *adj.* small. E. *small.*

Smarna, *str. s. f.* dung.

Smeitan, *str. v.* (smait, smitum, smitans), to smear. E. *smite.*

Smitha, *wk. s. m.* a smith. E. *smith.*

Smyrn, *str. s. n.* myrrh;—mith smyrna, mingled with myrrh, 15. 23. Gk. σμύρρον.

Snaga, *wk. s. m.* a garment, 2. 21.

Snaiws, *str. s. m.* snow, 9. 3. E. *snow.*

Snarpjan, *wk. v.* to bite, nip.

Sneithan, *str. v.* (snaith, snithum, snithans), to cut. A. S. *snidan.*

Sniumjan, *wk. v.* to hasten.

Sniumundo, *adv.* with haste, quickly, 6. 25; *compar.* sniumundos, with more haste. See above.

Sniwan, *str. v.* (snau, snewum, sniwans), to go, proceed, come. Cf. A. S *snéome,* quickly.

Snorjo, *wk. s. f.* a basket.

Snutrs, *adj.* wise. A.S. *snotor.*

So, *fem. of* **Sa,** she, this, the, 1. 27, 31.

Sokjan, *wk. v.* to question with, dispute. 1. 27; 9. 10; to seek, desire, long for, 1. 37; 3.ʾ32; 8. 11; samana sokjan, to talk together, discuss, 12. 28. E. *seek.*

Sokun, they rebuked, 10. 13. See **Sakan.**

Spaikulatur, *s.* a spy, 'executioner' (A.V.), 6. 27. Lat. *speculator.*

Sparwa, *wk. s. m.* a sparrow. E. *sparwa.*

Spaurds, *str. s. f.* a stadium, furlong.

Speds, Speids, Spids, *adj.* late; *compar.* spediza, *superl.* spedists, spedumists, last, 12. 6, 22. Cf. G. *spät.*

Spewan, Speiwan, *str. v.* (*pt. t.* spaiw, *pl.* spiwum, *pp.* spiwans), to spit, 7. 33; 8. 23; 10. 34; 14. 65. E. *spew.*

Spilda, *str. s. f.* a writing-tablet.

Spill, *str. s. n.* a fable, tale. E. *spell.*

Spillon, *wk. v.* to tell a tale, narrate, 5. 16; 9. 9.

Spinnan, *str. v.* (spann, spunnum, spunnans), to spin. E. *spin.*

Sprauto, *adv.* quickly, soon, 9. 39.

Spyreida, *wk. s. m.* a large basket, 8. 8, 20. Gk. σπυρίς.

Stabs, *str. s. m.* a letter. E. *staff.*

Stadim, *dat. pl. of* **Staths,** q. v.

Staiga, *str. s. f.* a path, way, 1. 3. E. *sty.*

Stainahs, *adj.* stony, 4. 5, 16.

Stains, *str. s. m.* a stone, rock, 5. 5; 12. 10; stainam wairpan, to stone, 12. 4. E. *stone.*

Stairno, *wk. s. f.* a star, 13. 25. E. *star.*

Staks, *str. s. m.* a mark, stigma.

Stamms, *adj.* stammering, with an impediment in the speech, 7. 32. Cf. E. *stamm-er.*

Standan, *str. v.* (stoth, stothans), to stand, stand firm, 11. 5. E. *stand.*

Staths, *str. s. m.* (*pl.* stadeis), a stead, a place, 1. 35; 15. 22; 16. 6; land, shore, 4. 1; jainis stadis, the other side (of the lake), 4. 35. E. *stead.*

Staua, *str. s. f.* judgment, 6. 11.

Staua, *wk. s. m.* a judge.

Stautan, *str. v.* (staistaut, stautans), to strike, smite. Cf. E. *stutt-er.*

Steigan, *str. v.* (staig, stigum, stigans), to mount up, ascend. A.S. *stigan.*

Stibna, *str. s. f.* a voice, 1. 3. A.S. *stefn.*

Stiggkwan, *str. v.* to strike, smite, thrust. Cf. E. *stink.*

Stikls, *str. s. m.* a cup, 7. 4; 9. 41; 10. 38.

Stiks, *str. s. m.* a point, moment.

Stilan, *str. v.* (stal, stelum, stulans), to steal. E. *steal.*

Stiur, *str. s. m.* a calf. E. *steer.*

Stiurjan, *wk. v.* to steer, govern. E. *steer.*

Stojan, *wk. v.* to judge. *From* staua.

Stols, *str. s. m.* seat. E. *stool.*

Straujan, *wk. v.* to strew, straw, 11. 8; to prepare, 14. 15. E. *strew.*

Striks, *str. s. m.* a stroke, mark. Cf. E. *stroke.*

Stubjus, *str. s. m.* dust. Cf. G. *staub.*

Suljo, *str. s. f.* a sole of a shoe, sandal, 6. 9.

Sums, *adj.* (*f.* suma, *n.* sumata), some one, some, 2. 6; one, 14. 43; sums—sumsuh, the one—the other, 12. 5; *pl.* sumai, some, certain, 7. 1. E. *some.*

Sundro, *adv.* asunder, alone, privately, 4. 10; 7. 33. A.S. *sundor.*

Sunja, *str. s. f.* the sooth, the truth, 5. 33; bi sunjai, truly, verily, 12. 14, 32. Cf. E. *sooth.*

Sunjeins, *adj.* true, 12. 14.

Sunna, *wk. s. m.* the sun, 4. 6; 16. 2. E. *sun.* (Also found in the form *sunno,* wk. s. f.)

Suns, *adv.* soon, at once, immediately, 1. 9; 4. 5. E. *soon.*

Suns-aiw, *adv.* soon, immediately, straightway, 3. 6; 5. 29; 6. 25; 9. 15; 15. 1.

Sunus, *str. s. m.* a son, 1. 1; 2. 10. E. *son.*

Supon, *wk. v.* to season, 9. 50.

Suthjon, *wk. v.* to itch.

Suts, *adj.* sweet; *hence* patient, peaceable; *compar.* sutiza, more tolerable, 6. 11. E. *sweet.*

Swa, *conj.* so, just so, also, 2. 6; 4. 40. E. *so.*

Swaei, *conj.* so that, that, 1. 27; 2. 27. *For* swa ei.

Swaihro, *wk. s. f.* mother-in-law, 1. 30. A. S. *sweger,* fem. of *sweor.*

Swairban, *str. v.* (swarf, swaurbum, swaurbans), to wipe.

Swa-leiks, *adj.* such, 4. 33; 6. 2; 7. 8; 9. 3. E. *such.*

Swamms, Swams, *str. s. m.* a sponge, 15. 36. A. S. *swamm.*

Swaran, *str. v.* (swor, sworum, swarans), to swear, 6. 23. E. *swear.*

Sware, Swarei, *adv.* without a cause, in vain, 7. 7.

Swarts, *adj.* black. E. *swart.*

Swaswe, *adv.* as, just as, as it were, in like manner as, 1. 22; so that, 4. 32. *From* swa *and* swe.

Swe, *adv.* as, just as, 1. 2, 10; 4. 27.

Swegnjan, *wk. v.* to rejoice, triumph.

Sweiban, *str. v.* (*pt. t.* swaif), to cease.

Swein, *str. s. n.* a swine, pig. 5. 11. E. *swine.*

Sweran, *wk. v.* to honour, esteem, glorify, 7. 6, 10. *From* swers.

Swers, *adj.* heavy, grave, honoured. A. S. *swâr,* G. *schwer.*

Swes, *adj.* one's own, 15. 20. A. S. *swæs.*

Swe-thauh, *conj.* although, however, but, 9. 12.

Swibls, *str. s. m.* brimstone. A. S. *swefel.*

Swigljon, *wk. v.* to pipe.

Swikns, *adj.* pure, innocent.

Swi-kunthaba, *adv.* openly, manifestly, S. 32.

Swi-kunths, *adj.* manifest, evident, spread abroad. 6. 14; swikunths wairthan, to come abroad, 4. 22. *From* swe *and* kunnan.

Swiltan, *str. v.* (swalt, swultum, swultans), to die. A.S. *sweltan.*

Swinths, *adj.* strong, healthy, whole, 2. 17; 3. 27; *comp.* swinthoza, mightier, 1. 7. A.S. *swið.*

Swistar, *str. s. f.* a sister, 3. 32; 6. 3; 10. 30. E. *sister.*

Swogatjan, *wk. v.* to sigh, groan.

Swor, he swore, 6. 23. See Swaran.

Synagoga-faths, *str. s. m.* the ruler of a synagogue, 5. 22.

Synagoge, *s. f.* a synagogue, 1. 21; 6. 2. Gk. συναγωγή.

Ta-, Te-.

Tagl, *str. s. n.* hair, 1. 6. E. *tail.*

Tagr, *str. s. n.* a tear, 9. 24. E. *tear.*

Tahjan, *wk. v.* to tear, rend, 1. 26; 9. 20.

Taihswa, *wk. s. f.* the right hand, 16. 5.

Taihsws, *adj.* the right, on the right hand, 14. 47; *fem.* taihswo, the right hand, 10. 37. Cf. Lat. *dex-ter.*

Taihun, *num.* ten, 10. 41. E. *ten.*

Taihun-taihund, a hundred.

Tainknjan, *wk. v.* to betoken, point out, shew, 14. 15. See below.

Taikns, *str. s. f.* a token, sign, wonder, miracle, 8. 11; 13. 22. E. *token.*

Tainjo, *wk. s. f.* a basket of twigs, a light basket, 8. 19. *From* tains.

Tains, *str. s. m.* a twig. A.S. *tán.*

Tairan, *str. v.* (tar, terum, tauraus), to tear. E. *tear.*

Talzjan, *wk. v.* to teach, instruct.

Tamjan, *wk. v.* to tame. E. *tame.*

Tandjan, *wk. v.* to kindle. Cf. E. *tinder.*

Tarnjan, *wk. v.* to hide. Cf. E. *tarn-ish.*

Taui, *str. s. n.* a work, deed.

Taujan, *wk. v.* to do, make, 2. 24; *pt. t.* tawida, did, 3. 8. E. *taw,* to dress leather.

Tekan, Teikan, *str. v.* (taitok, tekans), to touch, 5. 30. E. *take.*

Tewa, *str. s. f.* order, arrangement.

TH.

Thadei, *adv.* where, wheresoever, whither, 6. 55; 14. 14; thishwad-uh thadei, whithersoever, 6. 56.

Thagkjan, thaggkjan, *wk. v.* (thata, thahts), to think, consider, reason, 2. 6; 8. 16. E. *think.*

Thagks, *str. s. m.* thank. E. *thank.*

Thahan, *wk. v.* to be silent, be still, hold one's peace, 1. 25; 3. 4; 14. 61. Cf. Lat. *tacere.*

Thaho, *wk. s. f.* clay. A.S. *þó.*

Thai, the; *pl. nom. masc. of art.* sa, so, thata, 1. 22, 36; *dat.* thaim, 1. 27. E. *they,* dat. *them.*

Thaih, whoever, *put for* thai uh, 3. 11.

Thairh, *prep.* by, *title*; through, by means of, 2. 23; 6. 2. E. *through.*

Thairh-bairan, *str. v.* to carry through, 11. 16.

Thairh-gaggan, *anom. v.* to go through, come through, 2. 23.

Thairko, *wk. s. n.* a hole through anything, the eye of a needle, 10. 25.

Thairsan, *str. v.* (thars, thaursum, thaursans), to dry up, thirst. E. *thirs-t.*

Thamma, to the, from the, *dat. s. m. and n. of the art.* sa, so, thata, 1. 10, 20. A.S. *ðám.*

Thammei, whom, which, *dat. s. of* sa-ei, 2. 4. *Put for* thamma ei.

Than, *adv.* then, thereupon, 1. 28; 2. 20; but, and, however, 1. 6; 4. 5. E. *then.*

Thana, the; *acc. s. m. of* sa, 1. 19. A.S. *ðone.*

Thana-mais, *adv.* more, still, further, 5. 35; 14. 63.

Thana-seiths, *adv.* more, longer; ni thana-seiths, no longer, 9. 8; 10. 8; 11. 14.

Thannu, *conj.* therefore, then, 4. 41; for, 14. 6.

Thans, the, those, them; *acc. m. pl. of* sa, 1. 19.

Thanuh, *conj.* then, 4. 29; 10. 13; therefore, 12. 6.

Thanzei, *rel. pron.* whom, which, *acc. pl. m. of* sa-ei, 2. 26; whomsoever, 3. 15. *For* thans ei.

Thar, *adv.* there, 6. 10. E. *there.*

Tharba, *wk. s. m.* a beggar, poor man, 10. 21.

Tharba, *str. s. f.* want, need.

Tharbs, *adj.* needy, in want. See **Thaurban.**

Tharei, *adv.* where, 2. 4. *For* thar ei.

Tharuh, *adv.* there; but, 10. 20; and, 16. 6. *For* thar uh.

Thata, (*neut. of* sa), the, that, this, 1. 15. E. *that.*

Thatainei, Thataine, *adv.* only, 5. 36. *From* thata *and* ains.

Thatei, *rel. pron. neut.* that. *Neut. of* sa-ei; *put for* thata ei.

Thatei, *conj.* because, if, that, 1. 37; 2. 8; afar thatei, after that, 1. 14. See above.

Thathroh, Thathro, *adv.* thence; afterward, after that, thenceforth, 4. 17; afterwards, 4. 28.

That-ist, *for* thata ist, that is, 7. 2.

Thau, *conj.* than, 2. 9; 9. 43.

Thaurban, *str. v.* (*pt. t. as pres.* tharf, *pl.* thaurbum, *pt. t.* thaurfta), to need, want, lack, 2. 17; *pt. s.* thaurfta, had need, 2. 25.

Thaurfts, *str. s. f.* need; *adj.* needy.

Thaurneins, *adj.* thorny, made of thorns, 15. 17.

Thaurnus, *str. s. m.* a thorn, 4. 7. E. *thorn.*

Thaurp, *str. s. n.* a field. E. *thorp.*

Thaursjau, *impers. v.* to thirst.

Thaurstei, *wk. s. f.* thirst. E. *thirst.*

Thaursus, *adj.* dry, withered, parched up, 11. 20. *From* thairsan.

The, *instrumental case of* sa, so, thata, that, 2. 15. *Hence* bi-the, du-the, jath-the, the-ei.

The-ei, *conj.* that.

Thei, *conj.* that, 6. 10; 9. 18.

Theihan, *str. v.* (thaih, thaihans), to thrive. M. E. *thee,* to thrive.

Theihs, *str. s. n.* time, season.

Theihwo, *wk. s. f.* thunder, 3. 17.

Theins, *poss. pron.* thy, 1. 2; 2. 5; 5. 9. E. *thine, thy.*

Thewis, *str. s. n.* a slave, servant. A.S. *þeow.* See Thius.

This, of the; *m. and n. sing. of* sa, so, thata, 1. 16.

This-hwaduh, *adv.* wheresoever, 6. 10, 56.

This-hwah, *pron.* whatsoever, whatever, 6. 23; 7. 11. See This-hwazuh.

This-hwaruh, *adv.* wheresoever, 9. 18; 14. 9. *From* this, hwar, *and* uh.

Thishwazuh, *pron.* whoever, (*followed by* ei) 11. 23; *gen.* thishwizuh thei, 6. 22; *neut. acc.* thishwah, thishwah thei, whatever, 6. 23; 11. 23. *From* this, hwas, *and* uh.

Thiubi, *str. s. n.* a theft, 7. 22.

Thiubs, *str. s. m.* a thief. E. *thief.*

Thiuda, *str. s. f.* a people, a nation; *in pl.* the Gentiles, nations, 10. 42; 11. 17. A.S. *þeod.*

Thiudan-gardi, *str. s. f.* a kingdom, 1. 14; 3. 24.

Thiudans, *str. s. m.* a king, 6. 14. A.S. *þeoden.*

Thiudinassus, *str. s. m.* kingdom, 9. 1.

Thiujo, *acc. of* thiwi, a maid-servant, 14. 66.

Thius, *str. s. m.* a servant. A.S. *þeow.* See Thewis.

Thiuth, *str. s. n.* good;—thiuth taujan, to do good, 3. 4.

Thiutheigs, *adj.* good, 10. 17; blessed, 14. 61.

Thiuthjan, *wk. v. with dat. and acc.* to bless, 10. 16; 11. 9.

Thiwi, *str. s. f.* (*gen.* thiujos), a maid-servant, handmaid, 14. 66. A.S. *þeowe.*

Thizai, *pron.* (*dat. of fem.* so), the, 1. 13; at the, 1. 22; in the, 1. 23; with the, 7. 13.

Thize, of the, of them, *g. pl. m. of* sa, 2. 6.

Thizei, of whom, whose; *gen. of* saei, 1. 7. *Put for* this ei.

Thizozei, of her who, whose, *gen. s. f. of* sa-ei, 7. 25. *Put for* thizos ei.

Thlaihan*, *v.* to cherish, foudle.

Thlakwus, *adj.* flaccid, tender, 13. 28. Cf. Lat. *flaccus.*

Thlauhs, *str. s. m.* flight, 13. 18.

Thliuhan, *str. v.* (thlauh, thlauhans), to flee.

Tho, her, it, this, the, that, *acc. f. s. and acc. n. pl. of* sa, 1. 18, 31; 4. 30. A.S. *ðá.*

Thoei, her who, that which, whom, which; *acc. f. s. and acc. n. pl. of* sa-ei, 7. 13. *Put for* tho ei.

Thos, them, the; *acc. f. pl. of* sa, 1. 34.

Thrafstjan, *wk. v.* to console, comfort; *refl.* to take courage, be of good cheer, 10. 49.

Thragjan, *wk. v.* to run, 15. 36. Cf. A.S. *þrag, þrah,* a running, course.

Thramstei, *wk. s. f.* a locust, 1. 6.

Threihan, *str. v.* (thraih, thraihum, thraihans), to throng, crowd round, press upon, 3. 9; 5. 24.

Threis, *num.* (*neut.* thrija, *gen.* thrije. *dat.* thrim, *acc.* thrins), three, 8. 2. 31. E. *three.*

Thridja, *adj.* the third, 9. 31 : 12. 21 ; *fem.* thridjo, 15. 25. E. *third.*

Thrins; see **Threis.**

Thriskan, *str. v.* (thrask, thruskum, thruskans), to thresh, thrash. E. *thresh.*

Thriutan, *str. v.* (thraut, thrutum, thrutans), to urge, threaten, vex. E. *threat-en.*

Throthjan, *wk. v.* to exercise.

Thru's-fill, *str. s. n.* leprosy, 1. 42 ; thr. habands, a leper, 1. 40. *From* thriutan *and* fill.

Thu, *pers. pron.* thou, 1. 11 ; *gen.* theina, *dat.* thus, 1. 2 ; *acc.* thuk, 1. 24 ; 4. 38 ; 8. 29. E. *thou.*

Thuggkjan, Thugkjan, *wk. v.* to seem, 10. 42 ; 14. 64. Cf. E. *me-thinks.*

Thuhtus, *str. s. m.* thought, wisdom.

Thuk; see **Thu.**

Thulan, *wk. v.* to tolerate, suffer, put up with, endure, 9. 19. A. S. *folian.*

Thus; see **Thu.**

Thusei, *pron.* (*put for* thus ei), i. e. thee in whom, 1. 11.

Thusundi, *num.* a thousand, 5. 13 ; 8. 9. E. *thousand.*

Thusundi-faths, *str. s. m.* a leader of a thousand men, 6. 21.

Thut-haurn, *str. s. n.* a horn, trumpet.

Thwahan, *str. v.* (*pt. t.* thwoh, *pp.* thwahans), to wash, 7. 3. A. S. *þwéan.*

Thwairhs, *adj.* angry. A. S. *þweorh.*

Thwastjan, *wk. v.* to make safe, secure.

Ti–Tw.

Tigus, *num.* ten, 1. 13. *Hence* fidwor tigus, forty. E. *-ty* in *twen-ty,* &c.

Tils, *adj.* suitable, fit. A. S. *til.*

Timrja, *wk. s. m.* a builder, carpenter, 6. 2 ; 12. 10.

Timrjan, *wk. v.* to build. Cf. E. *timber.*

Tiuhan, *str. v.* (tauh, tauhum, tauhans), to tow, tug. pull ; *hence* to lead, to guide, to lead away, 14. 44. Cf. E. *tow.*

Trauan, *wk. v.* to trow, be persuaded. E. *trow.*

Trausti, *str. s. n.* a covenant.

Triggws, *adj.* true, faithful.

Trimpan, *str. v.* (*pt. t.* tramp), to tread.

Triu, *str. s. n.* (*gen.* triwis), a tree ; *hence* a piece of wood, a staff, 14. 43. 48. E. *tree.*

Trudan, *v.* to tread. E. *tread.*

Tuggl, *wk. s. n.* a star.

Tuggo, *wk. s. f.* a tongue, 7. 33. E. *tongue.*

Tulgus, *adj.* steadfast, sure.

Tundnan, *wk. v.* to burn, be on fire. See **Tandjan.**

Tunthus, *str. s. m.* a tooth, 9. 18. E. *tooth.*

Tuz-werjan, *wk. v.* to doubt, 11. 23. *From* tus (*a derivative of* twai) *and* werjan.

Twai, *num.* (*fem.* twos, *neut.* twa ; *gen.* twaddje, *dat.* twaim, *acc.* twans, twos, twa), two, 5. 13 ; 9. 43. 47. E. *two.*

Twalib, Twalif, *num.* twelve, 3. 14 ; 7. 31 ; *dat.* twalibim, 4. 10. E. *twelve.*

Tweifls, *str. s. m.* doubt. Cf. G. *zweifel.*

Tweihnai, *pl. adj.* two, 7. 31. See Mith. *From* twai. Cf. E. *twin.*

Twos, two, 5. 13. See **Twai.**

U.

Ubilaba, *adv.* evilly, ill, 2. 17.

Ubil-haban, *wk. v.* to be ill ; *from* ubils, evil, *and* haban, to have, 1. 32.

Ubil-kwithan, *str. v.* to speak evil of, curse, 7. 10. See **Ubils.**

Ubils, *adj.* evil, ill, bad, useless, 7. 23; ubil haban, to be ill, 6. 55; ubil kwithan, to speak evil against, to curse, 7. 10; ubil-waurdjan, to speak evil of, 9. 39. A. S. *yfel,* E. *evil.*

Ubil-waurdjan, *wk. v.* to speak evil of, 9. 39. *From* waurd.

Ubizwa, *str. s. f.* a porch. E. *eaves.*

Uf, *prep. with dat. and acc.* under, beneath, in the time of, 2. 26. *Occurs as a prefix in numerous compounds.*

Ufar, *prep. with dat. and acc.* over, beyond. E. *over.*

Ufarassus, *str. s. m.* overflow, abundance, superfluity; ufarassau sildaleikidedun, greatly wondered, were beyond measure astonished, 7. 36.

Ufar-gudja, *wk. s. m.* a chief-priest, 10. 33.

Ufar-meleins, *str. s. f.* superscription, 12. 16.

Ufar-meli, *str. s. n.* superscription, 15. 26.

Ufar-meljan, *wk. v.* to write over, 15. 26.

Ufar-munnon, *wk. v.* to forget, 8. 14.

Ufar-skadwjan, *wk. v.* to overshadow, 9. 7.

Ufar-steigan, *str. v.* (staig, stigum, stigans), to mount up, grow up, 4. 7.

Uf-brikan, *str. v.* (brak, brekum, brukans), to reject, 6. 26; to despise.

Uf-brinnan, *str. v. neut.* (brann, brunnum, brunnans), to be burnt up, be scorched, 4. 6.

Uf-hausjan, *wk. v.* lit. to hear under, to obey, submit to, 1. 27; 4. 41.

Uf-hropjan, *wk. v.* to cry out, 1. 23.

Uf-kunnan, *wk. v.* to know, perceive, recognise, 2. 8; *pt. s.* ufkuntha, knew, felt, 5. 29.

Uf-ligan, *str. v.* (lag, legum, ligans), to lie under; *hence* to faint, 8. 3.

Uf-rakjan, *wk. v.* to stretch out, 1. 41; 3. 5.

Uf-swogjan, *wk. v.* to sigh deeply, 8. 12.

Ufta, *adv.* oft, often, 5. 4. E. *oft.*

Uggkis, Ugkis, *dual. dat.* for us two, 10. 35, 37. A. S. *unc,* we two.

Uh, *conj.* but, and; *an enclitic particle like the Latin* que; *it takes the form* uth *before* th, ul *before* l, uk *before* k; *also a demonstrative particle, like Latin* -ce, *as in* sah, *put for* sa-uh; *also, an indefinite particle, as in* hwazuh, *put for* hwas uh. Hence swah = swa uh, &c.

Uhtedun, *for* Ohtedun, feared, 11. 32. See **Ogan.**

Uhteigs, *adj.* at leisure for.

Uhtwo, *wk. s. f.* early morn, 1. 35. Cf. A. S. *uhte.*

Ulbandus, *str. s.* a camel, 1. 6; 10. 25. A. S. *olfend.* Gk. ἐλέφας.

Un-, *negative prefix.* E. *un-.*

Und, *prep. with dat. but more often with acc.* unto, until, as far as, up to, 6. 23; 15. 33; und hwa, how long, 9. 19; und thatei, while, 2. 19. E. *un-* in *un-til, un-to.*

Undar, *prep. with acc.* under, 4. 21. E. *under.*

Undaro, *prep. with dat.* under, 6. 11; 7. 28.

Undaurni-mats, *str. s. m.* morning meal. Cf. E. *undern.*

Und-greipan, *str. v.* to grip, to lay hold of, 1. 31; 12. 8; 15. 21; *pt. pl.* undgripun, 14. 46.

Un-galaubeins, *str. s. f.* unbelief, 6. 6; 9. 24.

Un-galaubjands, *pres. pt. as from* un- *and* galaubjan, unbelieving, 9. 19.

Un-handuwaurhts, *adj.* not hand-wrought, not made with hands, 14. 58.

Un-hrains, *adj.* unclean, 1. 23.

Un-hultho, *wk. s. f.* (*or* unhultha), an evil spirit, unclean spirit, devil, 1. 32, 34.

Un-hwapnands, *pres. pt. as from* un- *and* hwapnan, unquenchable, that is not quenched, 9. 43.

Un-karja, *adj.* careless, neglectful, 4. 15. *From* kara.

Un-leds, *adj.* poor, 14. 5.

Un-mahteigs, *adj.* un - mighty, weak ; impossible, 10. 27.

Un-rodjands, *pres. pt. as from* un *and* rodjan, not speaking, speechless, dumb, 7. 37 ; 9. 17, 25.

Uns, *pron.* us ; *from* ik, 1. 24. E. *us.*

Un-saltans, *pp. as from* un- *and* saltan, unsalted, 9. 50.

Unsar, *pron. possess.* our, ours, 1. 3; 12. 7. E. *our.*

Un-selei, *wk. s. f.* wickedness, evil, injustice, unrighteousness, 7. 22.

Un-sels, *adj.* evil, wicked, unholy, 7. 22.

Un-sibis, *adj.* lawless, impious, a transgressor, 15. 28.

Unsis, *pron.* us, 5. 12. *From* ik.

Un-swers, *adj.* without honour, 6. 4.

Unte, *conj.* for, because, 1. 22 ; since, because that, 1. 34. *From* und.

Un-thiuth, *str. s. n.* evil ; unthiuth taujan, to do evil, 3. 4.

Un-thwahans, *pp. as if from* un- *and* thwahan, unwashen, 7. 2.

Un-werjan, *wk. v.* to be unable to endure, to be displeased, 10. 14, 41.

Un-witi, *str. s. n.* foolishness, ignorance, 7. 22.

Un-wits, *adj.* without understanding, foolish, 7. 18.

Ur-raisjan, *wk. v.* to raise up, 1. 31 ; to rouse up, wake, 4. 38. (*Ur-* = *us.*)

Ur-reisan, *str. v.* (rais, risum, ris-ans), to arise, 2. 9; 4. 39 ; *pt. s.* urrais, 2. 12 ; 5. 42. (*Ur-* = *us.*)

Ur-rinnan, *str. v.* to go out, come out, come forth, 4. 3 : to rise (of the sun), 4. 6 ; to spring up, 4. 5 ; *pt. pl.* urrunnun, 8. 11. (*Ur-* = *us.*)

Ur-runs, *str. s. m.* a running out, departure ; the draught, 7. 19. (*Ur-* = *us.*)

Us, *prep. with dat.* out, out of, forth, from, 1. 11 ; 3. 7; 7. 15. *It changes into* ur *before* r ; *and into* uz *in* uz-u *and* uz-uh, 11. 30; *also in* uz-on, q. v.   A. S. *á-*, G. *er-*, prefix ; E. *a-*, prefix, in *a-*rise.

Us-agjan, *wk. v.* to frighten utterly ; *pp.* usagiths, sore afraid, 9. 6.

Us-anan, *str. v.* to breathe out, expire ; *pt. s.* uzon, 15. 37, 39.

Us-bairan, *str. v.* to bear out, carry out ; to bear, to bring forth ; to answer. 11. 14.

Us-bauhtedun, they bought, 16. 1.   See **Us-bugjan.**

Us-bliggwan, *str. v.* to beat exceedingly, scourge ; *pt. pl.* us-bluggwun, 12. 3.

Us-bugjan, *wk. v.* to buy out, buy, 15. 46; 16. 1.

Us-dreiban, *str. v.* to drive out, send away, 5. 10; *pt. pl.* usdriban, 6. 13 ; *pt. pl. subj.* usdreibeina, *put for* usdribeina, 9. 18.

Us-filh, *str. s. n.* a hiding altogether, a burial, 14. 8.

Us-filmei, *wk. s. f.* amazement, 16. 8.

Us-films, *adj.* amazed, astonished, 1. 22.

Us-fullnan, *wk. v.* to become full, to be filled, to be fulfilled, 1. 15.

Us-gaggan, *anom. v.* (usiddja, us-iddjedum, usgaggans), to go out, come out, go forth, go up, 1. 5, 10, 26.

Us-gaisjan, *wk. v.* to make aghast; *hence pass.* to be beside oneself, 3. 21.   Cf. E. *aghast.*

Us-geisnan, *wk. v.* to be aghast, be amazed, 2. 12; 5. 42; 10. 26.

Us-giban, *str. v.* to give away, give, restore, pay, 12. 17.

Us-graban, *str. v.* (grof, grobum, grabans), to dig out, 12. 1; to break through, 2. 4.

Us-gutnan, *wk. v.* to be poured out, to gush out, 2. 22.

Us-hafjan, *str. v.* to heave up, lift, take up, 2. 12; 11. 23.

Us-hlaupan, *s'r. v.* (hlaihlaup), to leap up, rise quickly, 10. 50.

Us-hramjan, *wk. v.* to crucify, 15. 13.

Us-hrisjan, *wk. v.* to shake out, shake off, 6. 11.

Us-iddja, is gone out, 7. 29; went out, 1. 26; *pl.* usiddjedun, 1. 5. See **Us-gaggan.**

Us-keinan, *wk. v.* to spring up, grow up; to produce, put forth, 13. 28.

Us-kiusan, *str. v.* (kaus, kusum, kusans), to choose out; to reject, 8. 31.

Us-kwiman, *str. v.* to kill, destroy, 3. 6; 6. 19; 8. 31; *pt. pl.* uskwemun, 12. 8.

Us-kwistjan, *wk. v.* to destroy, kill, 3. 4; 9. 22; 12. 9.

Us-kwithan, *str. v.* to proclaim, blaze abroad, 1. 45.

Us-lagjan, *wk. v.* to lay on, lay upon, 14. 46.

Us-laubjan, *wk. v.* to permit, suffer, 5. 13.

Us-leithan, *str. v.* (laith, lithans), to come out, go out, 4. 35; 5. 21; *pt. s.* uslaith, went away, 8. 13.

Us-litha, *wk. s. m.* one who has useless limbs, a paralytic person, 2. 3. *From* lithus.

Us-lukan, *str. v.* (lauk, lukum, lukans), to unlock, open; to unsheath (a sword), 14. 47.

Us-luknan, *wk. v.* to become unlocked, to be opened, to open, 1. 10; 7. 34.

Us-niman, *str. v.* to take away, 4. 15; 6. 29; to take down, 15. 46; *pt. pl.* usnemun, took away, 8. 8.

Us-saihwan, *str. v.* to look up, 7. 34; to regain one's sight, 8. 25; 10. 51; to look on, 3. 5. See **Saihwan.**

Us-sandjan, *wk. v.* to send out, send forth, send away, 1. 43.

Us-satjan, *wk. v.* to set on, place upon; to set, plant, 12. 1.

Us-siggwan, *str. v.* to read; *pt. pl.* 2 *p.* ussuggwuth, 2. 25; 12. 10. Lit. 'to sing out' or aloud. See **Siggwan.**

Us-standan, *str. v.* to stand up, rise up, 1. 35; to rise again, 8. 31; *pt. s.* usstoth, went out, 6. 1; rose up against, 3. 26; *pt. s. subj.* usstothi, should rise, were risen, 9. 9.

Us-stass, *str. s. f.* a rising up, resurrection, 12. 18.

Us-steigan, *str. v.* (staig, stigum, stigans), to mount up, go up, 3. 13.

Us-stoth, Us-stothi; see **Us-standan.**

Us-suggwuth, ye have read, 2. 25; 12. 10. See **Us-siggwan.**

Us-tiuhan, *str. v.* to lead out, drive forth; *pt. s.* ustauh, 1. 11; 8. 23.

Us-thriutan, *str. v.* (thraut, thrutum, thrutans), to threaten, use despitefully; to trouble, 14. 6.

Us-waltjan, *wk. v.* to overthrow, overturn, 11. 15.

Us-wairpan, *str. v.* to cast out, 1. 34; 5. 40; to reject, 12. 10; *pt. s.* uswarp, cast out, 16. 9; *pt. s. subj.* uswaurpi, 7. 26.

Us-warp, Us-waurpi; see **Us-wairpan.**

Us-waurhts, *adj.* just, righteous, 2. 17. Lit. 'wrought out.'

Us-windan, *str. v.* (wand, wundum, wundans), to wind in and out, to plait. 15. 17.

H 2

Ut, *adv.* out, 1. 25; 11. 19. E. *out.*

Uta, *adv.* out, without, 1. 45; 3. 31.

Utana, *adv. and prep. with gen.* out, out of, 8. 23.

Utathro, *adv. and prep. with gen.* from without, 7. 15, 18.

Uz-on, gave up the ghost, 15. 37, 39. See **Us-anan.**

Uzuh, *prep.* whether from, 11. 30. *From* us *and* uh.

W.

Waddjus, *str. s. f.* a wall.

Wadi, *str. s. n.* a pledge. E. *wed.*

Waggari, *str. s. n.* a pillow, 4. 38. A. S. *wangere.*

Waggs, *str. s. m.* a field, Paradise. A. S. *wang.*

Wagjan, *wk. v.* to wag, shake. E. *wag. Causal of* wigan.

Wahsjan, *str. v.* (wohs, wahsans). to wax, grow, increase, 4. 8. E. *wax.*

Wahstus, *str. s. m.* a waxing, growth. E. *waist.*

Wahtwo, *wk. s. f.* a watch. *From* wakan.

Wai, *interj.* woe! 13. 17. E. *woe.*

Waian, *str. v.* (*pt. t.* waiwo), to blow, as the wind. Cf. G. *wehen.*

Wai-dedja, *wk. s. m.* a woe-doer, evil-doer, malefactor, robber, 11. 17.

Wai-fairhwjan, *wk. v.* to lament loudly, wail greatly, 5. 38. *From* wai *and* fairhwus.

Waihsta, *wk. s. m.* a corner, 12. 10.

Waihts, *str. s. f.* (*also* waiht *neut.*), a whit, a thing, 1. 44; ni waiht or waiht ni, no whit, naught, nothing, not at all, 5. 26. E. *whit, wight.*

Waila, *adv.* well, 1. 11; 7. 6; 12. 28. E. *well.*

Wainags, *adj.* miserable, wretched.

Waips, *str. s. m.* a crown, fillet. E. *wisp. From* weipan.

Wair, *str. s. m.* a man, 6. 20. A. S. *wer.*

Wairdus, *str. s. m.* a host (who receives guests).

Wairilo, *wk. s. f.* a lip, 7. 6. A. S. *weler.*

Wairpan, *str. v.* (warp, waurpum, waurpans, *with acc. and dat.*; *also with preps.* af, ana, in), to cast, 1. 16; to cast stones, 12. 4. A. S. *weorpan.*

Wairs, *adv.* worse, 5. 26. E. *worse.*

Wairsiza, *adj. compar.* worser, worse, 2. 21. E. *worser.*

Wairthan, *str. v.* (warth, waurthum, waurthans), to become, to happen, to come to pass, 1. 17, 41; 4. 11, 32; *pt. s.* warth, became, 1. 42; came to pass, 1. 9; 2. 15; was, 1. 14; *pt. pl.* waurthun, were, 1. 22, 36; *pp.* waurthans, 1. 32. A. S. *weorðan.*

Wairths, *adj.* worthy, 1. 7. A. S. *weorð.*

Wairths, *str. s. m.* worth.

Wait, I know, he knows, 4. 27. See **Witan** (1). E. *wot.*

Waja-mereins, *str. s. f.* blasphemy, 7. 22; 14. 64.

Waja-merjan, *wk. v.* to blaspheme, 3. 29; 15. 29. *From* wai.

Wakan, *str. v.* (wok, wakans), to wake, watch. E. *wake.*

Waldan, *v.* to rule, govern. E. *wield.*

Waldufni, *str. s. n.* power, might, authority, 1. 22.

Waljan, *wk. v.* to choose. Lowl. Sc. *wale,* to choose.

Waltjan, *wk. v.* to beat upon, clash against, 4. 37.

Walus, *str. s. m.* a staff, wand. Cf. E. *wale, goal.*

Walwison, *wk. v.* to wallow, 9. 20. See **Walwjan.**

Walwjan, *wk. v. (in compounds)* to roll. Cf. E. *wallow.*

Wamba, *str. s. f.* the belly, 7. 19. E. *womb.*

Wamm, *str. s. n.* a spot, blemish. A. S. *wamm.*

Wandjan, *wk. v.* to wend, turn. E. *wend.*

Wandus, *str. s. m.* a wand, rod. E. *wand.*

Wans, *adj.* waning, lacking, wanting; — wan wisan, to lack, 10. 21. Cf. E. *wane.*

Wardja, *wk. s. m.* a guard. E. *ward.*

Wargitha, *str. s. f.* condemnation. Cf. M. E. *warien,* to curse.

Warjan, *wk. v.* to bid to beware, to forbid, 9. 38; 10. 14. *From* wars.

Warmjan, *wk. v.* to warm, cherish; *refl.* to warm oneself, 14. 54. E. *warm.*

Wars, *adj.* wary. E. *war-y.*

Warth, became, 1. 42; was, 1. 14; came to pass, 2. 15. See **Wairthan.**

Was, was. See **Wisan.** E. *was.*

Wasjan, *wk. v.* to vest, clothe, be clad, 6. 9; *pp.* wasids, clothed.

Wasti, *str. s. f.* vesture, clothing, 5. 27; 6. 56. Cf. Lat. *vestis.*

Was-uth-than, *put for* was uh than, however he was, however she was, *lit.* but he (or she) was then, 1. 6; 7. 26.

Wato, *wk. s. n.* (*pl.* watna), water, 1. 8; 9. 22. E. *water.*

Waurd, *str. s. n.* a word, tale, 1. 45; the word, 4. 14. E. *word.*

Waurdjan, *wk. v.* to speak; — w. ubil, to speak evil, 9. 39.

Waurkjan, *wk. v.* (waurhta, waurhtedum, waurhts), to work, do, make, 1. 3; *neut.* to become operative, 6. 14. E. *work.*

Waurms, *str. s. m.* a serpent. E. *worm.*

Waurstw, *str. s. n.* a work, deed, 14. 6.

Waurstwja, *wk. s. m.* a workman, labourer, husbandman, 12. 1.

Waurthans, *pp. of* wairthan, 1. 32. See note, p. 44.

Waurthun, *used as auxiliary verb,* 1. 36. See **Wairthan.**

Waurts, *str. s. f.* a wort, root, 4. 6. E. *wort.*

Wegs, *str. s. m.* a wagging, violent movement; *hence* a tempest, raging, violent movement; *pl.* wegos (*dat. pl.* wegim), waves, 4. 37. See **Wagjan.**

Weigan, Weihan, *str. v.* (waih, wigum, wigans), to fight, contend. A. S. *wigan.*

Weihs, *adj.* holy, 1. 8, 24; 6. 20. A. S. *wig.*

Weihs, *str. s. m.* a wick, *i. e.* a town, village, 6. 6; 8. 23. Cf. Lat. *vicus.*

Wein, *str. s. n.* wine, 2. 22. Lat. *vinum.*

Weina-gards, *str. s. m.* a vineyard, 12. 1. Lit. *wine-yard.*

Weipan, *str. v.* (waip, wipum, wipans), to crown.

Weis, *pron.* we; *from* ik, 10. 28. E. *we.*

Weitan*, *str. v.* (*pt. t.* wait, *pl.* witum, *pp.* witans), to see; *whence* witan, *vb.* to know.

Weit-woditha, *str. s. f.* witness, testimony, 1. 44; 6. 11.

Weit-wodjan, *wk. v.* to witness, to testify; galiug weitwodjan, to bear false witness, 14. 56.

Weit-wods, *str. s. m.* a witness, 14. 63.

Wenjan, *wk. v.* to ween, hope. E. *ween.*

Wens, *str. s. f.* a weening, hope.

Wepna, *str. s. n. pl.* weapons. E. *weapon.*

Wesi, Wesun; see **Wisan.**

Widan, *str. v.* (wath, wedum, widans), to bind. Cf. E. *with-y.*

Widuwo, Widowo, *wk. s. f.* a widow. E. *widow*.

Wigan*, *str. v.* (wag, wegum, wigans), to shake, move.

Wigs, *str. s. m.* a way, 1. 2; 4. 4. E. *way*.

Wiko, *wk. s. f.* order (τάξις). E. *week*?

Wilja, *wk. s. m.* the will, 3. 35. E. *will*.

Wiljan, *v. anom.* (*pres.* wiljau, *pt. t.* wilda, *pl.* wildedum), to will, wish; *pres.* wiljau, 1. 41; 2 *p.* wileis, thou wilt, 1. 40; *pt. s.* wilda, would, wished, 3. 13; 6. 19. E. *will*, v.

Wiltheis, *adj.* wild. E. *wild*.

Wilwan, *str. v.* (*pt. t.* walw, *pp.* wulwans), to take by force, 3. 27.

Windan, *str. v.* (wand, wundum, wundans), to wind. E. *wind*.

Winds, *str. s. m.* the wind, 4. 37. E. *wind*.

Winja, *str. s. f.* pasture.

Winnan, *str. v.* (wann, wunnum, wunnans), to suffer, 8. 31. E. *win*.

Wintrus, *str. s. m.* a winter, 13. 18. E. *winter*.

Wipja, Wippja, *str. s. f.* a crown, 15. 17. *From* weipan.

Wis, *str. s. n.* a calm, 4. 39.

Wisan, *v.* (*pres.* im, is, ist, sijum, sijuth, sind; *pt. t.* was, wast, was, wesum, wesuth, wesun; *pres. subj.* sijau, *pt. subj.* wesjau), to be, 8. 1, etc. *Hence* im, 1. 7; is, 1. 11; ist, 1. 2; was, 1. 4; *pt. s. subj.* wesi, 3. 9; 5. 18; 9. 34. *Also* wesun-uth, but there were, 2. 6; sec **Uh.** A. S. *wesan*.

Witan (1), *anom. v.* (*pres. sing.* wait, *pl.* witum; *pt. t.* wissa), to know, 2. 10; *pr. s.* wait, 4. 27; *pt. s.* wissa, 9. 6. E. *wit*.

Witan (2), *wk. v.* (*pt. t.* witaida), to watch, observe, 3. 2; *pt. s.* witaida, 6. 20.

Withon, *wk. v.* to shake, wag, 15. 29.

Withra, *prep. with acc.* over against, against, 3. 24; 9. 40; in return for, in reply to, for; near, 4. 1; on account of, 10. 5. A. S. *wiðer*.

Withra-wairths, *adj.* opposite, that which is over against, 11. 2.

Withrus, *str. s. m.* a wether, lamb. E. *wether*.

Witoth, *str. s. n.* law. Du. *wet*.

Wizon, *wk. v.* to live.

Wlaiton, *wk. v.* to look round about, 5. 32. A. S. *wlitan*.

Wlits, *str. s. m.* the face, 14. 65. A. S. *wlite*.

Wods, *adj.* mad, possessed, 5. 15, 16, 18. A. S. *wód*.

Wokrs, *str. s. m.* usury. A. S. *wócer*. Icel. *okr*.

Wopjan, *wk. v.* to cry aloud, cry out, call, 1. 3; to crow, 14. 68. E. *weep*.

Wotheis, *adj.* sweet, pleasant.

Wraikws, *adj.* wry, crooked. E. *wry*.

Wraka, *str. s. f.* a wreaking (vengeance), persecution, 10. 30. A.S. *wræc*. *From* wrikan.

Wrakja, *str. s. f.* (*the same as* wraka), persecution, 4. 17.

Wraton, *wk. v.* to go, journey.

Wrikan, *str. v.* (wrak, wrekum, wrikans), to persecute. A. S. *wrecan*.

Writhus, *str. s. f.* a herd, flock. Cf. A. S. *wriða*, a ring.

Writs, *str. s. m.* the stroke of a pen. A. S. *writ*, writing.

Wrohjan, *wk. v.* to accuse, 3. 2; 15. 3.

Wrohs, *str. s. f.* accusation. A. S. *wróht*.

Wulan, *str. v.* to boil, be fervent. E. *well*.

Wulfila, *proper name*, lit. 'little wolf'; usually written in the Graecised form Ulphilas.

Wulfs, *str. s. m.* a wolf. E. *wolf.*

Wulla, *str. s. f.* wool. E. *wool.*

Wullareis, *str. s. m.* one who whitens wool, a fuller, 9. 3.

Wulthus, *str. s. m.* glory, 8. 38; 10. 37. A.S. *wuldor.*

Wulwa, *str. s. f.* robbery. *From* wilwan.

Wunds, *adj.* wounded; haubith wundan briggan, to wound in the head (lit. make one wounded in the head), 12. 4. Cf. E. *wound.*

Wundufni, *str. s. f.* a wound, a plague, 3. 10.

Wunns, *str. s. f.* affliction, suffering.

THE END.